Azizollah

L.B.C. Ad Bio

A. Borrows L6

INTRODUCTION TO ELEMENTARY VECTOR ANALYSIS

INTRODUCTION TO ELEMENTARY VECTOR ANALYSIS

BY

J. C. TALLACK

Head of the Mathematics Department,
West Norfolk and King's Lynn High School

CAMBRIDGE
AT THE UNIVERSITY PRESS
1966

PUBLISHED BY
THE SYNDICS OF THE CAMBRIDGE UNIVERSITY PRESS

Bentley House, 200 Euston Road, London, N.W. 1
American Branch: 32 East 57th Street, New York, N.Y. 10022
West African Office: P.M.B. 5181, Ibadan, Nigeria

Printed in Great Britain at the University Printing House, Cambridge
(Brooke Crutchley, University Printer)

LIBRARY OF CONGRESS CATALOGUE
CARD NUMBER: 66–11036

CONTENTS

PREFACE

The aim of this book is to provide an easy introduction to the algebra of vectors and to the application of vectors in geometry and mechanics. Although the material is of an elementary nature it has been developed rigorously. It is hoped that by so doing an understanding of the concept of a vector and an appreciation of the procedure necessary in creating the algebra applicable to vectors will be achieved in the mind of the student.

The idea of a vector is introduced in chapter 1 by discussing displacements. In chapter 2 the algebra of vectors is developed from the definition of the addition of two vectors. Later chapters cover differentiation, integration and the scalar product of vectors but not the vector product.

A feature of the book is the number of worked examples, particularly geometrical, and these it is hoped will be of special value to those who are working on their own.

The book should appeal to the following groups:

a. scientists and mathematicians in the sixth form;
b. first year university students of mathematics, science (particularly physics) and engineering, who wish for an easy introduction to the fundamental principles during the first term;
c. students in training and technical colleges, and
d. students taking 'Modern' mathematics with vectors in the syllabus.

Although the text has not been written for any particular examination syllabus, it covers the topics for applied mathematics set by the University of Cambridge Local Examinations Syndicate, to whom I acknowledge permission for the use of recent examination questions. My thanks are due to Mrs K. A. Neale who patiently and carefully typed out the manuscript and to the staff of the Cambridge University Press for their helpful advice at all stages and for the excellence of their printing.

J.C.T

King's Lynn
January, 1966

1

INTRODUCTION TO VECTORS THROUGH DISPLACEMENTS

Introduction

We shall, in what follows, introduce the idea of a vector and indicate why a special branch of analysis or algebra has to be developed to deal with operations involving vectors. In this chapter the algebra of vectors will be developed by recourse to geometrical drawing and to number-pair form.

Concept of a displacement

An aeroplane starts from London at noon and in half an hour flies 100 miles in a straight line. A person wishes to pin-point its exact position at 12.30 p.m. on a map. Now it is obvious that this cannot be done since the information given is insufficient. We have a number 100 representing the distance gone in miles but we have no idea of the direction taken by the aeroplane. The information we need is a combined distance–direction or a combined number–direction since the distance in miles is expressed as a number. This leads to the idea of displacement as distinct from distance and we may think of a displacement as the distance gone considered together with the direction taken.

We shall now discuss displacements in detail since they will help us to obtain an understanding of vectors in general.

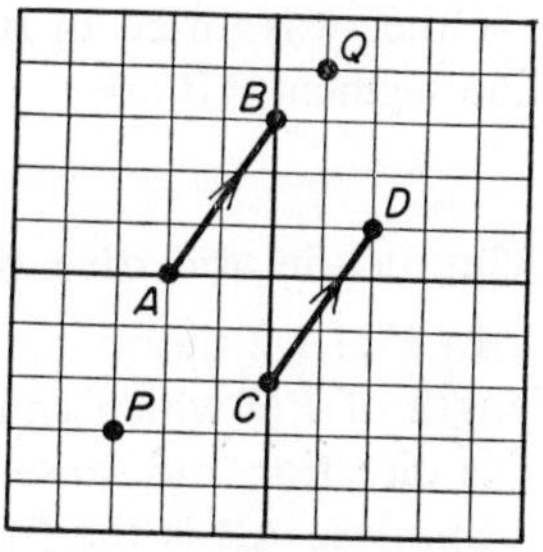

Fig. 1.1

The representation of displacements

In Fig. 1.1 if we start at P and move 1 unit to the right and 3 units up we arrive at A. We can represent this movement in a shorthand way by the ordered number-pair (1, 3). If we start at Q and move 1 unit to the right and 3 units down we arrive at D and we can denote this by $(1, -3)$. Again if we start at Q and move 1 unit to the left and 1 unit down we arrive at B and we denote this by $(-1, -1)$.

The movement or displacement in going from A to B can be described as moving 2 units to the right and 3 units up or (2, 3). The displacement from B to A is the result of moving 2 units to the left and 3 units down or $(-2, -3)$.

The displacement from C to D in number-pair form is (2, 3). This is also the displacement from A to B. Can we make any conclusions about these two displacements? We can say that they are the same since they are equal in length and have the same direction and sense, or we can say they are the same since they are both represented by the same number-pair. However, there is an objection to this equality since it may be argued that they are not the same because they each have different starting-points and ending-points. Thus it seems that when we are considering a displacement we should make it clear whether we wish its location to be included or not. Now if we wish to specify the location of a displacement we use the term 'located' or 'localized' displacement. The displacement itself with no regard to its position is called a 'free' displacement.

We now introduce the notation **PQ** in bold type to denote the directed line segment which represents the free displacement whose magnitude is the length of the line segment PQ, whose direction is that of the line PQ and whose sense is the direction of travel from P to Q, i.e. the sense is given by the order of the letters in **PQ**.

With this notation we can say that for the above displacements **AB, CD**

$$\mathbf{AB} = \mathbf{CD}.$$

Other ways used in printing and writing to indicate the directed line segment **AB** are $\overrightarrow{AB}$, $\underrightarrow{AB}$, $\overline{AB}$, $\underline{AB}$ $\underset{\sim}{AB}$.

Magnitude and direction of displacements

In Fig. 1.2 the magnitude of the located displacement **PQ** is the length of PQ which can be associated with the positive number 5. The direction and sense of **PQ** is along PQ and from P to Q.

Suppose **AB** is the free displacement whose number-pair form is (3, 4). **PQ** and **RS** also have the same number-pair form and are therefore the associated located displacements of **AB**. This means that the magnitude, direction and sense of **PQ, RS** and all associated located displacements of **AB** are the same as the magnitude, direction and sense of **AB**. Thus the terms magnitude, direction and sense of **AB** will mean the magnitude, direction and sense of all associated located displacements. In passing we note that we can always associate a displacement with a positive number which defines its magnitude or length.

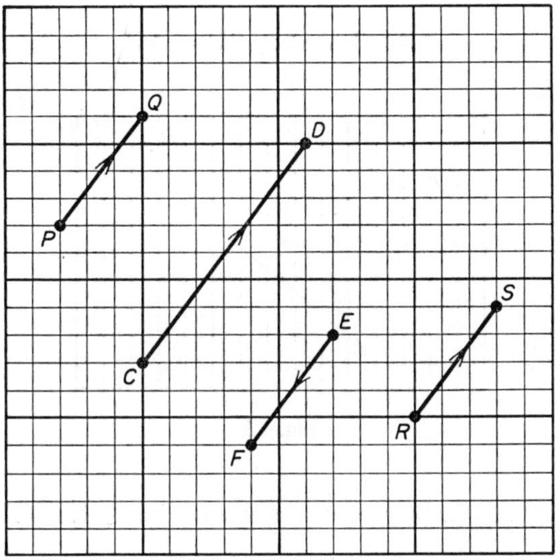

Fig. 1.2

Unless we state otherwise 'displacement' in future will imply 'free displacement'.

The located displacements **PQ**, **CD**, **EF** have all the same direction, that is, they are parallel. Writing them in number-pair forms **PQ** = (3, 4), **CD** = (6, 8), **EF** = (−3, −4) we see that the condition for them to be parallel is given by the relation

$$\frac{3}{4} = \frac{6}{8} = \frac{-3}{-4}$$

between the number-pairs. However, the complete reversal of signs of (3, 4), (−3, −4) indicates that **PQ**, **EF** are opposite in sense.

Successive displacements

Suppose in Fig. 1.3 we start at A and we make a displacement **AB** = (1, 3) followed by a displacement **BC** = (4, 1). We now note that a displacement (5, 4) will take us directly from A to C. Thus we conclude that a displacement from A to B followed by one from B to C is equivalent to one from A to C. This can be symbolized as

$$\mathbf{AB} \text{ followed by } \mathbf{BC} = \mathbf{AC}.$$

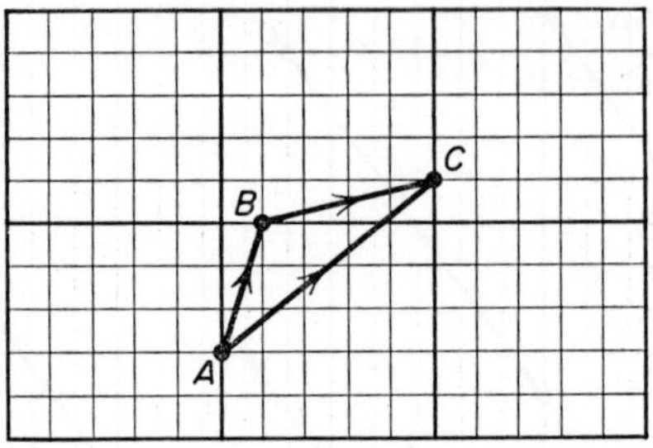

Fig. 1.3

To shorten this further let us use the symbol $\oplus$ for 'followed by'. Thus

$$\mathbf{AB} \oplus \mathbf{BC} = \mathbf{AC}.$$

However, is it really necessary to introduce a new symbol $\oplus$? We already have the four symbols $+$, $-$, $\times$, $\div$ which indicate the names of familiar operations in arithmetic and which have been sufficient for doing all that we require. To answer our question we have another look at

$$\mathbf{AB} \oplus \mathbf{BC} = \mathbf{AC}. \qquad (1)$$

We write the displacements in number-pair form

$$\mathbf{AB} = (1, 3),$$

$$\mathbf{BC} = (4, 1),$$

$$\mathbf{AC} = (5, 4).$$

$$\therefore \quad (1, 3) \oplus (4, 1) = (5, 4), \text{ by substituting in (1).}$$

We note that if we add the 1 and the 4 we get the 5, and similarly adding the 3 and 1 gives us the 4.

Let us try again with the following displacements **PQ, QR** as in Fig. 1.4.

The symbolic description of the successive displacements **PQ, QR** is

$$\mathbf{PQ} \oplus \mathbf{QR} = \mathbf{PR}. \qquad (2)$$

Again $\mathbf{PQ} = (3, 5),$

$\mathbf{QR} = (2, -1),$

$\mathbf{PR} = (5, 4).$

$\therefore \quad (3, 5) \oplus (2, -1) = (5, 4),$

by substituting in (2).

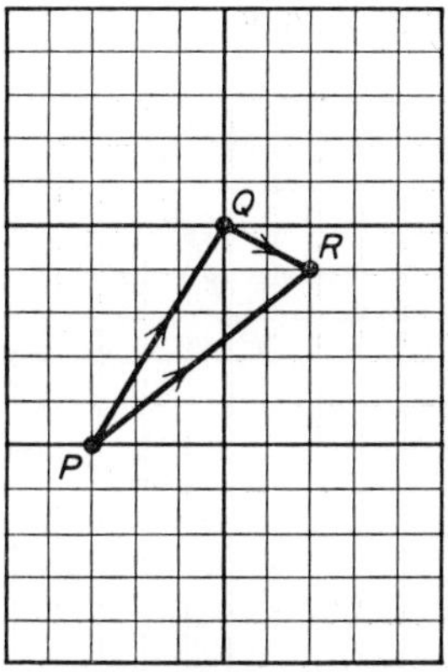

Fig. 1.4

We again see that by adding the 3 and 2 we get the 5 and by adding the 5 and -1 we get the 4.

This suggests the idea that the result of the successive displacements **AB, BC** can be regarded as an addition process, but the operation of addition is to be carried out in a special way. Thus we can discard the symbol $\oplus$ and write $+$ in its place, but we must understand that the $+$ indicates addition by an operation which is different from that for numbers. We now write

$$\mathbf{AB} + \mathbf{BC} = \mathbf{AC}$$

and this symbolic statement tells us the rule or law by which displacements and in general vectors are added. We shall in chapter 2 state this law formally as the triangle law of vector addition, and use this law as the starting-point of the development of vector analysis.

We shall see later that there are other physical quantities apart from displacement which have the combined number–direction property and which are added by the triangle law. We call such quantities by the general name of vectors. Thus we can say displacement is a vector.

In continuing our discussion on displacements we shall use 'vector' for 'displacement' whenever we want to emphasize the applicability of any statement to vectors in general. Referring to Fig. 1.5, since we have in number-pair forms **PQ** = (1, 2), **UV** = (3, −1), **MN** = (4, 1) and since the relation between the number-pairs is

$$(1, 2)+(3, -1) = (4, 1),$$

we can say **PQ**+**UV** = **MN**.

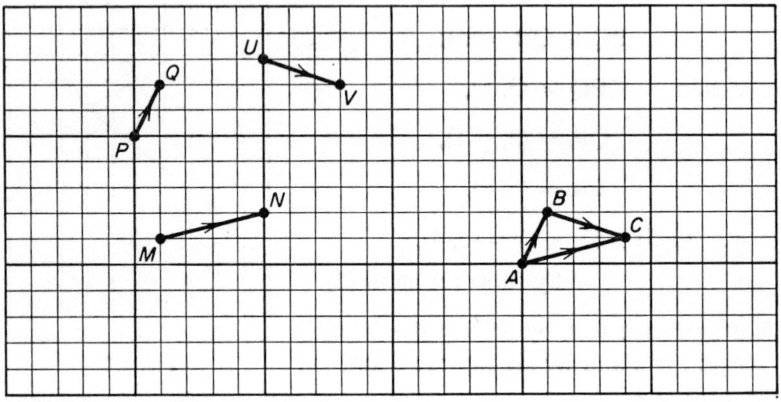

Fig. 1.5

The geometrical significance of this vector equation is that **PQ**+**UV** = **MN** if a triangle *ABC* exists where **PQ** = **AB**, **UV** = **BC**, **MN** = **AC**.

In order to appreciate further developments in our study of vectors we must now discuss symbols more thoroughly.

Symbols

When we use the symbols 3 and 7 in the normal way we understand them to represent the size of two numbers. The nature of our number system may be brought out by algebraic generalizations. For example, if we introduce the symbols x and y to denote two numbers then we can write

$$x+y = y+x.$$

However, is the statement $x+y = y+x$ always true if the symbols x and y do not stand for numbers? This question must be asked since in the study of displacements we have used symbols such as **AB**, **BC**, + and have connected them up as **AB**+**BC**. Thus since the symbols

AB, BC do not stand for numbers but for combined number–directions, can we conclude that **AB**+**BC** = **BC**+**AB**? Before answering the question we must remember that in the statement $x+y = y+x$ we have another symbol, namely +. The statement $x+y$ denotes the result of adding x to y and when x and y are numbers we clearly understand how we are to proceed and how we are to write down the result as a number symbol. The + sign is the name of the operation. It tells us what we are to do but it does not tell us how. How we are to add depends on what we are adding. As we have seen when we add vectors we must do it in a special way.

Now to get back to our question. Is $x+y = y+x$ true when x, y are not numbers and when + means we are to add x, y according to the operation defined for x, y?

Suppose A and B are two points (Fig. 1.6). Here we are using the symbols A, B to stand for two points.

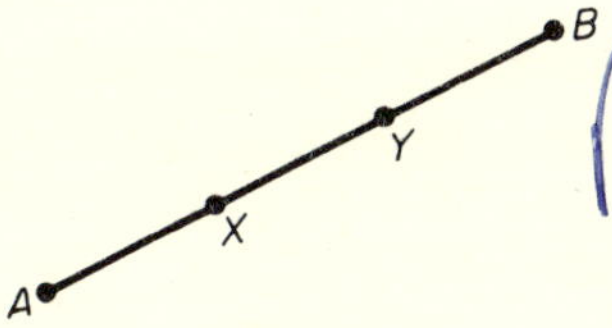

Fig. 1.6

Suppose we invent an algebra to enable us to 'add' two points. Let us define the addition of two points A and B as the point of trisection of AB nearer to the first of the points mentioned, i.e. the point X.

Therefore $A+B = X$.

Using the same definition, if we add point B to point A we obtain the point Y, the point of trisection of BA nearer to B.

Therefore $B+A = Y$.

Thus the addition of A to B and B to A gives two different points.

Thus with this algebraic system

$$A+B \neq B+A.$$

So we see that knowing $x+y = y+x$ is true for numbers we must not assume the statement is true for x and y when they are not numbers. In particular this means that if **AB, BC** are vectors we cannot conclude that **AB**+**BC** and **BC**+**AB** are the same.

Since the addition of vectors is an operation different from the addition of numbers the algebra developed for vectors will be a new algebra and the results for number algebra must not be assumed to apply for vector algebra. To make the point clear if x, y, z are symbols standing for numbers and **a**, **b**, **c** are symbols standing for vectors and if we know that

$$x+y = y+z,$$
$$(x+y)+z = x+(y+z),$$
$$xy = yx,$$
$$m(x+y) = mx+my \quad (m \text{ a constant number}),$$

we must not assume that the above are true when x, y, z are replaced by **a**, **b**, **c** respectively.

However, we now return to a further study of successive displacements.

Order of adding successive displacements

Consider the vectors **AB** = (4, 5), **BC** = (2, −2). Suppose we want to find **AB**+**BC** and **BC**+**AB** geometrically. Take any point O. Let **OP** = **AB** and **PQ** = **BC** (Fig. 1.7).

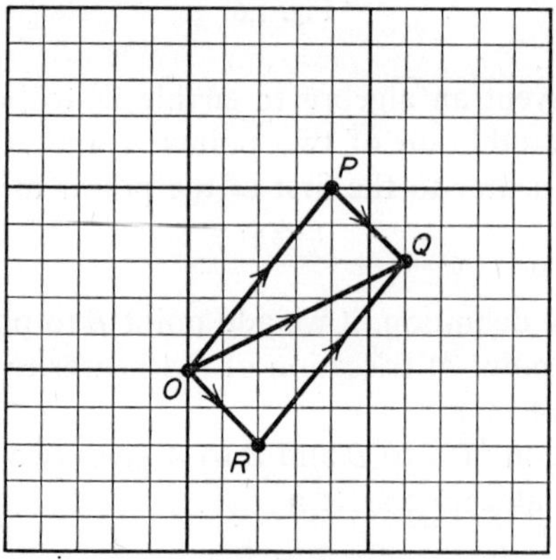

Fig. 1.7

Then $\quad$ **AB**+**BC** = **OP**+**PQ** = **OQ** = (6, 3).

Let **OR** = **BC**. Join **RQ**. We see that **RQ** = (4, 5) = **AB**.

Then $\quad$ **BC**+**AB** = **OR**+**RQ** = **OQ** = (6, 3).

From this we conclude that $(\mathbf{AB}+\mathbf{BC})$ and $(\mathbf{BC}+\mathbf{AB})$ are the same, which implies that the order of adding the vectors is immaterial. This is therefore the answer to one of our questions of the previous section.

We can, without drawing, show the equality by expressing the vectors in number-pairs:

$$\mathbf{AB} = (4, 5),$$

$$\mathbf{BC} = (2, -2),$$

$$\therefore \quad \mathbf{AB}+\mathbf{BC} = (4, 5)+(2, -2) = (6, 3),$$

and
$$\mathbf{BC}+\mathbf{AB} = (2, -2)+(4, 5) = (6, 3),$$

$$\therefore \quad \mathbf{AB}+\mathbf{BC} = \mathbf{BC}+\mathbf{AB}.$$

Now suppose we wish to add the three displacements **AB, MN, PQ**. The question immediately arises, which two of the three vectors do we add first? This difficulty is resolved by using brackets and giving them the same significance when grouping vectors as in number algebra.

Thus $(\mathbf{AB}+\mathbf{MN})+\mathbf{PQ}$ means that we must obtain the sum of the displacements **AB, MN** first and then add this result to **PQ**.

Another question now arises. Does the way in which we group the vectors affect the final result?

Let $\mathbf{AB} = (4, 8)$, $\mathbf{MN} = (12, 8)$, $\mathbf{PQ} = (-20, -4)$. To obtain $(\mathbf{AB}+\mathbf{MN})+\mathbf{PQ}$ geometrically take any point O and let $\mathbf{OC} = \mathbf{AB}$, $\mathbf{CD} = \mathbf{MN}$ (Fig. 1.8).

Then
$$(\mathbf{AB}+\mathbf{MN}) = (\mathbf{OC}+\mathbf{CD}) = \mathbf{OD}.$$

Now let
$$\mathbf{DE} = \mathbf{PQ}.$$

Then
$$\mathbf{OD}+\mathbf{PQ} = \mathbf{OD}+\mathbf{DE} = \mathbf{OE} = (-4, 12),$$

$$\therefore \quad (\mathbf{AB}+\mathbf{MN})+\mathbf{PQ} = \mathbf{OE} = (-4, 12).$$

To obtain $\mathbf{AB}+(\mathbf{MN}+\mathbf{PQ})$ geometrically let $\mathbf{OF} = \mathbf{MN}$, $\mathbf{FG} = \mathbf{PQ}$.

Then
$$(\mathbf{MN}+\mathbf{PQ}) = \mathbf{OF}+\mathbf{FG} = \mathbf{OG},$$

Now we see from the figure

$$\mathbf{GE} = (4, 8) = \mathbf{AB},$$

and
$$\mathbf{OG}+\mathbf{GE} = \mathbf{OE},$$

$$\therefore \quad \mathbf{GE}+\mathbf{OG} = \mathbf{OE}$$

(since we have seen the order of addition of two vectors is immaterial).

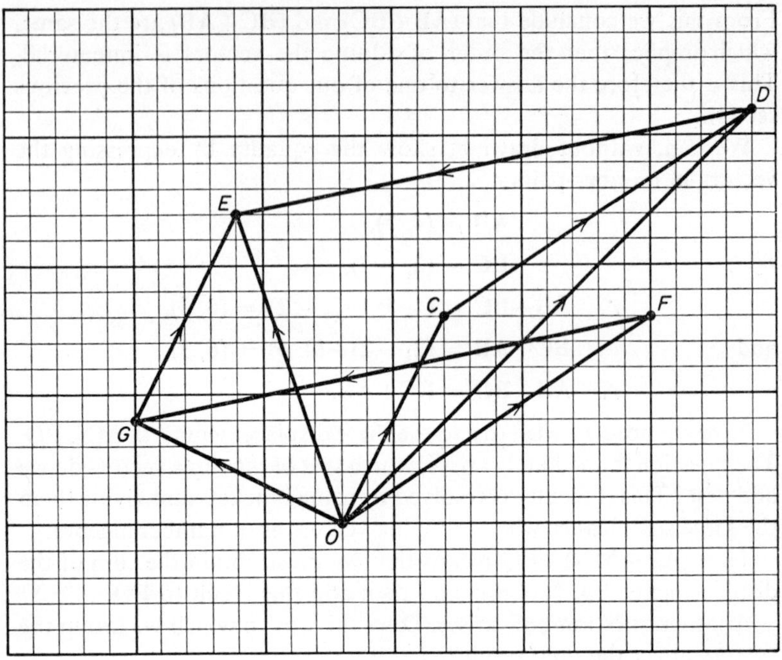

Fig. 1.8

$$\therefore \quad \mathbf{AB}+(\mathbf{MN}+\mathbf{PQ}) = \mathbf{OE} = (-4, 12),$$

$$\therefore \quad (\mathbf{AB}+\mathbf{MN})+\mathbf{PQ} = \mathbf{AB}+(\mathbf{MN}+\mathbf{PQ}).$$

Again we can obtain this result by expressing the vectors in number-pairs

$$\begin{aligned}(\mathbf{AB}+\mathbf{MN})+\mathbf{PQ} &= [(4, 8)+(12, 8)]+(-20, -4)\\ &= (16, 16)+(-20, -4)\\ &= (-4, 12).\\ \mathbf{AB}+(\mathbf{MN}+\mathbf{PQ}) &= (4, 8)+[(12, 8)+(-20, -4)]\\ &= (4, 8)+(-8, 4)\\ &= (-4, 12).\end{aligned}$$

$$\therefore \quad (\mathbf{AB}+\mathbf{MN})+\mathbf{PQ} = \mathbf{AB}+(\mathbf{MN}+\mathbf{PQ}).$$

Thus we conclude that the sum of three vectors is unaffected by the order of grouping.

The zero and inverse vectors

Suppose we start at A and carry out the following displacements **AB, BC, CA** (Fig. 1.9). We see that we end at the starting-point A, that is, the sum of the displacements, namely **AB**+**BC**+**CA** is a zero displacement.

Expressing this sum in number-pair form we have

$$\mathbf{AB}+\mathbf{BC}+\mathbf{CA} = (2, 3)+(5, 2)+(-7, -5)$$
$$= (0, 0).$$

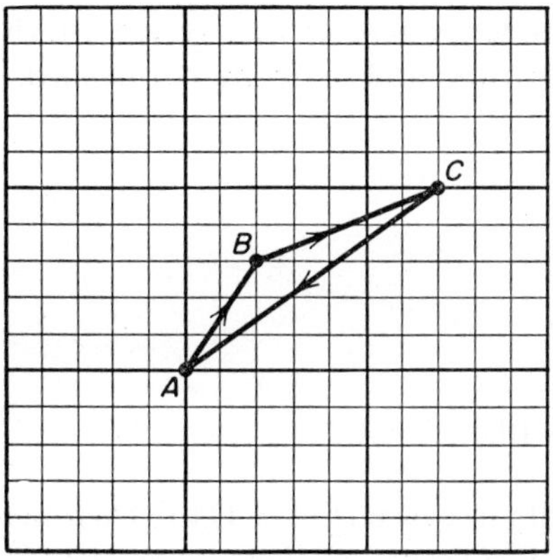

Fig. 1.9

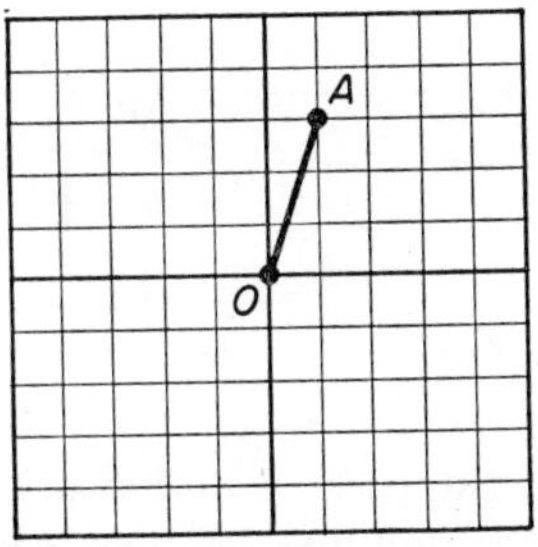

Fig. 1.10

Thus we can interpret the number-pair (0, 0) to imply that we are back at where we started, and also to stand for zero displacement. The number-pair (0, 0) is more generally called the zero vector or the null vector.

Suppose we make a displacement **OA** = (1, 3) (Fig. 1.10). The displacement **AO** necessary to bring us back to the original position denoted by the zero vector (0, 0) is given by the number-pair $(-1, -3)$.

We define $(-1, -3)$ as the inverse of (1, 3) and **AO** as the inverse of **OA**.

Vectors

We shall end this chapter by restating some of the facts we have learnt about vectors through the study of displacements. Also we shall give various definitions.

Representation of vectors

We have seen that a vector has the following essential features: (1) a magnitude or length given by a positive number; (2) a direction in space; (3) a sense.

The only exception to the above is the zero or null vector, which has zero magnitude and whose direction and sense are not defined.

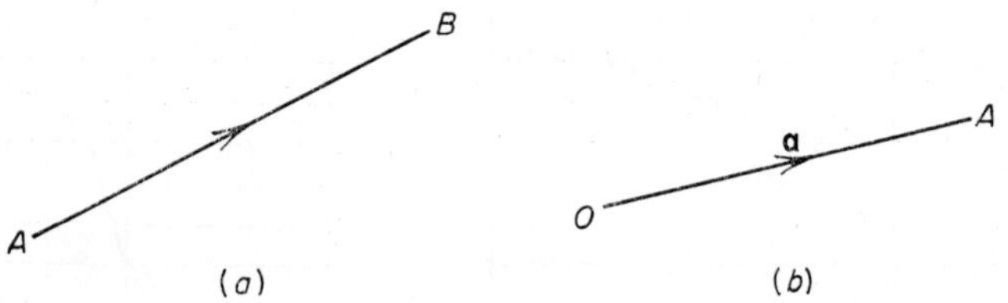

Fig. 1.11

Suppose A and B are two points in space (Fig. 1.11a). Then the directed line segment **AB** represents a vector of length or magnitude AB, the direction of the vector being that of the line AB and the sense of the vector being the direction of travel from A to B. On diagrams the sense of direction can be indicated by an arrow.

Suppose the point B approaches the point A. When B reaches A we have the vector **AA** whose magnitude is zero and whose direction and sense are not specified. Thus **AA** represents the zero vector which is denoted by **0**.

The vector **BA** represents a vector in the opposite sense to the vector **AB** but whose magnitude and direction are the same.

Often a vector is denoted by a single small letter if there is no ambiguity about its direction.

The vector **OA** (Fig. 1.11b) can be denoted thus:

In printing: **a**.

In writing: $\bar{\text{a}}$, $\underline{\text{a}}$, $\underset{\sim}{\text{a}}$.

Magnitude of vectors

The magnitude or modulus of a vector **AB**, denoted by |**AB**|, is the length of the straight line AB.

Thus |**AB**| $= AB$ and |**a**| $= a$, where length $OA = a$.

A vector whose modulus is 1 is defined as a unit vector. We shall denote the unit vector having the same direction and sense as **a** by **â**.

Like and unlike vectors

Definition. *Vectors having the same direction and sense are said to be like and those which have the same direction but opposite sense are said to be unlike.*

Equal vectors

Definition. *Two vectors are said to be equal if they have the same magnitude, direction and sense.*

Thus the statement **AB** = **PQ** means, providing the vectors are not zero vectors;

(1) the two vectors are equal in magnitude, i.e. $AB = PQ$;

(2) the two vectors have the same direction, i.e. they are parallel;

(3) the sense of direction from A to B is the same as the sense of direction from P to Q.

It must be realized that the converse of (1) is not true, i.e. if the moduli of 2 vectors are equal it does not follow that the vectors are equal since their directions may not be the same. Thus if $AB = PQ$ it does not necessarily follow that **AB** = **PQ**.

All zero vectors are equivalent to one another no matter what their directions may be.

Addition of vectors

We define the addition of two vectors by the triangle law.

Later on we shall see that before a physical quantity can be called a vector it must be shown to obey the triangle law of addition even though it is a combined number–direction quantity. It therefore follows that any physical quantity such as displacement which can be represented in magnitude, direction and sense by a directed line segment and which obeys the triangle law of addition, belongs to the class of vectors of which the directed line segment itself can be regarded as the prototype.

Free and localized vectors

We have seen that if we wish to specify the location of a vector then the term 'localized' or 'located' vector is used. Otherwise we refer to the vector as a 'free' vector. As we shall be concerned with free vectors it is important to understand thoroughly the concept of a free vector.

Consider a rigid body which is displaced a given distance in a given direction, without the body undergoing any rotation (Fig. 1.12).

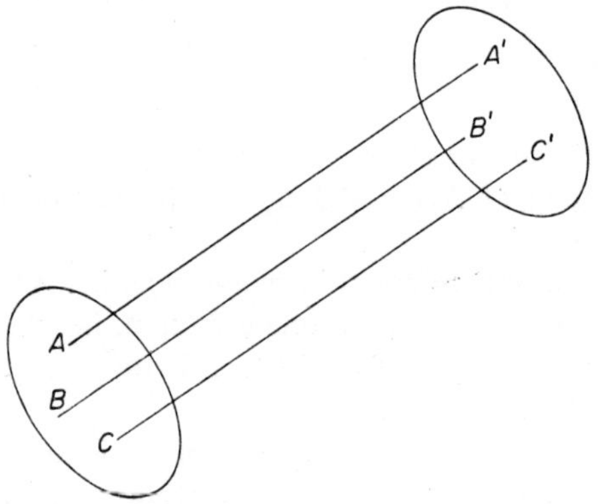

Fig. 1.12

Each point A, B, C moves to a new position A', B', C' in space. The movement of the points is given by the displacement vectors $\mathbf{AA'}$, $\mathbf{BB'}$, $\mathbf{CC'}$. Now it will be clear that any one of these displacements, such as $\mathbf{AA'}$, is sufficient to describe the displacement of the body, i.e. the vector describing the displacement of the body is independent of its location and in this sense is a free vector. It therefore follows that a free vector can be represented by many different parallel and equal directed line segments. Furthermore, we see that free vectors can be transferred from one place to another and providing their magnitude, direction and sense remain the same we consider them not only to be equal but equivalent vectors.

Sometimes it is important to know the location of a vector. We shall later show that force is a vector. If a force is acting on a rigid body its effect is dependent on its line of action. Hence we must treat the force as a localized vector or as it is sometimes called a 'line' or 'sliding' vector. Another example of a localized vector is an electric or magnetic field whose effect is fully known when it is specified with respect to some given point. In such a case the vector is sometimes called a 'tied' vector.

We shall in future use the term 'vector' to imply a 'free' vector, unless we state otherwise. Thus when we refer to the vector **AB** we are not inferring that it is located at *A* or that its line of action is along *AB*.

Exercise 1

The object of this exercise is to extend the previous work into three dimensions.

(1) See Fig. 1.13.

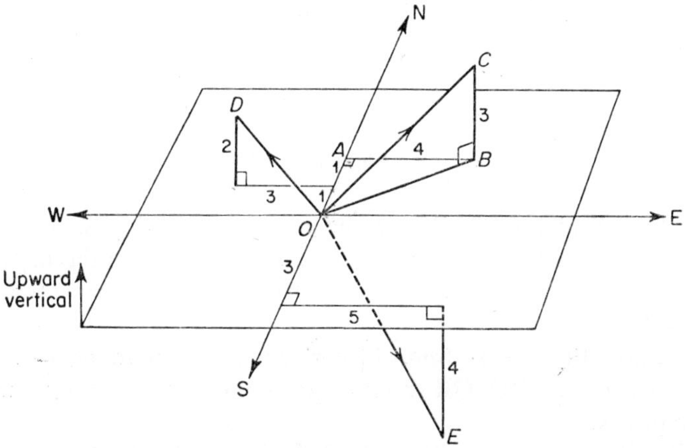

Fig. 1.13

(i) Express as a single vector **OA**+**AB**, **OB**+**BC**. Hence express **OA**+**AB**+**BC** as a single vector.

(ii) The vector **OC** can be regarded as moving 2 units N., 4 units E., 3 units vertically up and can be written as the ordered number-triple (2, 4, 3). What are the vectors **OD**, **OE** as number-triples?

(iii) **OB** is known as the projection of **OC** on the horizontal plane. What is the length of **OB**? Hence what is the length of **OC**?

If **OP** = (a_1, a_2, a_3) in number-triple form deduce the length of the projection of **OP** on the horizontal plane and the length of **OP**.

The numbers a_1, a_2, a_3 are known as the components of the vector **OP**.

(2) See Fig. 1.14.

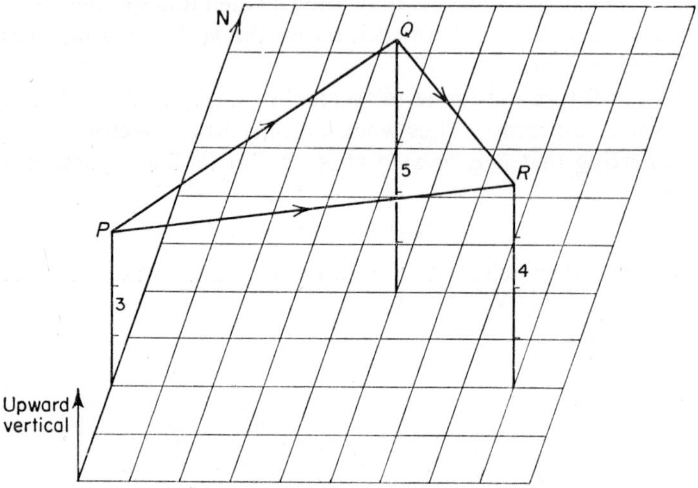

Fig. 1.14

(i) The displacement **PQ** is the result of moving 2 units N., 5 units E., 2 units vertically up and can be written as the number-triple (2, 5, 2). What are the displacements in number-triple form of **QR, PR**?

(ii) Show that the addition of corresponding components of the number-triples of **PQ, QR** results in the components of the number-triple of **PR**.

(iii) **AB** = (2, 3, −1), **BC** = (−2, 0, 4). What is **AC**?

(3) See Fig. 1.15.

(i) Express as number-triples **OA, OB, OC, AB, AC**.

(ii) What can we say about **OB, AC**? Hence prove that the vector sum of **OA, OB** is obtained by adding the corresponding components of the number-triples of **OA, OB**.

(iii) Subtract the components of **OA** from the corresponding components of **OB**. What vector has these components?

Hence express **AB** in terms of **OA, OB**.

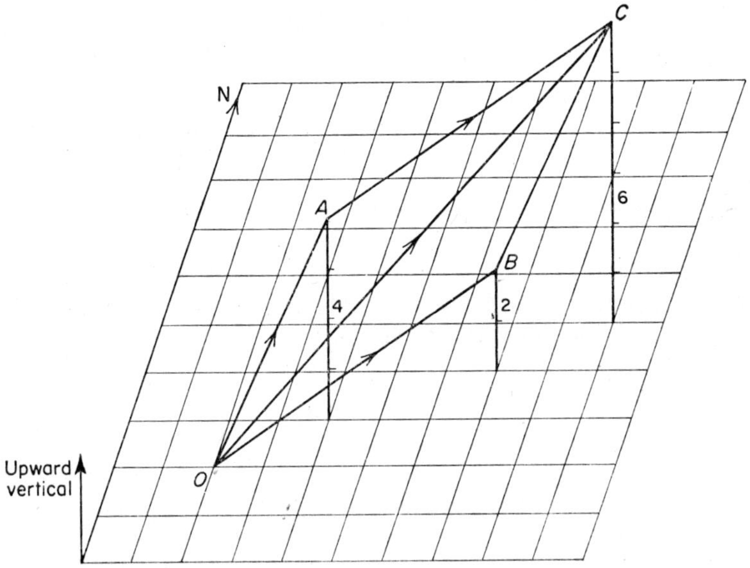

Fig. 1.15

(iv) If **OP** = (2, −4, 5), **OQ** = (7, 1, −3) what are **OP** + **OQ** and **PQ** in number-triple form?

2

ADDITION AND SUBTRACTION OF VECTORS

In this chapter the ideas already developed from the study of displacements will be redeveloped, but in a formal way, taking as our starting-point the definition of vector addition.

The addition of two vectors

Two vectors are added by either the triangle law of vector addition or the parallelogram law of vector addition. We shall define addition by each of these two laws and also show their equivalence.

(1) *The triangle law*

Suppose **a** and **b** are two vectors (Fig. 2.1).

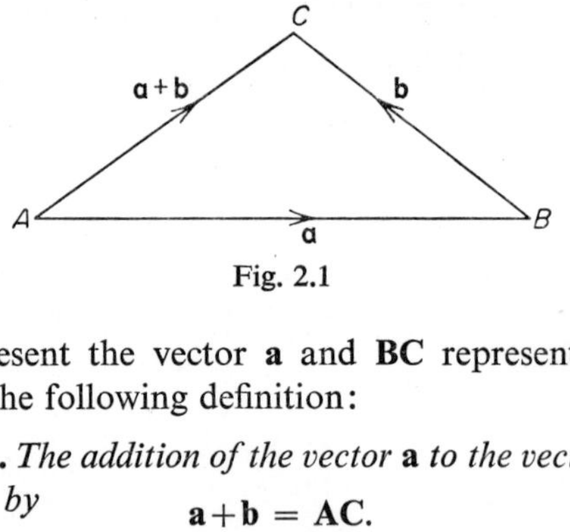

Fig. 2.1

Let **AB** represent the vector **a** and **BC** represent the vector **b**. Then we have the following definition:

***Definition* 1.** *The addition of the vector* **a** *to the vector* **b**, *written as* $\mathbf{a}+\mathbf{b}$, *is defined by*

$$\mathbf{a}+\mathbf{b} = \mathbf{AC}.$$

This sum is unique since all triangles ABC with **AB**, **BC** representing **a** and **b** in size and direction are congruent. Hence **AC** will be of fixed length and direction, i.e. **AC** is unique.

Also since $AC < AB+BC$ we have $|\mathbf{a}+\mathbf{b}| < |\mathbf{a}|+|\mathbf{b}|$, i.e. the modulus of the sum of two vectors is less than the sum of the moduli of the two vectors. There is an exception to this, as will be seen later.

Applying this definition to Fig. 2.2 we have

$$\mathbf{PQ}+\mathbf{QR} = \mathbf{PR},$$

and

$$\mathbf{a}+\mathbf{b} = \mathbf{c}.$$

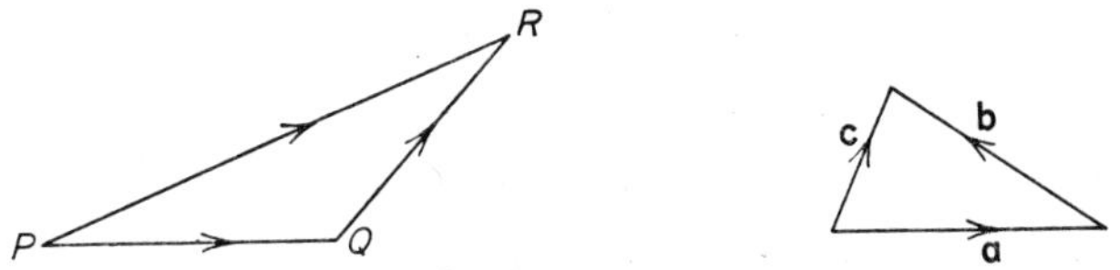

Fig. 2.2

From a geometrical point of view, $\mathbf{p}+\mathbf{q} = \mathbf{r}$ (Fig. 2.3) if a triangle OAB exists where $\mathbf{OA} = \mathbf{p}$, $\mathbf{AB} = \mathbf{q}$ and $\mathbf{OB} = \mathbf{r}$.

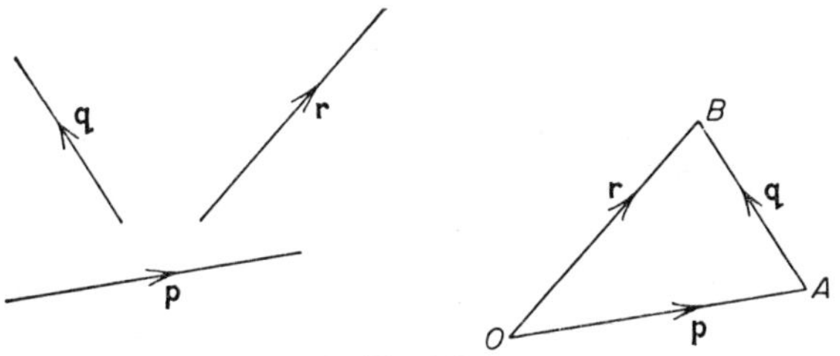

Fig. 2.3

Definition 1 agrees with the way in which two displacements are added (chapter 1) and it also represents mathematically how the vector quantities in physics and mathematics are added.

(2) *The parallelogram law*

Suppose $\mathbf{a}$ and $\mathbf{b}$ are two vectors (Fig. 2.4).

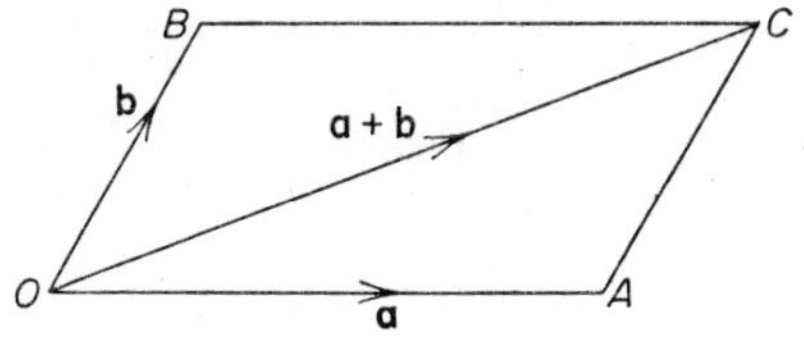

Fig. 2.4

Let $\mathbf{OA}$ and $\mathbf{OB}$ represent the vectors $\mathbf{a}$ and $\mathbf{b}$ respectively. Complete the parallelogram $OACB$. Then we have the following definition:

Definition **2.** *The addition of the vector* **a** *to the vector* **b**, *written* **a**+**b**, *is defined by*

$$\mathbf{a}+\mathbf{b} = \mathbf{OC}.$$

We shall now show that this definition gives the same sum as that defined by the triangle law of addition.

By the triangle law, $\mathbf{a}+\mathbf{AC} = \mathbf{OC}.$

But $\mathbf{AC} = \mathbf{OB} = \mathbf{b},$

$$\therefore \quad \mathbf{a}+\mathbf{b} = \mathbf{OC}.$$

Thus the equivalence is shown.

We shall as a rule prefer the triangle law to the parallelogram law.

Special cases of the addition of two vectors

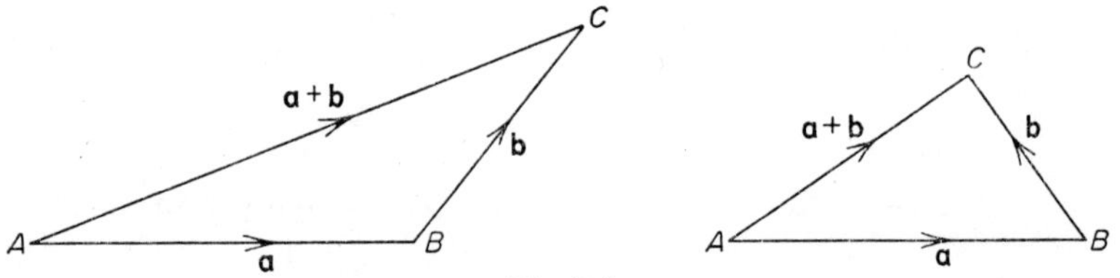

Fig. 2.5

The triangles *ABC* of Fig. 2.5 exists if **a**, **b** are not parallel or if neither **a** nor **b** is the zero vector **0**. If **a** and **b** are parallel or if $\mathbf{a} = \mathbf{0}$ or $\mathbf{b} = \mathbf{0}$ then the triangle degenerates to a straight line but definition 1 can still be applied. We shall now consider these cases:

(1)

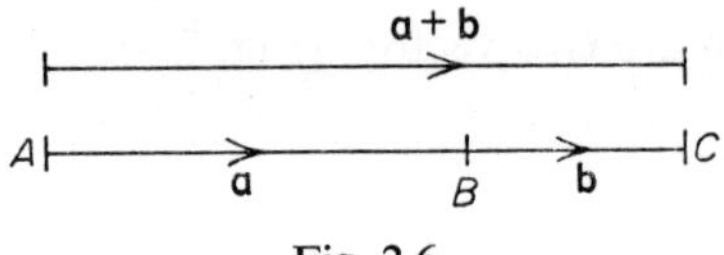

Fig. 2.6

Suppose **a** and **b** have the same direction and sense as in Fig. 2.6.

From the triangle law $\mathbf{a}+\mathbf{b} = \mathbf{AC}.$

Thus **AC** has the same direction and sense as **a** and **b**. Now

$$AC = AB+BC,$$

i.e. $|\mathbf{a}+\mathbf{b}| = |\mathbf{a}|+|\mathbf{b}|.$

Thus the modulus of the sum of two like vectors is equal to the sum of the moduli of the vectors.

(2)

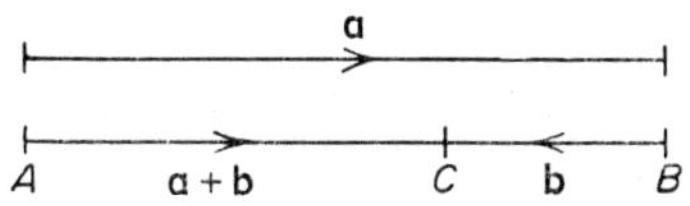

Fig. 2.7

Suppose **a** and **b** have the same direction but opposite sense and suppose that C is between A and B as in Fig. 2.7.

From the triangle law

$$\mathbf{a}+\mathbf{b} = \mathbf{AC}.$$

Thus **AC** has the same direction and sense as **a**.

Since

$$AC = AB - BC,$$

$$|\mathbf{a}+\mathbf{b}| = |\mathbf{a}| - |\mathbf{b}|.$$

Thus the modulus of the sum of two unlike unequal vectors is equal to the difference of the moduli of the vectors.

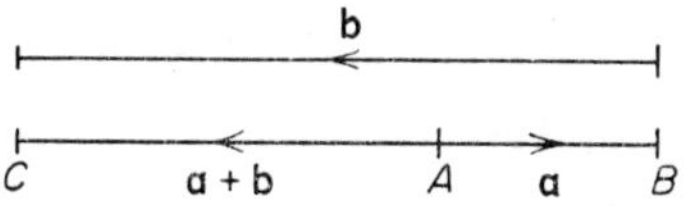

Fig. 2.8

Suppose **a** and **b** have the same direction but opposite sense and suppose C is on BA produced as in Fig. 2.8.

From the triangle law

$$\mathbf{a}+\mathbf{b} = \mathbf{AC}.$$

Thus **AC** has the same direction and sense as **b**.

Since

$$AC = BC - AB,$$

$$|\mathbf{a}+\mathbf{b}| = |\mathbf{b}| - |\mathbf{a}|.$$

Thus, as before, the modulus of the sum of two unlike unequal vectors is equal to the difference of the moduli of the vectors.

(3)

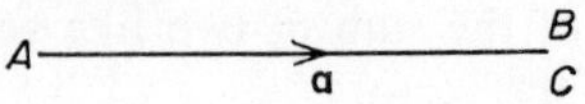

Fig. 2.9

Suppose $\mathbf{b} = \mathbf{BC} = \mathbf{0}$, that is B and C coincide as in Fig. 2.9.

From the triangle law
$$\mathbf{a}+\mathbf{b} = \mathbf{AC},$$
$$\therefore \quad \mathbf{a}+\mathbf{0} = \mathbf{a}.$$

In general, there is a vector $\mathbf{0}$ such that for all $\mathbf{p}$,
$$\mathbf{p}+\mathbf{0} = \mathbf{p}.$$

Suppose $\mathbf{a} = \mathbf{AB} = \mathbf{0}$, that is B and A coincide as in Fig. 2.10.

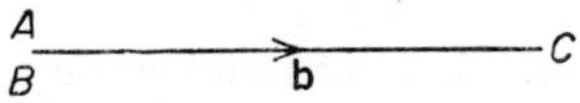

Fig. 2.10

From the triangle law $\qquad \mathbf{a}+\mathbf{b} = \mathbf{AC},$
$$\therefore \quad \mathbf{0}+\mathbf{b} = \mathbf{b}.$$

The statements $\qquad \mathbf{a}+\mathbf{0} = \mathbf{a}$ and $\mathbf{0}+\mathbf{b} = \mathbf{b}$

have their analogy in the identities
$$x+0 = x \quad \text{and} \quad 0+y = y$$
from the algebra of numbers.

(4)

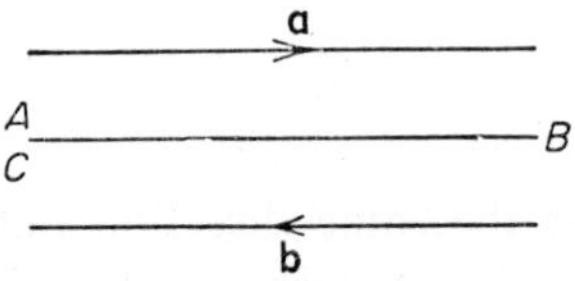

Fig. 2.11

Suppose $\mathbf{a}$ and $\mathbf{b}$ have the same direction but are opposite in sense (Fig. 2.11). Further suppose that their moduli are equal, i.e. A and C coincide.

From the triangle law $\qquad \mathbf{a}+\mathbf{b} = \mathbf{AC},$
$$\therefore \quad \mathbf{AB}+\mathbf{BA} = \mathbf{0}.$$

This means that the sum of two vectors of equal magnitude and direction but of opposite sense is the zero vector.

If we now define the vector $-\mathbf{AB}$ (known as the inverse or negative of $\mathbf{AB}$) as the vector having the same magnitude and direction as $\mathbf{AB}$ but of opposite sense we then have

$$-\mathbf{AB} = \mathbf{BA},$$

and
$$\mathbf{AB}+(-\mathbf{AB}) = \mathbf{0}.$$

Thus, in general, for all $\mathbf{p}$ there is an inverse or negative vector $-\mathbf{p}$ such that

$$\mathbf{p}+(-\mathbf{p}) = \mathbf{0}.$$

Since by definition $\qquad -\mathbf{AB} = \mathbf{BA}$

we have $\qquad -(-\mathbf{BA}) = \mathbf{BA}$

or, in general, $\qquad \mathbf{p} = -(-\mathbf{p}).$

The order of adding two vectors

The Commutative Law

We now return to the question asked in chapter 1. In number algebra the result of adding a number y to a number x is the same as adding the number x to the number y, i.e. the numbers x, y obey the Commutative Law:

$$x+y = y+x.$$

Now is the result of adding a vector $\mathbf{a}$ to a vector $\mathbf{b}$ the same as adding $\mathbf{b}$ to $\mathbf{a}$?

Suppose we represent the vectors $\mathbf{a}$ and $\mathbf{b}$ by $\mathbf{AB}$ and $\mathbf{BC}$ (Fig. 2.12).

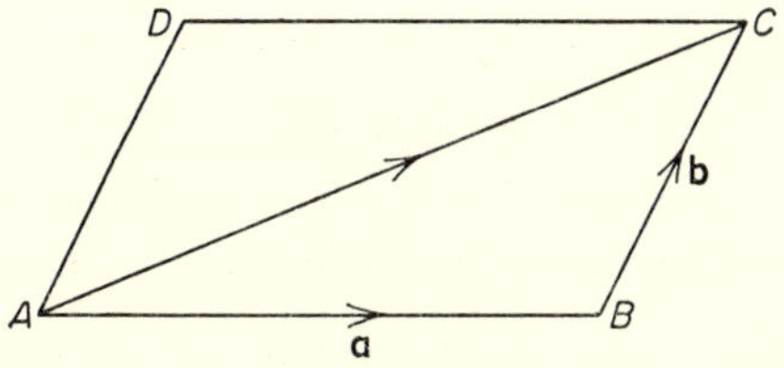

Fig. 2.12

Applying the triangle law of addition

$$\mathbf{a}+\mathbf{b} = \mathbf{AC}.$$

Now $\mathbf{a}$, $\mathbf{b}$ do not enter symmetrically into this relation, since the starting-point of $\mathbf{b}$ coincides with the end-point of $\mathbf{a}$. Thus we cannot conclude that **a** and **b** are interchangeable in the above relation. In other words, it is not obvious that

$$\mathbf{a}+\mathbf{b} = \mathbf{b}+\mathbf{a} = \mathbf{AC}.$$

To obtain **b**+**a** the parallelogram *ABCD* is completed and the triangle law is applied to the triangle *ADC*.

$$\mathbf{AD}+\mathbf{DC} = \mathbf{AC}.$$

But $$\mathbf{AD} = \mathbf{b} \quad \text{and} \quad \mathbf{DC} = \mathbf{a},$$

$$\therefore \quad \mathbf{b}+\mathbf{a} = \mathbf{AC}.$$

Thus we conclude $$\mathbf{a}+\mathbf{b} = \mathbf{b}+\mathbf{a}.$$

This has shown that vectors obey the Commutative Law when they are added by the triangle law.

Now consider the alternative method of addition, i.e. by the parallelogram law.

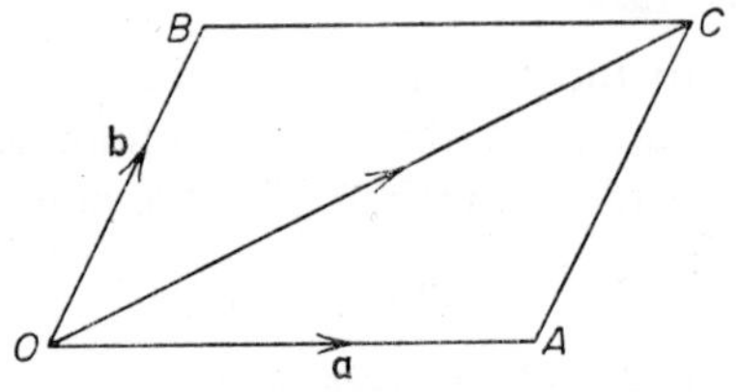

Fig. 2.13

Let **a** and **b** be represented by **OA** and **OB** (Fig. 2.13). Complete the parallelogram *OACB*. Then by the parallelogram law

$$\mathbf{a}+\mathbf{b} = \mathbf{OC}.$$

Now **a, b** enter symmetrically in this relation since the initial points of **a, b** coincide. This means that **a, b** are interchangeable and thus it is obvious that

$$\mathbf{a}+\mathbf{b} = \mathbf{b}+\mathbf{a}.$$

Alternatively by the parallelogram law

$$\mathbf{b}+\mathbf{a} = \mathbf{OC},$$

$$\therefore \quad \mathbf{a}+\mathbf{b} = \mathbf{b}+\mathbf{a}.$$

Thus addition defined by both the triangle and parallelogram laws leads to the same result

$$\mathbf{a}+\mathbf{b} = \mathbf{b}+\mathbf{a}.$$

This is to be expected in any case for we have shown the equivalence of the two definitions.

The order of adding several vectors

The Associative Law

We now discuss the addition of the vectors **a, b, c.** Suppose x, y, z are numbers. Consider adding x and y and then adding z to the result. This is denoted symbolically by using brackets as $(x+y)+z$. Now consider adding y and z and then adding the result to x, i.e. $x+(y+z)$.

The Associative Law for number–algebra states that

$$(x+y)+z = x+(y+z).$$

Now do vectors obey the same law? Is $(\mathbf{a}+\mathbf{b})+\mathbf{c}$ the same as $\mathbf{a}+(\mathbf{b}+\mathbf{c})$?

Suppose the result of $(\mathbf{a}+\mathbf{b})$ is **d,** and the result of $(\mathbf{b}+\mathbf{c})$ is **e.**

Then $$(\mathbf{a}+\mathbf{b})+\mathbf{c} = \mathbf{d}+\mathbf{c},$$

and $$\mathbf{a}+(\mathbf{b}+\mathbf{c}) = \mathbf{a}+\mathbf{e}.$$

It is by no means obvious that these last two results are the same.

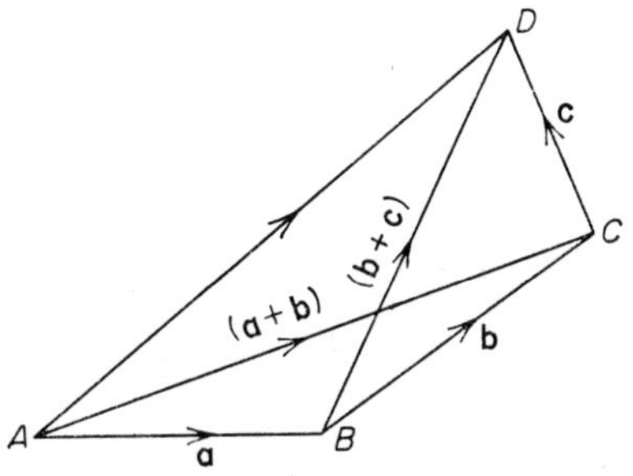

Fig. 2.14

Let **a, b, c,** not necessarily in the same plane, be represented by **AB, BC, CD** (Fig. 2.14). Then

$$\mathbf{a}+\mathbf{b} = \mathbf{AC},$$

and $$\mathbf{b}+\mathbf{c} = \mathbf{BD},$$

$$\therefore \quad (\mathbf{a}+\mathbf{b})+\mathbf{c} = \mathbf{AC}+\mathbf{c} = \mathbf{AD},$$

and $$\mathbf{a}+(\mathbf{b}+\mathbf{c}) = \mathbf{a}+\mathbf{BD} = \mathbf{AD},$$

$$\therefore \quad (\mathbf{a}+\mathbf{b})+\mathbf{c} = \mathbf{a}+(\mathbf{b}+\mathbf{c}).$$

Therefore the addition of three vectors obeys the Associative Law. This means that the order of adding is unimportant and we may omit the brackets, writing the vector sum as $\mathbf{a}+\mathbf{b}+\mathbf{c}$.

Extending this idea to several vectors $\mathbf{a}+\mathbf{b}+\mathbf{c}+\mathbf{d}+\mathbf{e}+\ldots$ we conclude that the sum of several vectors is independent of the order in which we add them.

Subtraction of vectors

Definition. *The subtraction of* **b** *from* **a** *is defined as the addition of the negative or inverse of* **b** *to* **a**, *i.e.*

$$\mathbf{a}-\mathbf{b} = \mathbf{a}+(-\mathbf{b}).$$

Thus to subtract **b** from **a** reverse the direction of **b** and add to **a**. Fig. 2.15 compares geometrically the processes of addition and subtraction of two vectors.

Let $\mathbf{OA} = \mathbf{a}$, $\mathbf{AB} = \mathbf{b}$. Then $\mathbf{OB} = \mathbf{a}+\mathbf{b}$.

Now to subtract **b** from **a** draw **AC** to represent **b** but in the opposite sense, i.e. draw $-\mathbf{b}$.

Then $$\mathbf{OC} = \mathbf{a}-\mathbf{b}.$$

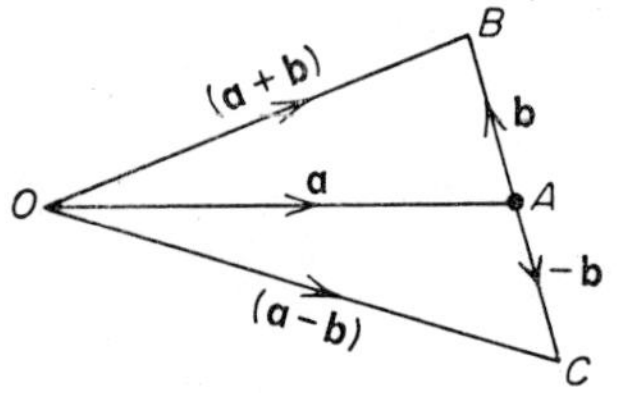

Fig. 2.15

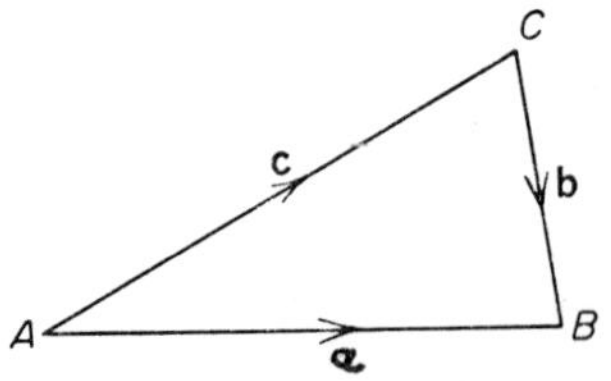

Fig. 2.16

Transposition of a vector in an equation

In Fig. 2.16, $\mathbf{AB} = \mathbf{a}$, $\mathbf{CB} = \mathbf{b}$, $\mathbf{AC} = \mathbf{c}$.

$$\left.\begin{aligned} \mathbf{AB}+\mathbf{BC} &= \mathbf{AC} \\ \therefore \quad \mathbf{a}-\mathbf{b} &= \mathbf{c}. \end{aligned}\right\} \qquad (1)$$

Also
$$\left.\begin{aligned} \mathbf{AB} &= \mathbf{AC}+\mathbf{CB} \\ \therefore \quad \mathbf{a} &= \mathbf{c}+\mathbf{b}. \end{aligned}\right\} \qquad (2)$$

From equations (1) and (2) we see that a vector may be transposed from one side of an equation to the other side providing the rules of algebra are obeyed.

Addition by inspection

It is not always necessary to draw a diagram to add two vectors. For example

$$\mathbf{PQ}+\mathbf{QR} = \mathbf{PR},$$

and

$$\mathbf{CD}-\mathbf{FD} = \mathbf{CD}+\mathbf{DF} = \mathbf{CF}.$$

We see that when the two inner letters are the same the vector representing the sum is given by the outer letters. This can be verified by drawing the appropriate diagrams.

Examples

(1) *Prove* $\mathbf{AB}-\mathbf{CB} = \mathbf{AC}$.

From Fig. 2.17,

$$\begin{aligned}\mathbf{AB}-\mathbf{CB} &= \mathbf{AB}+(-\mathbf{CB})\\ &= \mathbf{AB}+\mathbf{BC}\\ &= \mathbf{AC}.\end{aligned}$$

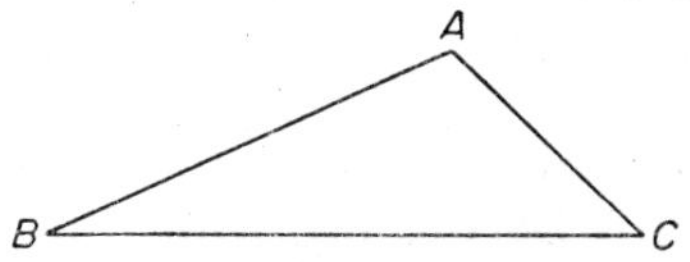

Fig. 2.17

(2) *ABCD is a quadrilateral. P and Q are the mid-points of AD and DC respectively. Show that* $\mathbf{PQ} = \mathbf{AP}+\mathbf{QC}$.

From Fig. 2.18,

$$\mathbf{PQ} = \mathbf{PD}+\mathbf{DQ}.$$

But

$$\mathbf{PD} = \mathbf{AP} \quad \text{and} \quad \mathbf{DQ} = \mathbf{QC},$$

$$\therefore \quad \mathbf{PQ} = \mathbf{AP}+\mathbf{QC}.$$

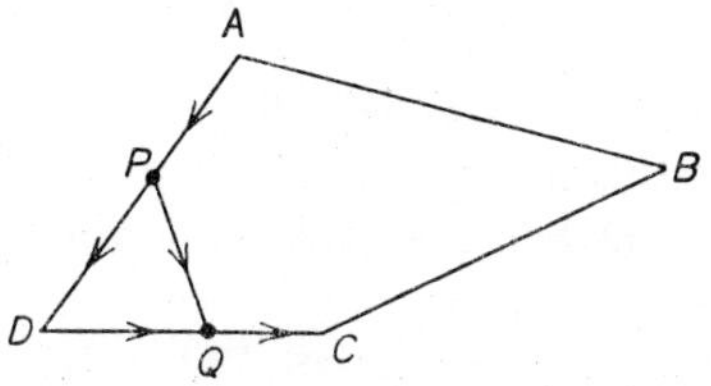

Fig. 2.18

3-2

(3) *ABCD is a quadrilateral. Show that* **BD** − **AC** = **CD** − **AB**.

Referring to Fig. 2.19 we see that **AD** can be expressed in two ways bringing in the required vectors:

$$\mathbf{AD} = \mathbf{AB}+\mathbf{BD}.$$

Also
$$\mathbf{AD} = \mathbf{AC}+\mathbf{CD},$$

$$\therefore \quad \mathbf{AB}+\mathbf{BD} = \mathbf{AC}+\mathbf{CD},$$

$$\therefore \quad \mathbf{BD}-\mathbf{AC} = \mathbf{CD}-\mathbf{AB}.$$

N.B. Instead of **AD** we can use **BC**.

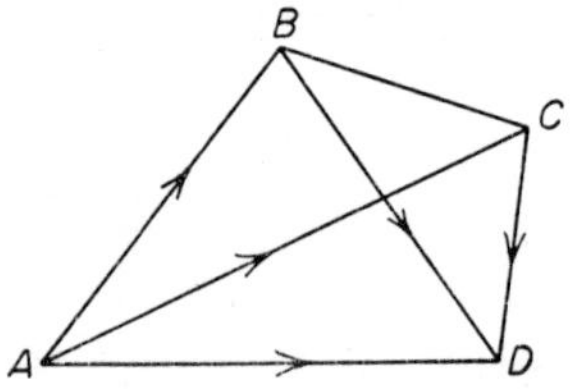

Fig. 2.19

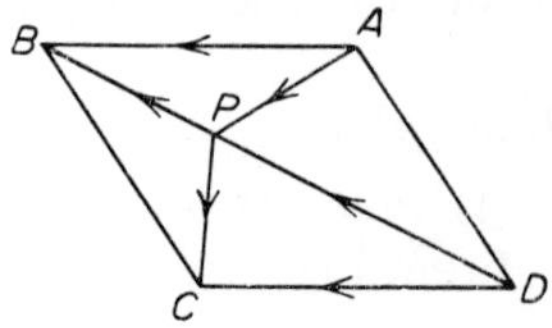

Fig. 2.20

(4) *ABCD is a quadrilateral and P is any point on BD. If*

$$\mathbf{AP}+\mathbf{PB}+\mathbf{PD} = \mathbf{PC}$$

prove that ABCD is a parallelogram.

We aim to get **AB** = **DC** (see Fig. 2.20).

$$\mathbf{AP}+\mathbf{PB}+\mathbf{PD} = \mathbf{PC} \text{ (given)},$$

$$\therefore \quad \mathbf{AP}+\mathbf{PB} = \mathbf{PC}-\mathbf{PD}$$

$$= \mathbf{PC}+\mathbf{DP},$$

$$\therefore \quad \mathbf{AB} = \mathbf{DC}.$$

Similarly,
$$\mathbf{AD} = \mathbf{BC}.$$

∴ *AB* is parallel to *DC* and *AD* is parallel to *BC*.

∴ *ABCD* is a parallelogram.

Note (*a*) In fact **AB** = **DC** is sufficient to prove *ABCD* is a parallelogram since this means that *AB* is parallel and equal to *DC* which leads to *ABCD* being a parallelogram by the well-known theorem in elementary geometry.

(*b*) The geometrical significance of **PQ** = **RS** is that *PQSR* is a parallelogram.

(5) *ABCDEF is a hexagon. If* **AB** = **a**, **BC** = **b**, **CD** = **c**, **DE** = **d**, *and* **EF** = **e**, *show that* **AF** = **a**+**b**+**c**+**d**+**e**.

From Fig. 2.21,

$$\begin{aligned} \mathbf{AC} &= \mathbf{AB}+\mathbf{BC} \\ &= \mathbf{a}+\mathbf{b}, \\ \mathbf{AD} &= \mathbf{AC}+\mathbf{CD} \\ &= \mathbf{a}+\mathbf{b}+\mathbf{c}, \\ \mathbf{AE} &= \mathbf{AD}+\mathbf{DE} \\ &= \mathbf{a}+\mathbf{b}+\mathbf{c}+\mathbf{d}, \\ \mathbf{AF} &= \mathbf{AE}+\mathbf{EF} \\ &= \mathbf{a}+\mathbf{b}+\mathbf{c}+\mathbf{d}+\mathbf{e}. \end{aligned}$$

This example shows how several vectors can be added by means of repeated applications of the triangle law. We shall now state this formally.

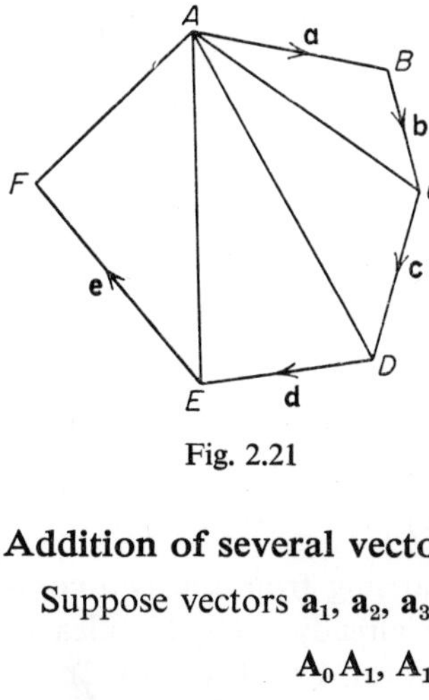

Fig. 2.21

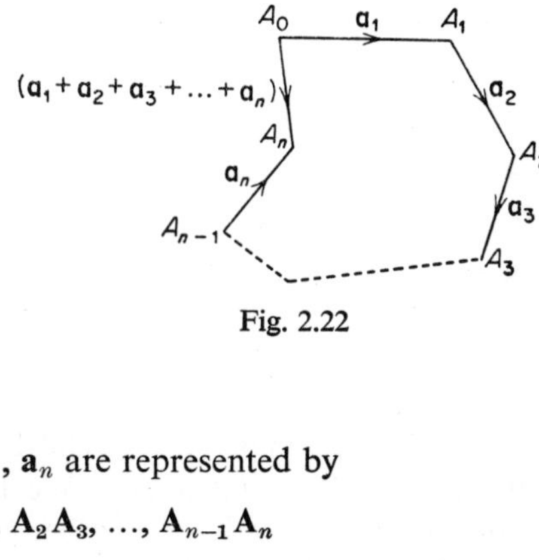

Fig. 2.22

Addition of several vectors

Suppose vectors $\mathbf{a}_1$, $\mathbf{a}_2$, $\mathbf{a}_3$, ..., $\mathbf{a}_n$ are represented by

$$\mathbf{A}_0\mathbf{A}_1,\ \mathbf{A}_1\mathbf{A}_2,\ \mathbf{A}_2\mathbf{A}_3,\ \ldots,\ \mathbf{A}_{n-1}\mathbf{A}_n$$

(Fig. 2.22). It is clear that A_0, A_1, A_2, ..., A_n are not necessarily points in the same plane.

The addition of the vectors is given by the law

$$\mathbf{a}_1+\mathbf{a}_2+\mathbf{a}_3+\ldots+\mathbf{a}_n = \mathbf{A}_0\mathbf{A}_n.$$

The vector $\mathbf{A}_0\mathbf{A}_n$ is sometimes known as the resultant of the vectors and $A_0A_1A_2A_3 \ldots A_n$ as the vector polygon.

Components of a vector

If the resultant of vectors **a** and **b** is **c**, i.e. $\mathbf{a}+\mathbf{b} = \mathbf{c}$, then the vectors **a** and **b** are known as the components in their particular directions of the vector **c**.

Suppose **AB** is a given vector and we require its components in two given directions.

Draw straight lines through A and B in the given directions (Fig. 2.23). Let the straight lines meet at C. Then since by construction,

$$\mathbf{AC}+\mathbf{CB} = \mathbf{AB},$$

the required components are **AC** and **CB.**

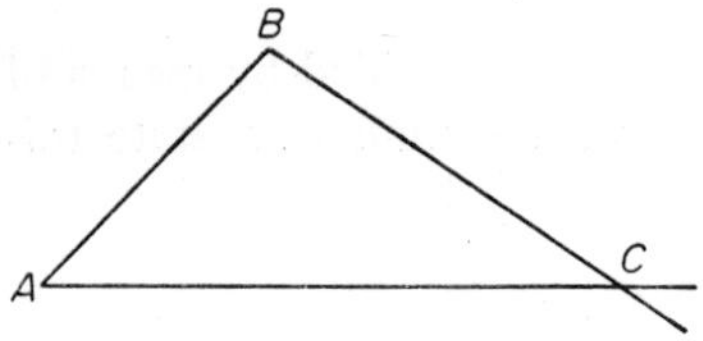

Fig. 2.23

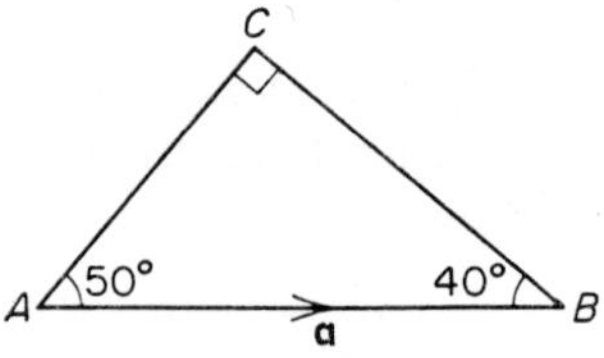

Fig. 2.24

Example

Obtain the moduli of the components of a vector **a** *which are inclined at* 50° *and* 40° *with it.*

Let $$\mathbf{AB} = \mathbf{a} \quad \text{(Fig. 2.24)}.$$

$$\therefore \quad |\mathbf{AB}| = |\mathbf{a}|.$$

Since $\mathbf{AC}+\mathbf{CB} = \mathbf{AB}$, **AC** and **CB** are the components.

$$|\mathbf{AC}| = |\mathbf{a}| \cos 50°,$$

and $$|\mathbf{CB}| = |\mathbf{a}| \cos 40°.$$

Note. This example is a special case arising from the two components being at right angles. We have already used this idea in writing vectors in ordered number-pair form, e.g. if $\mathbf{a} = (3, 2)$ the 3 and 2 can be regarded as the components of **a** in two particular directions. We shall develop this further in chapter 5.

Vector equations of a triangle and quadrilateral

The equations $$\mathbf{AB}+\mathbf{BC}+\mathbf{CA} = 0$$

and $$\mathbf{AB}+\mathbf{BC}+\mathbf{CD}+\mathbf{DA} = 0,$$

are the vector equations of a triangle ABC and a quadrilateral $ABCD$ respectively (Fig. 2.25).

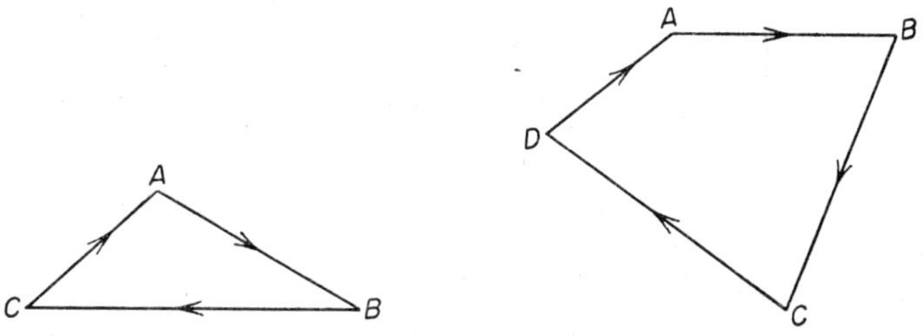

Fig. 2.25

Their proofs are left as an exercise (see Ex. 2, Question 1). These equations should be remembered since they are often useful as a starting-point in the solution of problems involving a triangle or quadrilateral (see Ex. 2, Question 8).

Similar vector equations hold for polygons of five or more sides. Thus in general the sum of the vectors forming the sides of a polygon taken in order is zero.

Exercise 2

(1) Prove: (i) $\mathbf{AB}+\mathbf{BC}+\mathbf{CA} = 0$, and (ii) $\mathbf{AB}+\mathbf{BC}+\mathbf{CD}+\mathbf{DA} = 0$.

(2) If $\mathbf{BC} = \mathbf{BA}+\mathbf{PQ}-\mathbf{CB}$ show that $\mathbf{AB}$ is parallel to $\mathbf{PQ}$.

(3) Prove that P coincides with R if $\mathbf{PQ}+\mathbf{PS} = \mathbf{RQ}+\mathbf{RS}$.

(4) O is any point within a triangle ABC. Prove that

$$\mathbf{OA}+\mathbf{CO} = \mathbf{CB}+\mathbf{BA}.$$

(5) **ABCD** is a parallelogram. If $\mathbf{AB} = \mathbf{a}$ and $\mathbf{BC} = \mathbf{b}$ show that $\mathbf{AC} = \mathbf{a}+\mathbf{b}$ and $\mathbf{BD} = \mathbf{b}-\mathbf{a}$.

(6) Show that the moduli of the components of a vector $\mathbf{r}$ which are inclined at 30° and 60° to it are

$$\frac{\sqrt{3}}{2}|\mathbf{r}| \quad \text{and} \quad \tfrac{1}{2}|\mathbf{r}|$$

respectively.

(7) If $\mathbf{AO}+\mathbf{OB} = \mathbf{BO}+\mathbf{OC}$ prove that A, B and C are collinear (i.e. they lie in a straight line).

(8) $ABCD$ is a quadrilateral with $\mathbf{AB} = \mathbf{DC}$. Prove that $ABCD$ is a parallelogram.

(9) Prove that a quadrilateral whose diagonals bisect each other is a parallelogram.

3

MULTIPLICATION AND DIVISION OF A VECTOR BY A NUMBER

Multiplication of a vector by a number

In number–algebra the repeated addition of x, for example $x+x+x+x+x$, is contracted to $5x$. We can extend this idea to the repeated addition of a vector. The vector $4\mathbf{p}$ represents $\mathbf{p}+\mathbf{p}+\mathbf{p}+\mathbf{p}$. Referring to Fig. 3.1,

$$
\begin{aligned}
\mathbf{AC} &= \mathbf{AB}+\mathbf{BC} \\
&= \mathbf{a}+\mathbf{a}+\mathbf{a}+\mathbf{a}+\mathbf{b}+\mathbf{b}+\mathbf{b} \\
&= 4\mathbf{a}+3\mathbf{b}.
\end{aligned}
$$

In the same way we can shorten $-\mathbf{a}-\mathbf{a}-\mathbf{a}-\mathbf{a}-\mathbf{a}$ to $(-5)\mathbf{a}$.

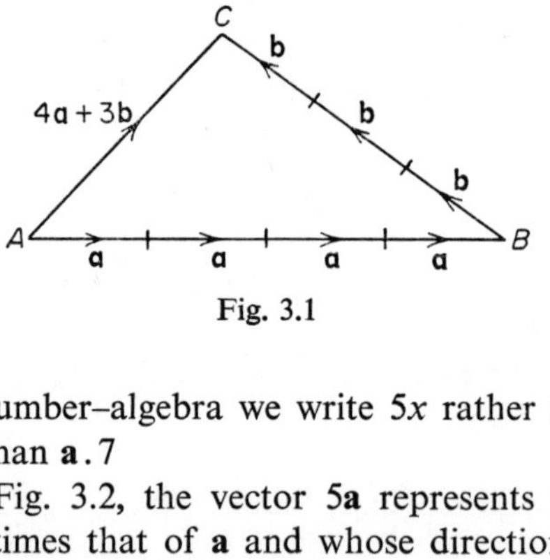

Fig. 3.1

Note. As in number–algebra we write $5x$ rather than $x.5$ so we write $7\mathbf{a}$ rather than $\mathbf{a}.7$

Referring to Fig. 3.2, the vector $5\mathbf{a}$ represents a vector whose magnitude is 5 times that of $\mathbf{a}$ and whose direction and sense are those of $\mathbf{a}$. The vector $(-4)\mathbf{a}$ represents a vector whose magnitude is 4 times that of $\mathbf{a}$ and whose direction is that of $\mathbf{a}$ but whose sense is opposite to that of $\mathbf{a}$.

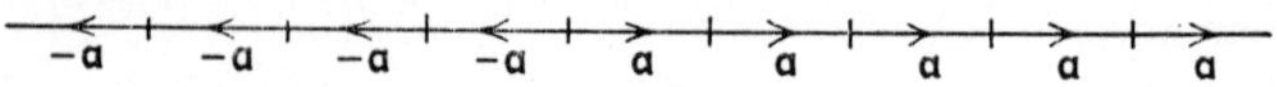

Fig. 3.2

Extending this idea if m is a positive integer then $m\mathbf{a}$ and $(-m)\mathbf{a}$ will represent vectors with magnitudes m times that of $\mathbf{a}$, with direction the same as that of $\mathbf{a}$, and in the case of $m\mathbf{a}$ with the same sense as $\mathbf{a}$ but in the case of $(-m)\mathbf{a}$ with the opposite sense as that of $\mathbf{a}$.

Now in order to further extend this idea to give a meaning to $\sqrt{3}\mathbf{a}$ or $\frac{3}{4}\mathbf{a}$ which cannot be shown geometrically by successive additions of $\mathbf{a}$ we make the following general definition.

Definition. *If m is any real number (positive or negative) and $\mathbf{a}$ a vector then $m\mathbf{a}$ is defined as the vector whose magnitude is $|m|$ times that of $\mathbf{a}$, whose direction is the same as that of $\mathbf{a}$ and with the same sense as $\mathbf{a}$ if m is positive but with opposite sense if m is negative.*

This definition does not apply when $\mathbf{a}$ is the zero vector or m is zero, in which case $m\mathbf{a}$ is the zero vector whose direction and sense are not defined. Thus

$$0\mathbf{a} = m\mathbf{0} = \mathbf{0}.$$

We have already defined a unit vector $\hat{\mathbf{a}}$ as the vector of modulus 1 and with the same sense and direction as that of $\mathbf{a}$. It therefore follows that

$$\mathbf{a} = |\mathbf{a}|\hat{\mathbf{a}} = a\hat{\mathbf{a}}$$

and

$$m\mathbf{a} = m|\mathbf{a}|\hat{\mathbf{a}} = ma\hat{\mathbf{a}}.$$

Division of a vector by a number

The definition of $m\mathbf{a}$ covers any real number. So if $m = 1/n$ where m is any real number then

$$m\mathbf{a} = (1/n)\mathbf{a} = \mathbf{a}/n.$$

We define the division of the vector $\mathbf{a}$ by the number n as the multiplication of $\mathbf{a}$ by $1/n$ resulting in a vector whose:

(1) magnitude is $1/|n|$ that of $\mathbf{a}$;

(2) direction is the same as that of $\mathbf{a}$;

(3) sense is the same as that of $\mathbf{a}$ if n is positive and opposite to that of $\mathbf{a}$ if n is negative.

This definition excludes the case of $\mathbf{a}$ being the zero vector.

We point out at this stage that if $\mathbf{a} = k\mathbf{b}$ then it is not correct to write $\mathbf{a}/\mathbf{b} = k$ since no division of vectors as an operation inverse to multiplication is possible. We can write $\mathbf{a}/k = \mathbf{b}$, however. We shall later show that we can attach a meaning to multiplication of two vectors.

Parallel vectors

In Fig. 3.3, $\mathbf{a} = 3\mathbf{b}$. This represents two parallel vectors of the same sense, the modulus of **a** being three times that of **b**, i.e. $|\mathbf{a}| = 3|\mathbf{b}|$. In the same way $\mathbf{p} = -5\mathbf{q}$ represents two parallel vectors of opposite senses, the modulus of **p** being five times that of **q**.

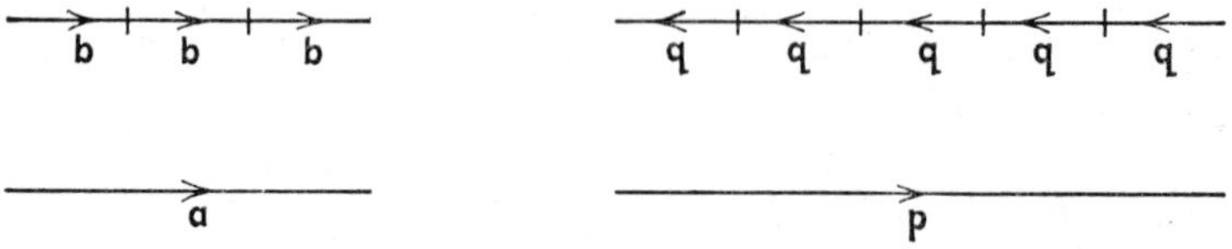

Fig. 3.3

In general $\mathbf{a} = m\mathbf{b}$ ($m \neq 0$, **a**, **b** not zero vectors) means that **a**, **b** are parallel vectors of the same sense if m is positive, but of opposite sense if m is negative, the modulus of **a** being $|m|$ times that of **b**.

Conversely, if **p** and **q** are two parallel vectors then **p** can be expressed as a multiple of **q**, i.e.

$$\mathbf{p} = k\mathbf{q}.$$

The value of k is given by $\pm|\mathbf{p}|/|\mathbf{q}|$, the plus sign to be taken if **p** and **q** have the same sense and the minus sign if they have opposite senses.

The laws of vector-number multiplication

In the algebra of numbers we have the following laws:

(1) *The Commutative Law:* $xy = yx$ which states the product of two numbers x, y, is independent of their order.

(2) *The Associative Law:* $x(yz) = (xy)z$ which states the order of multiplication of the numbers x, y, z does not matter. This law enables us to omit brackets in the product xyz.

(3) *The Distributive Law:* $(x+y)z = xz+yz$ which states the product of the sum of two numbers x, y and the number z is equal to the sum of the products xz and yz.

We have shown that numbers and vectors obey the Commutative and Associative Laws pertaining to addition. Now we shall show that vectors obey the same laws of number-multiplication. In terms of vectors **a**, **b** and numbers p, q, m, n these laws are

$$m\mathbf{a} = \mathbf{a}m \qquad \text{(Commutative Law),}$$

$$p(q\mathbf{a}) = (pq)\mathbf{a} \qquad \text{(Associative Law),}$$

$$\left.\begin{aligned}(p+q)\mathbf{a} &= p\mathbf{a}+q\mathbf{a}\\ n(\mathbf{a}+\mathbf{b}) &= n\mathbf{a}+n\mathbf{b}\end{aligned}\right\} \qquad \text{(Distributive Law).}$$

The Commutative Law

$m\mathbf{a} = \mathbf{a}m$

By definition the vector whose magnitude is $|m|$ times that of **a** and whose direction is the same as that of **a**, the sense of direction being determined by the sign of m, is written as $m\mathbf{a}$. However apart from the question of preference and analogy with number–algebra (5 times x written $5x$, not $x5$) there is no reason why it cannot be written as $\mathbf{a}m$. Thus by definition $m\mathbf{a} = \mathbf{a}m$.

The Associative Law

$p(q\mathbf{a}) = (pq)\mathbf{a}$

There are really five separate cases for the complete proof. We shall consider only two of them and leave the other three as an exercise.

(i) $p = 0$ or $q = 0$ or $\mathbf{a} = \mathbf{0}$.

In this case each side of $p(q\mathbf{a}) = (pq)\mathbf{a}$ is the zero vector and so the law is true for either $p = 0$ or $q = 0$ or $\mathbf{a} = \mathbf{0}$.

(ii) $p > 0$, $q > 0$, $\mathbf{a} \neq \mathbf{0}$.

$p(q\mathbf{a})$ is a vector of modulus $|p|\,|q\mathbf{a}|$, i.e. $|p|\,|q|\,|\mathbf{a}|$ and with the same direction and sense as $q\mathbf{a}$, i.e. with the same direction and sense as **a**.

$(pq)\mathbf{a}$ is a vector of modulus $|pq|\,|\mathbf{a}|$, i.e. $|p|\,|q|\,|\mathbf{a}|$ and with the same direction and sense as **a**.

Thus

$$p(q\mathbf{a}) = (pq)\mathbf{a}.$$

Exercise

Prove $p(q\mathbf{a}) = (pq)\mathbf{a}$ $(\mathbf{a} \neq \mathbf{0})$ for the following cases

(i) $p < 0$, $q < 0$;

(ii) $p > 0$, $q < 0$;

(iii) $p < 0$, $q > 0$.

The Distributive Laws

(1) $(p+q)\mathbf{a} = p\mathbf{a}+q\mathbf{a}$.

Again there are several cases and we shall prove three of them.

(i) $p = 0$, or $q = 0$, or $\mathbf{a} = \mathbf{0}$.

It immediately follows that $(p+q)\mathbf{a} = p\mathbf{a}+q\mathbf{a}$.

(ii) $p > 0, q > 0$.

Since p, q are both positive, $(p+q)$ is positive and hence $(p+q)\mathbf{a}$ has the same direction and sense as $\mathbf{a}$.

Modulus of $(p+q)\mathbf{a} = |p+q|\,|\mathbf{a}| = (p+q)\,|\mathbf{a}|$, since $p > 0, q > 0$.

Also since p, q are both positive, $p\mathbf{a}$ and $q\mathbf{a}$ have the same direction and sense as $\mathbf{a}$. Therefore the vector sum $p\mathbf{a}+q\mathbf{a}$ has the same direction and sense as $\mathbf{a}$.

Modulus of $(p\mathbf{a}+q\mathbf{a}) = |p\mathbf{a}|+|q\mathbf{a}|$ since we have shown the modulus of the sum of two like vectors is equal to the sum of their moduli.

$\therefore$ modulus of

$$(p\mathbf{a}+q\mathbf{a}) = |p|\,|\mathbf{a}|+|q|\,|\mathbf{a}| = (|p|+|q|)\,|\mathbf{a}| = (p+q)\,|\mathbf{a}|,$$

since $p > 0, q > 0$.

Hence $(p+q)\mathbf{a}$ and $(p\mathbf{a}+q\mathbf{a})$ both have the same modulus, direction and sense and therefore $(p+q)\mathbf{a} = p\mathbf{a}+q\mathbf{a}$.

(iii) $p < 0, q < 0, \mathbf{a} \neq \mathbf{0}$.

Since p, q are negative we can write $p = -m, q = -n$, where m, n are positive numbers.

From case (ii) since $m > 0, n > 0$,

$$(m+n)\,\mathbf{a} = m\mathbf{a}+n\mathbf{a},$$

$$\therefore\quad (-p-q)\,\mathbf{a} = -p\mathbf{a}-q\mathbf{a},$$

$$\therefore\quad (p+q)\,\mathbf{a} = p\mathbf{a}+q\mathbf{a}.$$

Exercise

Draw diagrams to illustrate $p\mathbf{a}+q\mathbf{a}$ $(\mathbf{a}\neq\mathbf{0})$ for

(i) $p < 0, q < 0$;

(ii) $p > 0, q < 0, |p| > |q|$;

(iii) $p > 0, q < 0, |p| < |q|$;

(iv) $p < 0, q > 0, |p| < |q|$;

(v) $p < 0, q > 0, |p| > |q|$;

(vi) $p = -q$.

Hence prove $(p+q)\,\mathbf{a} = p\mathbf{a}+q\mathbf{a}$ for each case. Also prove (ii)–(vi) using the method of case (iii).

(2) $n(\mathbf{a}+\mathbf{b}) = n\mathbf{a}+n\mathbf{b}$

This time there are three cases to be considered:

(i) $n = 0$ or $\mathbf{a} = \mathbf{0}$ or $\mathbf{b} = \mathbf{0}$.

It immediately follows that $n(\mathbf{a}+\mathbf{b}) = n\mathbf{a}+n\mathbf{b}$.

(ii) $n > 0$ $(\mathbf{a} \neq \mathbf{0}, \mathbf{b} \neq \mathbf{0})$.

Let OAC be a triangle with $\mathbf{OA} = \mathbf{a}$, $\mathbf{AC} = \mathbf{b}$ (Fig. 3.4).

$$\therefore \quad \mathbf{OC} = \mathbf{a}+\mathbf{b}.$$

Produce OA to B so that

$$\mathbf{OB} = n\mathbf{a} \quad (n>1).$$

From B draw BD parallel to AC, meeting OC produced at D.

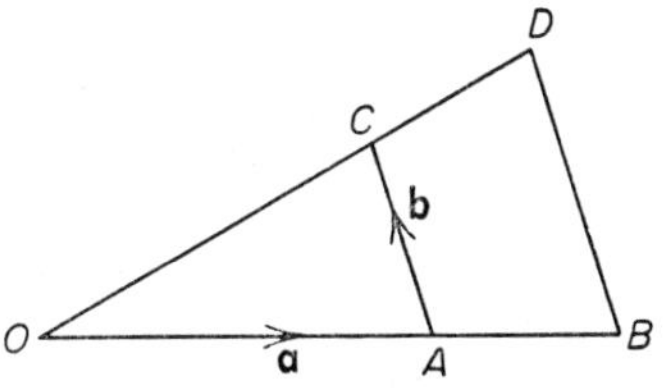

Fig. 3.4

Since triangles OAC, OBD are similar

$$\mathbf{BD} = n\mathbf{AC} = n\mathbf{b},$$

and

$$\mathbf{OD} = n\mathbf{OC} = n(\mathbf{a}+\mathbf{b}).$$

Also

$$\mathbf{OD} = \mathbf{OB}+\mathbf{BD} = n\mathbf{a}+n\mathbf{b},$$

$$\therefore \quad n(\mathbf{a}+\mathbf{b}) = n\mathbf{a}+n\mathbf{b}.$$

The proof is the same when $0 < n < 1$ but B is then on OA.

(iii) $n < 0$ $(\mathbf{a} \neq \mathbf{0}, \mathbf{b} \neq \mathbf{0})$.

Let $n = -m$ where $m > 0$.

Since $m > 0$ we can use the result of case (ii) and write

$$m(\mathbf{a}+\mathbf{b}) = m\mathbf{a}+m\mathbf{b},$$

$$\therefore \quad -n(\mathbf{a}+\mathbf{b}) = -n\mathbf{a}-n\mathbf{b},$$

$$\therefore \quad n(\mathbf{a}+\mathbf{b}) = n\mathbf{a}+n\mathbf{b}.$$

Summary

We have shown that the product of a vector and several numbers is independent of the order of multiplying. Also the product of a sum of numbers and a vector, or a sum of vectors and a number, is the same as the sum of the separate products obtained by the normal operation of removing brackets as in number–algebra.

Examples

(1) *If* $\mathbf{a}+2\mathbf{b} = \mathbf{c}$ *and* $\mathbf{a}-3\mathbf{b} = 2\mathbf{c}$ *show that* $\mathbf{a}$ *has the same sense as* $\mathbf{c}$ *and the opposite sense as* $\mathbf{b}$.

$$\mathbf{a}+2\mathbf{b} = \mathbf{c}, \quad \text{(i)}$$

$$\mathbf{a}-3\mathbf{b} = 2\mathbf{c}. \quad \text{(ii)}$$

Multiplying (i) by 3 and (ii) by 2 and adding we get

$$5\mathbf{a} = 7\mathbf{c},$$

$$\therefore \quad \mathbf{a} \text{ and } \mathbf{c} \text{ have the same sense.}$$

Multiplying (i) by 2 and subtracting (ii) we get

$$\mathbf{a}+7\mathbf{b} = 0,$$

$$\therefore \quad \mathbf{a} = -7\mathbf{b},$$

$$\therefore \quad \mathbf{a} \text{ and } \mathbf{b} \text{ have opposite senses.}$$

(2) *Prove that the opposite sides of a parallelogram are equal.*

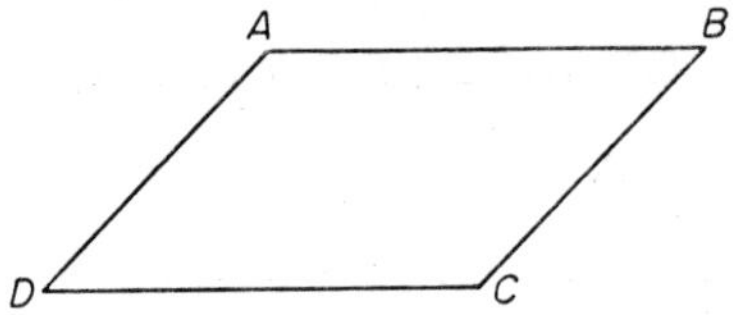

Fig. 3.5

Since AB and DC are parallel (Fig. 3.5),

$$\mathbf{AB} = x\mathbf{DC} \quad \text{where } x \text{ is a number.}$$

Similarly, $$\mathbf{BC} = y\mathbf{AD} \quad \text{where } y \text{ is a number.}$$

Now $$\mathbf{AB}+\mathbf{BC}+\mathbf{CD}+\mathbf{DA} = 0,$$

$$\therefore \quad x\mathbf{DC}+y\mathbf{AD}+\mathbf{CD}+\mathbf{DA} = 0,$$

$$\therefore \quad x\mathbf{DC}+y\mathbf{AD}-\mathbf{DC}-\mathbf{AD} = 0,$$

$$\therefore \quad (x-1)\,\mathbf{DC}+(y-1)\,\mathbf{AD} = 0,$$

$$\therefore \quad (x-1)\,\mathbf{DC} = -(y-1)\,\mathbf{AD}.$$

This implies that a vector parallel to **DC** is equal to a vector parallel to **AD** which is impossible unless both sides of the equation shown at bottom of page 38 are zero vectors.

$\therefore$ for the equation to hold true both $(x-1)$ and $(y-1)$ must be zero, since **DC**, **AD** are not zero vectors.

$$\therefore \quad x = 1 \quad \text{and} \quad y = 1,$$

$$\therefore \quad \mathbf{AB} = \mathbf{DC} \quad \text{and} \quad \mathbf{BC} = \mathbf{AD},$$

$$\therefore \quad AB = DC \quad \text{and} \quad BC = AD.$$

The vector median property of a triangle

AB+**AC** = 2**AO** where O is the mid-point of BC.

Proof

Let O be the mid-point of the side BC of the triangle ABC (Fig. 3.6):

$$\mathbf{AB} = \mathbf{AO}+\mathbf{OB},$$

$$\mathbf{AC} = \mathbf{AO}+\mathbf{OC},$$

$$\therefore \quad \mathbf{AB}+\mathbf{AC} = 2\mathbf{AO} \text{ (since } \mathbf{OB} = -\mathbf{OC}).$$

This important result should be remembered.

An alternative way of deriving it is to complete the parallelogram $ABDC$ and to use the parallelogram law of vector addition.

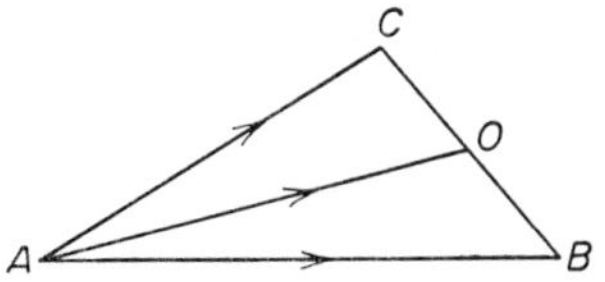

Fig. 3.6

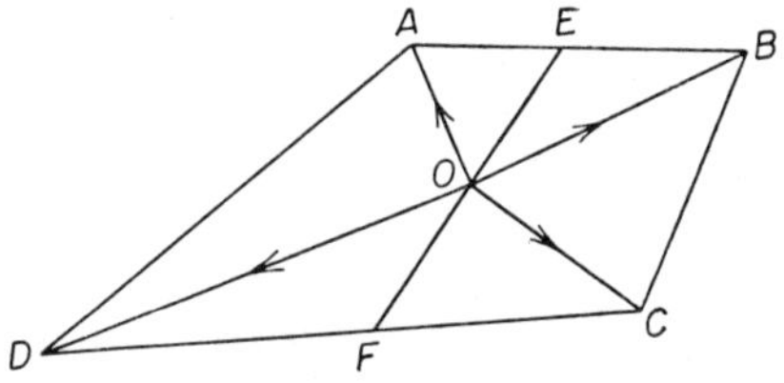

Fig. 3.7

Examples

(1) *ABCD is a quadrilateral and O is any point in its plane. Show that if* **OA**+**OB**+**OC**+**OD** = 0 *then O is the point of intersection of the lines joining the mid-points of the opposite sides of ABCD.*

Let E and F be the mid-points of AB and DC respectively (Fig. 3.7).

Then
$$\mathbf{OA}+\mathbf{OB} = 2\mathbf{OE},$$

and
$$\mathbf{OC}+\mathbf{OD} = 2\mathbf{OF},$$

$$\therefore \quad \mathbf{OA}+\mathbf{OB}+\mathbf{OC}+\mathbf{OD} = 2(\mathbf{OE}+\mathbf{OF}).$$

But $\quad \mathbf{OA}+\mathbf{OB}+\mathbf{OC}+\mathbf{OD} = 0$ (given),

$$\therefore \quad 2(\mathbf{OE}+\mathbf{OF}) = 0,$$

$$\therefore \quad \mathbf{OE} = -\mathbf{OF},$$

$$= \mathbf{FO}.$$

Therefore EOF is a straight line and O is the mid-point of EF. Similarly, O is the mid-point of GH where G and H are the mid-points of BC and AD respectively.

Therefore O is the point of intersection of the lines joining the mid-points of opposite sides of the quadrilateral.

(2) *$ABCDEF$ is a regular hexagon. If* $\mathbf{AB} = \mathbf{a}$ *and* $\mathbf{BC} = \mathbf{b}$, *show that* $\mathbf{AE} = 2\mathbf{b}-\mathbf{a}$ *and* $\mathbf{AF} = \mathbf{b}-\mathbf{a}$.

Referring to Fig. 3.8 since AD is parallel to BC and is twice BC

$$\mathbf{AD} = 2\mathbf{BC} = 2\mathbf{b},$$

$$\mathbf{DE} = -\mathbf{AB} = -\mathbf{a}.$$

Now $\quad \mathbf{AE} = \mathbf{AD}+\mathbf{DE},$

$$\therefore \quad \mathbf{AE} = 2\mathbf{b}-\mathbf{a}.$$

Also $\quad \mathbf{AF} = \mathbf{AE}+\mathbf{EF},$

$$= 2\mathbf{b}-\mathbf{a}-\mathbf{b} \quad (\text{since } \mathbf{EF} = -\mathbf{b}),$$

$$\therefore \quad \mathbf{AF} = \mathbf{b}-\mathbf{a}.$$

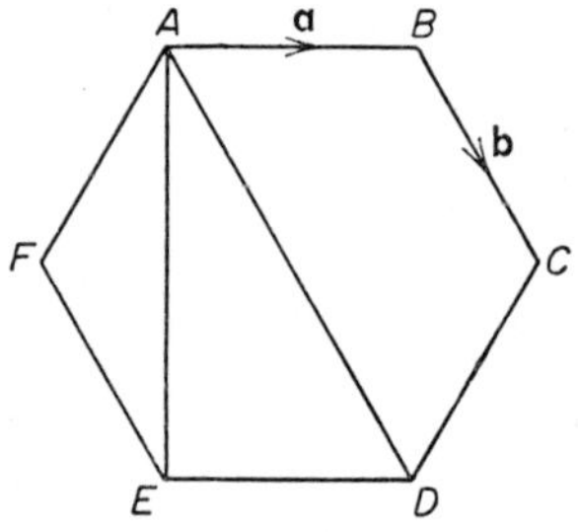

Fig. 3.8

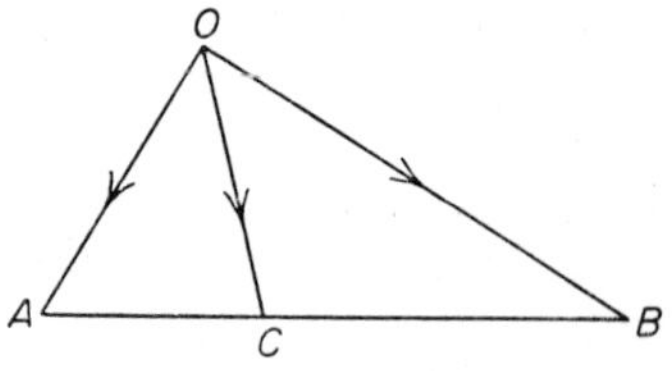

Fig. 3.9

(3) *Prove that* $m\mathbf{OA}+n\mathbf{OB} = (m+n)\,\mathbf{OC}$ *where C is a point dividing AB internally in the ratio of $n{:}m$ i.e. $AC{:}CB = n{:}m$ (m, n positive).*

From Fig. 3.9,

$$m\mathbf{OA}+n\mathbf{OB} = m(\mathbf{OC}+\mathbf{CA})+n(\mathbf{OC}+\mathbf{CB})$$

$$= (m+n)\,\mathbf{OC}+n\mathbf{CB}+m\mathbf{CA}.$$

But $$\frac{AC}{CB} = \frac{n}{m}$$

$$\therefore \quad m\mathbf{AC} = n\mathbf{CB},$$

$$\therefore \quad n\mathbf{CB} - m\mathbf{AC} = 0,$$

$$\therefore \quad n\mathbf{CB} + m\mathbf{CA} = 0,$$

$$\therefore \quad m\mathbf{OA} + n\mathbf{OB} = (m+n)\,\mathbf{OC}.$$

This result should be remembered.

(4) *ABCD is a parallelogram. E is the mid-point of AB. F is a point on DE such that DE = 3FE. Prove that A, F and C are collinear and that F is a point of trisection of AC.*

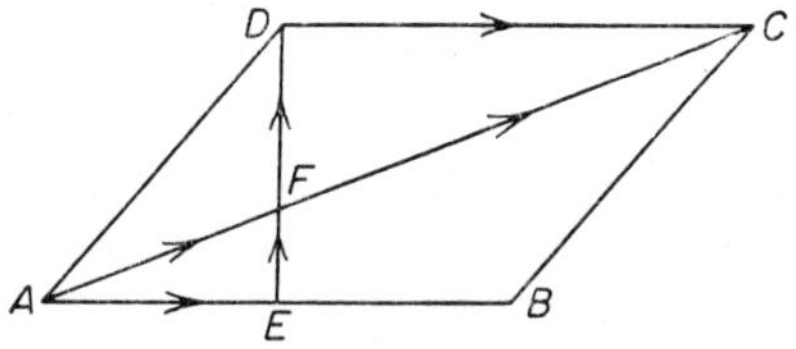

Fig. 3.10

Since $DE = 3FE,\ DF = 2FE$ (Fig. 3.10).

$$\mathbf{AF} = \mathbf{AE} + \mathbf{EF},$$

$$\mathbf{FC} = \mathbf{FD} + \mathbf{DC}.$$

But $$\mathbf{FD} = 2\mathbf{EF} \quad \text{and} \quad \mathbf{DC} = 2\mathbf{AE},$$

$$\therefore \quad \mathbf{FC} = 2\mathbf{AE} + 2\mathbf{EF},$$

$$\therefore \quad \mathbf{FC} = 2\mathbf{AF},$$

$\therefore$ A, F, C are collinear and $AC = 3AF$, i.e. F is a point of trisection of AC nearer to A.

Exercise 3

(1) Prove by completing the parallelogram $OADB$ that

$$\mathbf{OA} + \mathbf{OB} = 2\mathbf{OC},$$

where C is the mid-point of AB.

(2) Prove A, B and C are collinear if $2\mathbf{OA} - 3\mathbf{OB} + \mathbf{OC} = 0$.

(3) Prove that the line joining the mid-points of two sides of a triangle is parallel to the third side and equal to a half of it.

(4) *A, B, C* and *D* are any points. Prove

$$\mathbf{OA}+\mathbf{OB}+\mathbf{OC} = 3\mathbf{OD}+\mathbf{DA}+\mathbf{DB}+\mathbf{DC}.$$

(5) *ABCD* is a skew quadrilateral and *E, F, G* and *H* are the mid-points of *AB, BC, CD* and *DA* respectively. Prove *EFGH* is a parallelogram.

(6) *ABCD* is a quadrilateral with *E* and *F* the mid-points of *AB* and *DC* respectively. Show that $\mathbf{AD}+\mathbf{BC} = 2\mathbf{EF}$. Further if *X* and *Y* are the mid-points of *AC* and *BD* respectively show that

$$\mathbf{AB}+\mathbf{AD}+\mathbf{CB}+\mathbf{CD} = 4\mathbf{XY}.$$

(7) *ABC* is a triangle with *G* a point on the median *AD* such that $AG:GD = 2:1$. Prove that $\mathbf{BA}+\mathbf{BC} = 3\mathbf{BG}$.

(8) *ABCDEF* is a regular hexagon. If $\mathbf{AB} = \mathbf{a}$ and $\mathbf{BC} = \mathbf{b}$ show that $\mathbf{CD} = \mathbf{b}-\mathbf{a}$, $\mathbf{DE} = -\mathbf{a}$, $\mathbf{EF} = -\mathbf{b}$ and $\mathbf{FA} = \mathbf{a}-\mathbf{b}$.

(9) Prove that the diagonals of a parallelogram bisect one another. (*Hint.* Let *O* be the mid-point of one of the diagonals.)

(10) *ABC* is a triangle and *D* any point in *BC*. If

$$\mathbf{AD}+\mathbf{DB}+\mathbf{DC} = \mathbf{DE}$$

show that *ABEC* is a parallelogram and hence *E* is a fixed point.

(11) If *O* is the circumcentre of a triangle *ABC* and *H* the orthocentre prove that

$$\mathbf{OA}+\mathbf{OB}+\mathbf{OC} = \mathbf{OH} \quad \text{and} \quad \mathbf{HA}+\mathbf{HB}+\mathbf{HC} = 2\mathbf{HO}.$$

(*Hint.* Use geometrical fact $AH = 2OD$, where *D* is mid-point of *BC*.)

(12) *O* is a point within triangle *ABC* such that

$$\mathbf{OA}+\mathbf{OB}+\mathbf{OC} = 0.$$

Prove that *O* is the point of intersection of the medians.

4

POSITION VECTORS AND CENTROIDS

Definition. *If P is any point and O an origin then the position vector of P relative to O is the vector* **OP**.

We shall use **a**, **b**, **p**, **r**, ... to denote the position vectors of the points $A, B, P, R, \ldots$ relative to the origin O.

The use of position vectors enables vectors to be interpreted in algebraic terms resulting in a conciseness of expression.

The vector AB in terms of position vectors

Let the position vectors of A and B relative to the origin O be **a** and **b** (Fig. 4.1).

$$\mathbf{OA}+\mathbf{AB} = \mathbf{OB},$$

$$\therefore \quad \mathbf{AB} = \mathbf{OB}-\mathbf{OA},$$

$$\therefore \quad \mathbf{AB} = \mathbf{b}-\mathbf{a}.$$

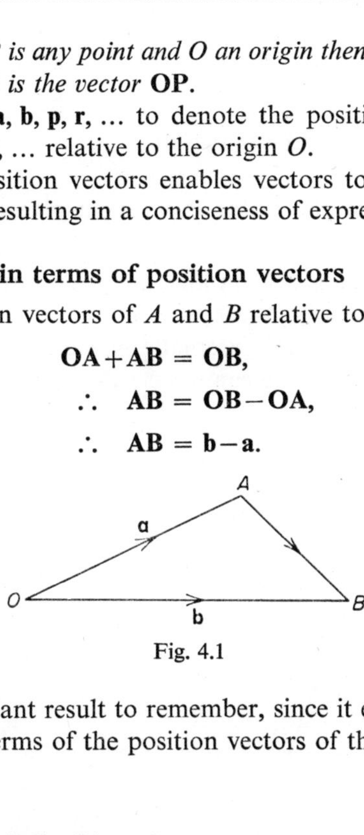

Fig. 4.1

This is an important result to remember, since it enables us to write a vector **AB** in terms of the position vectors of the points A and B.

Examples

(1) *Prove* $\mathbf{AB}+\mathbf{BC}+\mathbf{CA} = 0$.

Let the position vectors of A, B and C relative to an origin O be **a**, **b** and **c**.

Then $\quad \mathbf{AB}+\mathbf{BC}+\mathbf{CA} = \mathbf{b}-\mathbf{a}+\mathbf{c}-\mathbf{b}+\mathbf{a}-\mathbf{c} = 0.$

This is a result already known and proved without the use of position vectors in Ex. 2, Question 1.

(2) *If* **AB**$-$**BC**$-$**DC**$+$**AD** $= 0$ *prove ABCD is a parallelogram.*

Let the position vectors of A, B, C and D relative to an origin O be **a**, **b**, **c** and **d**.

$$\mathbf{AB}-\mathbf{BC}-\mathbf{DC}+\mathbf{AD} = 0,$$

$$\therefore\ \mathbf{AB}+\mathbf{CB}+\mathbf{CD}+\mathbf{AD} = 0,$$

$$\therefore\ (\mathbf{b}-\mathbf{a})+(\mathbf{b}-\mathbf{c})+(\mathbf{d}-\mathbf{c})+(\mathbf{d}-\mathbf{a}) = 0,$$

$$\therefore\ 2(\mathbf{b}-\mathbf{a})-2(\mathbf{c}-\mathbf{d}) = 0,$$

$$\therefore\ \mathbf{b}-\mathbf{a} = \mathbf{c}-\mathbf{d},$$

$$\therefore\ \mathbf{AB} = \mathbf{DC}.$$

Similarly, $$\mathbf{BC} = \mathbf{AD}.$$

Therefore *ABCD* is a parallogram.

Position vector of the point dividing a given straight line in a given ratio

A point can divide a straight line in a given ratio either internally or externally.

In Fig. 4.2 P divides AB internally in the ratio $m:n$. Taking the ratio $m:n$ to be positive we can write **AP** $= (m/n)$ **PB**.

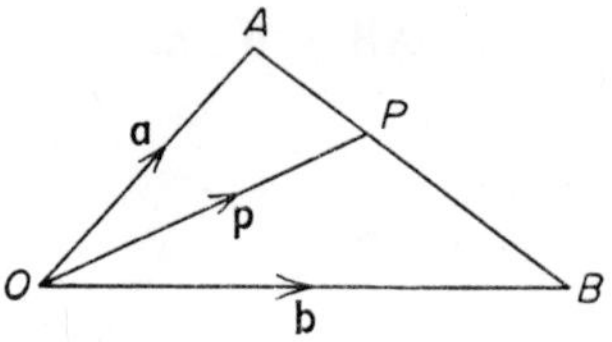

Fig. 4.2

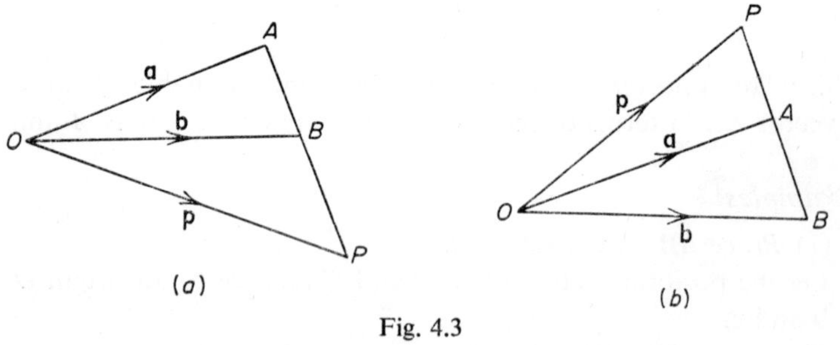

Fig. 4.3

In Fig. 4.3 (a) P divides AB externally and in Fig. 4.3 (b) P divides BA externally. Now if we take the ratio $m:n$ to be negative for the cases of external division we can still write $\mathbf{AP} = (m/n)\,\mathbf{PB}$. We note that in these cases if P is nearer to B then $m:n$ is between -1 and $-\infty$ and if P is nearer to A then $m:n$ is between 0 and -1.

Thus in all cases of division of a straight line into a given ratio by a point we have $\mathbf{AP} = (m/n)\,\mathbf{PB}$.

$$\therefore \quad n(\mathbf{p}-\mathbf{a}) = m(\mathbf{b}-\mathbf{p}),$$

where $\mathbf{a}$, $\mathbf{b}$, $\mathbf{p}$ are the position vectors of A, B, P relative to an origin O.

$$\therefore \quad n\mathbf{p}-n\mathbf{a} = m\mathbf{b}-m\mathbf{p},$$

$$\therefore \quad (m+n)\,\mathbf{p} = n\mathbf{a}+m\mathbf{b},$$

$$\therefore \quad \mathbf{p} = \frac{n\mathbf{a}+m\mathbf{b}}{m+n}. \qquad \text{(i)}$$

Thus (i) gives the required position vector whether the line is divided internally or externally. In the internal case $m:n$ is taken to be positive and in the external case $m:n$ is taken to be negative when substituting in (i).

A particular case of (i) occurs when $m = n = 1$, i.e. P is the mid-point of AB. We then have,

$$\text{position vector of mid-point of } AB = \frac{\mathbf{a}+\mathbf{b}}{2}. \qquad \text{(ii)}$$

The results (i) and (ii) should be remembered.

The result (i) can be written as

(*a*) $n\mathbf{OA}+m\mathbf{OB} = (m+n)\,\mathbf{OP}$ (see Ex. 3, p. 40),

or (*b*) $-(m+n)\,\mathbf{p}+n\mathbf{a}+m\mathbf{b} = 0$.

Writing $l = -(m+n)$ we have

$$l\mathbf{p}+n\mathbf{a}+m\mathbf{b} = 0.$$

Thus we see that if $\mathbf{p}$, $\mathbf{a}$, $\mathbf{b}$ are the position vectors of three distinct collinear points there are numbers l, m, n, different from zero, such that

$$l\mathbf{p}+n\mathbf{a}+m\mathbf{b} = 0 \quad \text{and} \quad l+m+n = 0.$$

The converse of this is true as now will be shown.

Condition for three points to be collinear

If $p\mathbf{a}+q\mathbf{b}+r\mathbf{c} = 0$ where $\mathbf{a}$, $\mathbf{b}$, $\mathbf{c}$ are the position vectors relative to an origin of the points A, B, C and $p+q+r = 0$ then A, B, C are collinear.

First proof. We have

$$p+q+r = 0 \text{ and } p\mathbf{a}+q\mathbf{b}+r\mathbf{c} = 0.$$

$$\therefore\quad p\mathbf{a}-(p+r)\,\mathbf{b}+r\mathbf{c} = 0,$$

$$\therefore\quad \mathbf{b} = \frac{p\mathbf{a}+r\mathbf{c}}{p+r}.$$

Therefore B is the point which divides the straight line AC internally or externally in the ratio $r:p$ according as whether $r:p$ is positive or negative.

Therefore A, B, C are collinear.

Second proof. Let the origin be O. Then

$$p\mathbf{OA}+q\mathbf{OB}+r\mathbf{OC} = 0.$$

$$\therefore\quad p(\mathbf{OB}+\mathbf{BA})+q(\mathbf{OB})+r(\mathbf{OB}+\mathbf{BC}) = 0,$$

$$\therefore\quad (p+q+r)\,\mathbf{OB}+p\mathbf{BA}+r\mathbf{BC} = 0.$$

But

$$p+q+r = 0,$$

$$\therefore\quad p\mathbf{BA}+r\mathbf{BC} = 0,$$

$$\therefore\quad p\mathbf{BA} = r\mathbf{CB}.$$

If $p:r$ is positive we have Fig. 4.4 (*a*).
If $p:r$ is negative we have Fig. 4.4 (*b*) or Fig. 4.4 (*c*).
Therefore A, B, C are collinear.

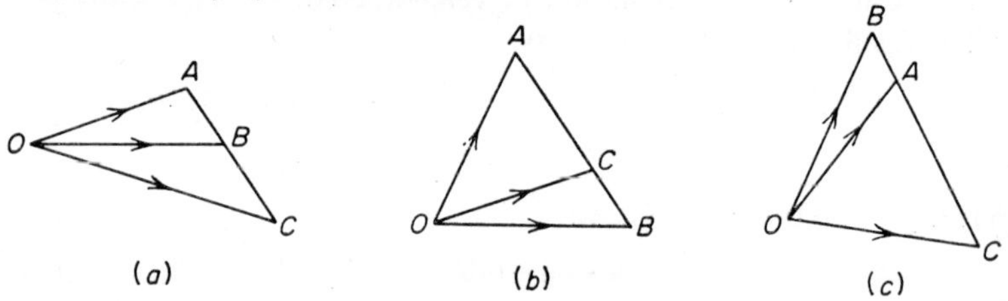

Fig. 4.4

Examples

(1) *ABC is a triangle with D the mid-point of BC and E a point on AC such that AE:EC* = 2:1. *Prove that the sum of the vectors* **BA, CA, 2BC** *is parallel to* **DE**.

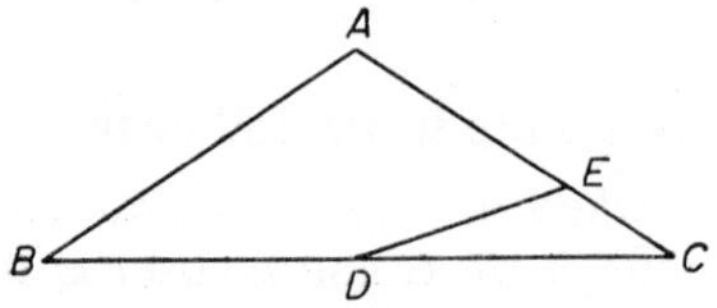

Fig. 4.5

Let **a**, **b**, **c**, **d** and **e** be the position vectors relative to an origin O of the points A, B, C, D and E (Fig. 4.5).

$$\mathbf{d} = \frac{\mathbf{b}+\mathbf{c}}{2},$$

$$\mathbf{e} = \frac{\mathbf{a}+2\mathbf{c}}{3}.$$

$$\begin{aligned}\mathbf{DE} &= \mathbf{e}-\mathbf{d}\\ &= \frac{\mathbf{a}+2\mathbf{c}}{3}-\frac{\mathbf{b}+\mathbf{c}}{2}\\ &= \frac{2\mathbf{a}-3\mathbf{b}+\mathbf{c}}{6}.\end{aligned}$$

$$\begin{aligned}\mathbf{BA}+\mathbf{CA}+2\mathbf{BC} &= (\mathbf{a}-\mathbf{b})+(\mathbf{a}-\mathbf{c})+2(\mathbf{c}-\mathbf{b})\\ &= 2\mathbf{a}-3\mathbf{b}+\mathbf{c}\\ &= 6\mathbf{DE}.\end{aligned}$$

Therefore $\mathbf{BA}+\mathbf{CA}+2\mathbf{BC}$ is parallel to **DE**.

(2) *Show that if* $7\mathbf{AB}-2\mathbf{AC}-5\mathbf{AD} = 0$ *the points B, C and D are collinear.*

Using the condition for collinearity since

$$7\mathbf{AB}-2\mathbf{AC}-5\mathbf{AD} = 0$$

and sum of coefficients $= 7-2-5$
$= 0,$

then B, C and D are collinear.

Centroid of a number of points

Definition. *The centroid or mean centre of n points* $A_1, A_2, \ldots, A_n$ *with position vectors* $\mathbf{a}_1, \mathbf{a}_2, \ldots, \mathbf{a}_n$ *respectively is the point with position vector*

$$\frac{\mathbf{a}_1+\mathbf{a}_2+\ldots+\mathbf{a}_n}{n}.$$

If $m_1, m_2, \ldots, m_n$ *are real numbers the point with position vector*

$$\frac{m_1\mathbf{a}_1+m_2\mathbf{a}_2+\ldots+m_n\mathbf{a}_n}{m_1+m_2+\ldots+m_n}$$

is defined as the centroid or weighted mean centre of the given points with associated numbers or weights $m_1, m_2, \ldots, m_n$.

There are two important theorems concerning centroids; the first showing that the position of the centroid is independent of the origin taken for the position vectors, and the second showing how the centroid of a number of points is obtained from a consideration of the centroids of systems forming the points.

Theorem I. *The centroid is independent of the origin.*

Proof. Consider points $A, B, C, \ldots$ with associated numbers $p, q, r, \ldots$. Let the position vector of point A relative to O be $\mathbf{a}$ and relative to O_1 be $\mathbf{a}_1$ (Fig. 4.6). Let position vector of O_1 relative to O be $\mathbf{h}$.

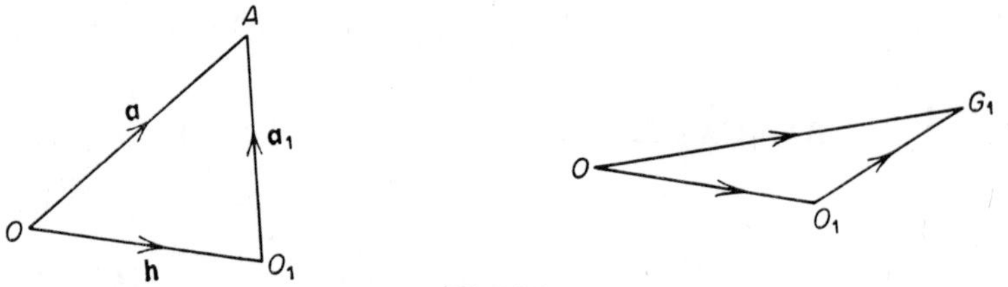

Fig. 4.6

Then
$$\mathbf{OO_1}+\mathbf{O_1A} = \mathbf{OA},$$
$$\therefore \quad \mathbf{h}+\mathbf{a}_1 = \mathbf{a},$$
$$\therefore \quad \mathbf{a}_1 = \mathbf{a}-\mathbf{h}.$$

Similarly, if $\mathbf{b}$, $\mathbf{c}$, ... are position vectors of the points B, C, ... relative to the origin O then $(\mathbf{b}-\mathbf{h})$, $(\mathbf{c}-\mathbf{h})$, ... are their position vectors relative to O_1.

Let G and G_1 be the centroids of the points with O and O_1 as origins respectively.

$$\therefore \quad \mathbf{OG} = \frac{p\mathbf{a}+q\mathbf{b}+r\mathbf{c}+\ldots}{p+q+r+\ldots},$$

and
$$\mathbf{O_1G_1} = \frac{p\mathbf{a}_1+q\mathbf{b}_1+r\mathbf{c}_1+\ldots}{p+q+r+\ldots}$$
$$= \frac{p(\mathbf{a}-\mathbf{h})+q(\mathbf{b}-\mathbf{h})+r(\mathbf{c}-\mathbf{h})+\ldots}{p+q+r+\ldots}$$
$$= \frac{(p\mathbf{a}+q\mathbf{b}+r\mathbf{c}+\ldots)-\mathbf{h}(p+q+r+\ldots)}{p+q+r+\ldots}$$
$$= \frac{p\mathbf{a}+q\mathbf{b}+r\mathbf{c}+\ldots}{p+q+r+\ldots}-\mathbf{h}.$$

Now $$\mathbf{OG_1} = \mathbf{OO_1}+\mathbf{O_1G_1},$$

$$\therefore\quad \mathbf{OG_1} = \mathbf{h}+\frac{p\mathbf{a}+q\mathbf{b}+r\mathbf{c}+\dots}{p+q+r+\dots}-\mathbf{h}$$

$$= \frac{p\mathbf{a}+q\mathbf{b}+r\mathbf{c}+\dots}{p+q+r+\dots},$$

$$\therefore\quad \mathbf{OG_1} = \mathbf{OG}.$$

Therefore G_1 coincides with G.

Therefore centroid is independent of the origin.

Theorem II. *If H is the centroid of a system of points $A, B, C, \dots$ with associated numbers $p, q, r, \dots$ and H' is the centroid of a second system of points $A', B'\ C' \dots$ with associated numbers $p', q'\ r', \dots$ then the centroid of all the points is the centroid of the two points H and H' with associated numbers $(p+q+r+\dots)$ and $(p'+q'+r'+\dots)$ respectively.*

Proof. Let the origin be O and G the centroid of all the points.

$$\mathbf{OH} = \frac{p\mathbf{a}+q\mathbf{b}+r\mathbf{c}+\dots}{p+q+r+\dots} = \frac{\Sigma(p\mathbf{a})}{\Sigma p},$$

$$\mathbf{OH'} = \frac{p'\mathbf{a}'+q'\mathbf{b}'+r'\mathbf{c}'+\dots}{p'+q'+r'+\dots} = \frac{\Sigma(p'\mathbf{a}')}{\Sigma p'},$$

$$\mathbf{OG} = \frac{(p\mathbf{a}+q\mathbf{b}+r\mathbf{c}+\dots)+(p'\mathbf{a}'+q'\mathbf{b}'+r'\mathbf{c}'+\dots)}{(p+q+r+\dots)+(p'+q'+r'+\dots)}.$$

$$\therefore\quad \mathbf{OG} = \frac{\Sigma(p\mathbf{a})+\Sigma(p'\mathbf{a}')}{\Sigma p+\Sigma p'}$$

$$= \frac{(\Sigma p)\,\mathbf{OH}+(\Sigma p')\,\mathbf{OH'}}{\Sigma p+\Sigma p'}.$$

But this represents the position vector of the centroid of points H and H' associated with the numbers Σp and $\Sigma p'$ respectively. Thus the theorem is proved.

The theorem can be extended for more than two systems, that is,

$$\mathbf{OG} = \frac{(\Sigma p)\,\mathbf{OH}+(\Sigma p')\,\mathbf{OH'}+(\Sigma p')\,\mathbf{OH''}+\dots}{\Sigma p+\Sigma p'+\Sigma p''+\dots}.$$

Examples

(1) *Show that the centroid of the points A and B with associated numbers p and q respectively is the point C on AB such that*

$$AC:CB = q:p.$$

Let **a** and **b** be the position vectors relative to a fixed origin of the points A and B respectively.

Position vector of centroid $= \dfrac{p\mathbf{a}+q\mathbf{b}}{p+q}$.

Position vector of point $C = \dfrac{p\mathbf{a}+q\mathbf{b}}{p+q}$.

Therefore centroid and the point C coincide.

Note. When $p = q = 1$, the centroid is the mid-point of AB.

(2) *Prove that the centroid of the vertices of a triangle is a point of trisection of a median and hence deduce that the medians are concurrent.*

Let D be the mid-point of BC and G the centroid of A, B and C (Fig. 4.7). Let **a**, **b** and **c** be the position vectors of A, B and C relative to a fixed origin.

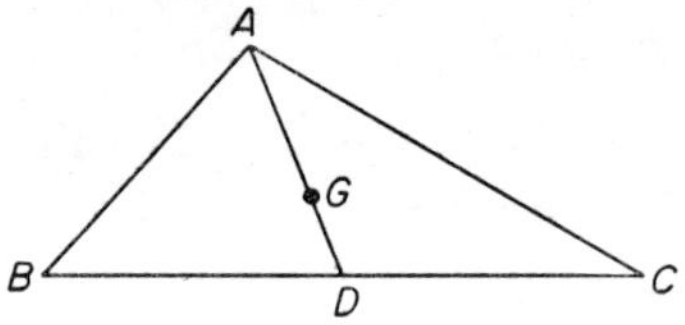

Fig. 4.7

Position vector of $G = \dfrac{\mathbf{a}+\mathbf{b}+\mathbf{c}}{3}$.

Position vector of $D = \dfrac{\mathbf{b}+\mathbf{c}}{2}$.

Position vector of centroid of B and $C = \dfrac{\mathbf{b}+\mathbf{c}}{2}$.

Therefore D is the centroid of B and C.

Therefore centroid of A, B and C must lie on AD, i.e. G is on AD.

Suppose

$$AG:GD = m:n.$$

Therefore position vector of $G = \dfrac{n\mathbf{a}+m\dfrac{\mathbf{b}+\mathbf{c}}{2}}{m+n}$,

$$\therefore \quad \frac{n\mathbf{a}+m\dfrac{\mathbf{b}+\mathbf{c}}{2}}{m+n} = \frac{\mathbf{a}+\mathbf{b}+\mathbf{c}}{3},$$

$$\therefore \quad m:n = 2:1.$$

Therefore centroid is a point of trisection of the median *AD*. Since the position vector of the centroid is symmetrical in **a**, **b** and **c** the centroid is a point of trisection of all the medians and thus all the medians are concurrent. The point of intersection of the medians, i.e. the centroid is one third of the way up each median from the base.

(3) *ABCD is a tetrahedron. Show that the lines joining the vertices of the tetrahedron to the centroids of opposite faces intersect in a point dividing these lines in the ratio* 3:1. *Also show that this point is the centroid of the vertices of the tetrahedron.*

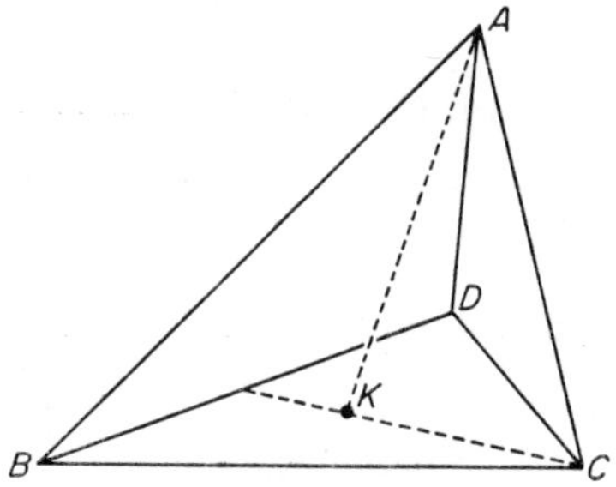

Fig. 4.8

Let the position vectors of *A*, *B*, *C* and *D* relative to a fixed origin be **a**, **b**, **c** and **d** (Fig. 4.8). Let centroid of face *BCD* be *K*.

Position vector of centroid of *B*, *C* and $D = \dfrac{\mathbf{b}+\mathbf{c}+\mathbf{d}}{3}$.

Centroid of vertices *A*, *B*, *C* and *D* must lie on *AK*.

But position vector of centroid of *A*, *B*, *C* and $D = \dfrac{\mathbf{a}+\mathbf{b}+\mathbf{c}+\mathbf{d}}{4}$

$$= \frac{1.\mathbf{a}+3\dfrac{\mathbf{b}+\mathbf{c}+\mathbf{d}}{3}}{4}.$$

But this is the position vector of a point *G* on *AK* such that $AG:GK = 3:1$.

By symmetry G must also lie on the corresponding lines through B, C and D.

Therefore the lines joining the vertices to the centroids of the opposite faces are concurrent at a point of quadrisection of each line, this point also being the centroid of the four vertices.

(4) *Prove that if G is the centroid of n points $A_1, A_2, \ldots, A_n$ and G' is the centroid of n points $B_1, B_2, \ldots, B_n$ then*

$$\mathbf{A_1B_1}+\mathbf{A_2B_2}+\ldots+\mathbf{A_nB_n} = n\mathbf{GG'}.$$

Let the position vectors of $A_1, A_2, \ldots, A_n$ and $B_1, B_2, \ldots, B_n$ relative to a fixed origin be

$\mathbf{a}_1, \mathbf{a}_2, \ldots, \mathbf{a}_n$ and $\mathbf{b}_1, \mathbf{b}_2, \ldots, \mathbf{b}_n$ respectively.

Then

$$\begin{aligned}\mathbf{A_1B_1}+\mathbf{A_2B_2}+\ldots+\mathbf{A_nB_n} &= (\mathbf{b}_1-\mathbf{a}_1)+(\mathbf{b}_2-\mathbf{a}_2)+\ldots+(\mathbf{b}_n-\mathbf{a}_n)\\ &= (\mathbf{b}_1+\mathbf{b}_2+\ldots+\mathbf{b}_n)-(\mathbf{a}_1+\mathbf{a}_2+\ldots+\mathbf{a}_n).\end{aligned}$$

Now position vector of $G = \dfrac{\mathbf{a}_1+\mathbf{a}_2+\ldots+\mathbf{a}_n}{n} = \mathbf{g}$, and position vector of $G' = \dfrac{\mathbf{b}_1+\mathbf{b}_2+\ldots+\mathbf{b}_n}{n} = \mathbf{g}'$.

$$\begin{aligned}\therefore\quad \mathbf{A_1B_1}+\mathbf{A_2B_2}+\ldots+\mathbf{A}_n\mathbf{B}_n &= n(\mathbf{g}'-\mathbf{g})\\ &= n\mathbf{GG'}.\end{aligned}$$

Exercise 4

(1) Prove that the position vector of the point Q which divides AB externally such that $AQ:QB = m:n$ ($m:n$ positive) is $\dfrac{n\mathbf{a}-m\mathbf{b}}{n-m}$, where $\mathbf{a}$ and $\mathbf{b}$ are the position vectors of A and B relative to a fixed origin.

(2) The position vectors of the points P and Q are $\mathbf{p}$ and $\mathbf{q}$ respectively. PQ is divided internally at R and externally at S so that $PR:RQ = PS:QS = m:1$. Show that $\mathbf{RS} = \dfrac{2m(\mathbf{p}-\mathbf{q})}{1-m^2}$.

(3) The medians of a triangle ABC intersect at G. Prove that $\mathbf{GA}+\mathbf{GB}+\mathbf{GC} = 0$.

(4) $OABC$ is a tetrahedron with $\mathbf{OA} = \mathbf{a}$, $\mathbf{OB} = \mathbf{b}$ and $\mathbf{OC} = \mathbf{c}$. P and Q are the mid-points of OA and BC respectively. Find in terms of $\mathbf{a}$, $\mathbf{b}$ and $\mathbf{c}$ the position vector of the mid-point of PQ relative to

O as the origin, and hence deduce that the joins of the mid-points of opposite edges of a tetrahedron are concurrent and bisect each other.

(5) G and G' are the mid-points of PQ and $P'Q'$ respectively. Prove that $\mathbf{PP}'+\mathbf{QQ}' = 2\mathbf{GG}'$.

(6) Prove that the diagonals of a parallelepiped are concurrent and bisect one another.

(7) The position vectors of four points P, Q, R and S are $\mathbf{a}$, $\mathbf{a}+\mathbf{p}$, $\mathbf{a}+\mathbf{q}$, and $\mathbf{a}+\mathbf{p}+\mathbf{q}$ respectively. Prove that $PQSR$ is a parallelogram.

(8) The position vectors of three points are $\mathbf{p}$, $\mathbf{q}$ and $5\mathbf{p}-4\mathbf{q}$. Show that the points are collinear.

(9) Show that the centroid of two points A and B associated with the numbers 3 and 1 respectively is the point of quadrisection of AB nearer to A.

(10) $ABCD$ is a quadrilateral with P and Q the mid-points of AB and DC respectively. Prove that the centroid of A, B, C and D is the mid-point of PQ. Hence deduce that the straight lines joining the mid-points of opposite sides and the straight line joining the mid-points of the diagonals are concurrent.

(11) $ABCD$ is a parallelogram. E is on AD such that

$AE:ED = 1:n-1$. BE meets the diagonal AC at P. If

$$AP:AC = 1:x$$

show that $\mathbf{AB}+n\mathbf{AE} = x\mathbf{AP}$. Hence show that BE divides AC in the ratio of $1:n$.

(12) Show that the centroid of the points A, B and C with associated numbers a, b and c respectively is the incentre of the triangle ABC with sides BC, CA and AB of length a, b and c respectively.

(13) Prove that $p_1\mathbf{A}_1\mathbf{B}_1+p_2\mathbf{A}_2\mathbf{B}_2+\ldots+p_n\mathbf{A}_n\mathbf{B}_n = N\mathbf{GG}'$ where $N = p_1+p_2+\ldots+p_n$, G is the centroid of $A_1, A_2, \ldots, A_n$ with associated numbers $p_1, p_2, \ldots, p_n$ respectively, and G' is the centroid of $B_1, B_2, \ldots, B_n$ with associated numbers $p_1, p_2, \ldots, p_n$ respectively.

5

PROJECTION AND COMPONENTS OF A VECTOR

Before we discuss what is meant by the projection of a vector we must define the angle between two vectors.

Angle between two vectors

Definition. *The angle between two vectors* **a**, **b** *is the angle AOB where* **OA** = **a**, **OB** = **b**.

Referring to Fig. 5.1 the angle between the vectors **a**, **b** is denoted by θ. The usual convention is used, i.e. angles measured in an anti-clockwise sense are positive.

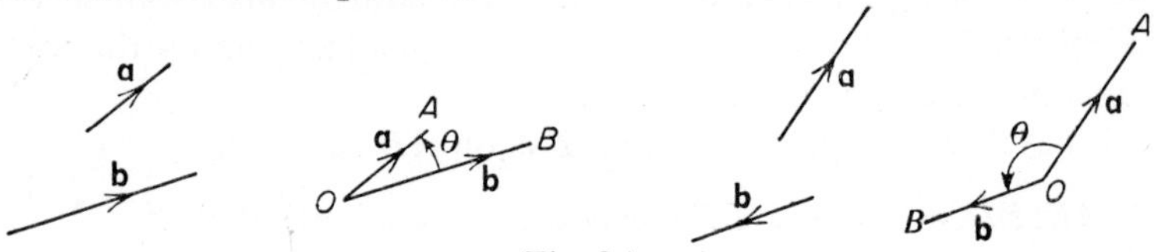

Fig. 5.1

Projection of a vector upon a vector

Definition. *The projection of a vector* **b** *upon a vector* **a** *is defined as the number* $|\mathbf{b}|\cos\theta$ *where* θ *is the angle between the vectors* **a**, **b**.

For convenience we shall denote the projection of a vector **b** upon another vector by $p(\mathbf{b})$. The geometrical significance of the definition is seen from Figs. 5.2 and 5.3.

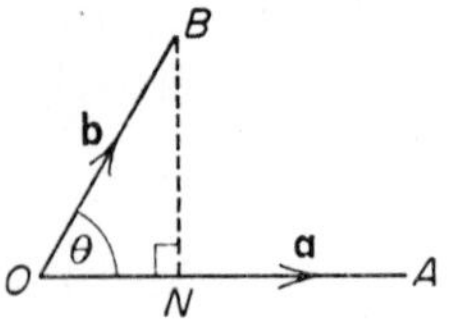

Fig. 5.2

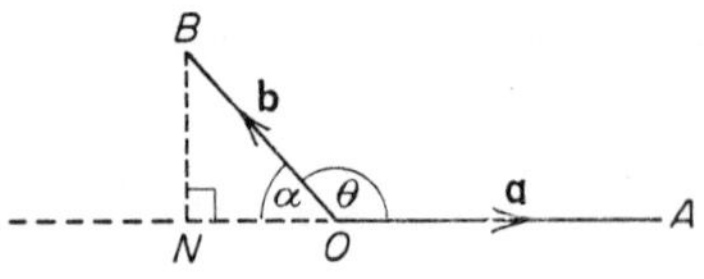

Fig. 5.3

Let **OA** = **a** and **OB** = **b**. From B draw BN perpendicular to OA or AO produced.

In Fig. 5.2

$$p(\mathbf{b}) \text{ on } \mathbf{a} = |\mathbf{b}|\cos\theta = OB\cos\theta = ON.$$

In Fig. 5.3

$$p(\mathbf{b}) \text{ on } \mathbf{a} = |\mathbf{b}|\cos\theta = OB\cos(180-\alpha) = -OB\cos\alpha = -ON.$$

From these it is seen that the projection is either a positive or negative number depending whether θ is acute or obtuse.

The projection of a vector **b** upon a vector **a** is also known as the resolute or resolved part of the vector **b** upon the vector **a**.

We now obtain an important theorem on the projection of the sum of several vectors.

The angle between **b** and **p** is acute in Fig. 5.4 and obtuse in Fig. 5.5. Hence the projections of **b** on **p** are opposite in signs in the two figures.

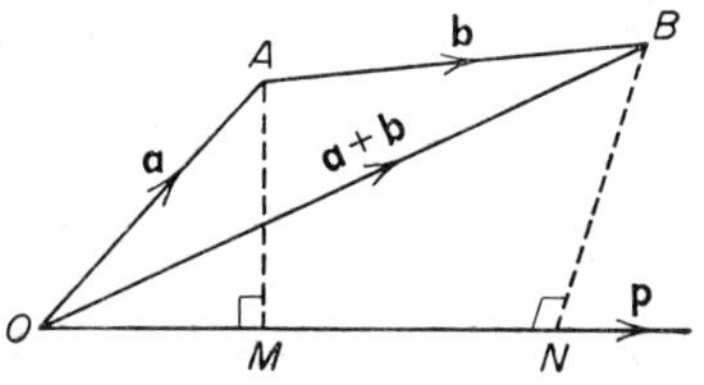

Fig. 5.4

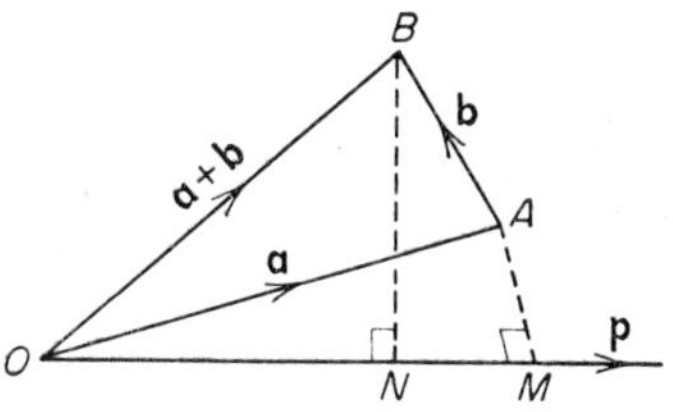

Fig. 5.5

From A, B draw perpendiculars AM, BN on to the vector **p**, the vectors not necessarily being in the same plane.

We shall consider the projections of **a**, **b** and **a**+**b** upon **p** in each case.

In Fig. 5.4, $\quad p(\mathbf{a}) = OM, \quad p(\mathbf{b}) = MN, \quad p(\mathbf{a}+\mathbf{b}) = ON.$

But $\quad ON = OM+MN,$

$$\therefore \quad p(\mathbf{a}+\mathbf{b}) = p(\mathbf{a})+p(\mathbf{b}).$$

In Fig. 5.5, $\quad p(\mathbf{a}) = OM, \quad p(\mathbf{b}) = -MN, \quad p(\mathbf{a}+\mathbf{b}) = ON.$

But $\quad OM = ON+NM,$

$$\therefore \quad p(\mathbf{a}) = p(\mathbf{a}+\mathbf{b})-p(\mathbf{b}),$$

$$\therefore \quad p(\mathbf{a}+\mathbf{b}) = p(\mathbf{a})+p(\mathbf{b}).$$

In the same way by extending the argument we can show that

$$p(\mathbf{a}+\mathbf{b}+\mathbf{c}\ldots) = p(\mathbf{a})+p(\mathbf{b})+p(\mathbf{c})+\ldots.$$

Thus the projection of a sum of vectors on a given vector is equal to the sum of the projections of the separate vectors on the given vector.

Projection of a vector upon a plane

In Fig. 5.6 we require the projection of the vector **AB** on the plane XY.

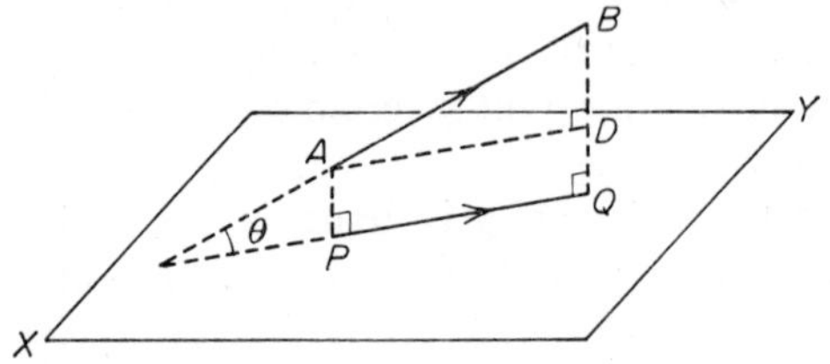

Fig. 5.6

Definition. *The projection of a vector* **AB** *on a plane is the vector* **PQ** *where P, Q are the feet of the perpendiculars from A, B respectively to the plane.*

Since the projection **PQ** is a vector we denote the projection of a vector **a** upon a plane by the bold type **P(a)**.

If θ is the angle between **AB** and the plane then

$$|\mathbf{PQ}| = AD = |\mathbf{AB}|\cos\theta,$$

where AD is perpendicular to BQ.

We now obtain a theorem about the projection of the sum of several vectors upon a plane.

In Fig. 5.7 **p, q, r** are the projections of the vectors **a, b, (a + b)** on the plane XY, i.e. $\mathbf{P}(\mathbf{a}) = \mathbf{p}$, $\mathbf{P}(\mathbf{b}) = \mathbf{q}$, $\mathbf{P}(\mathbf{a}+\mathbf{b}) = \mathbf{r}$.

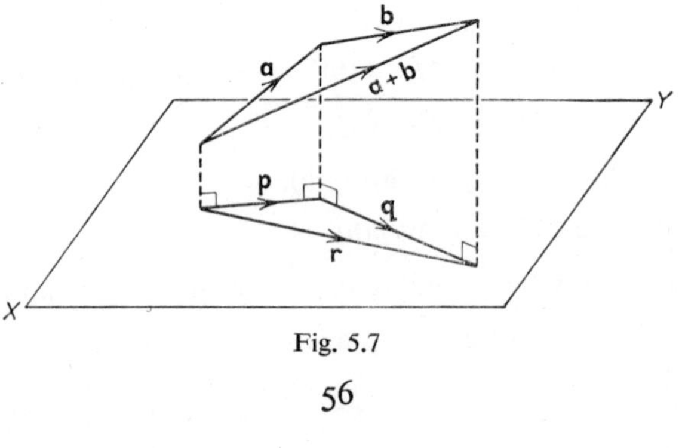

Fig. 5.7

Now $$\mathbf{r} = \mathbf{p}+\mathbf{q},$$

$$\therefore \quad \mathbf{P}(\mathbf{a}+\mathbf{b}) = \mathbf{P}(\mathbf{a})+\mathbf{P}(\mathbf{b}).$$

In the same way we can deduce that

$$\mathbf{P}(\mathbf{a}+\mathbf{b}+\mathbf{c}\ldots) = \mathbf{P}(\mathbf{a})+\mathbf{P}(\mathbf{b})+\mathbf{P}(\mathbf{c})+\ldots.$$

Thus the projection of a sum of vectors on a given plane is equal to the sum of the projections of the separate vectors on the plane.

Components of a vector

The position of a point P can be completely specified by the vector **OP** if we agree upon a fixed origin O. We have previously used the term position vector of P relative to the origin O for the vector **OP**. Furthermore, if we have agreed axes OX, OY the point P is completely specified in position by its co-ordinates, namely OA, AP (Fig. 5.8).

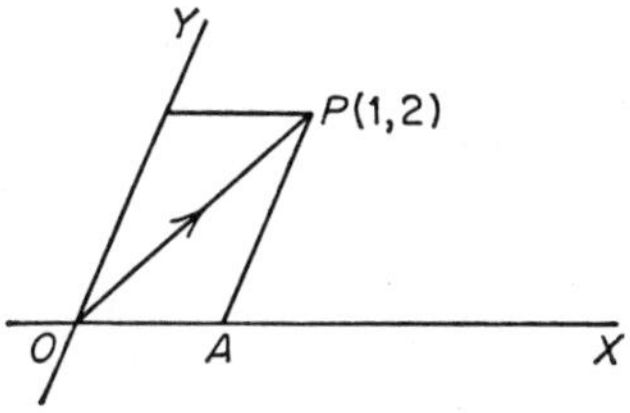

Fig. 5.8

Now since **OA**+**AP** = **OP**, **OA** and **AP** are the components parallel to the axes of the vector **OP**. In particular if P is the point (1, 2) then $OA = 1$ and $AP = 2$ and thus the co-ordinates of a point may be defined as the components of the position vector. This means that when we label a point $P(1, 2)$ we may think of the separate numbers 1, 2 as co-ordinates of the point P, or we may think of the number-pair (1, 2) as the position vector of P with the numbers 1, 2 referring to the components of **OP**.

We shall now show generally that a vector can be uniquely expressed in terms of two components in two given directions or three components in three given directions not parallel to the same plane.

The process of expressing a vector into components is known as the decomposition or resolution of the vector.

Decomposition of a vector in two directions

Suppose **r** is a given vector and $\hat{\mathbf{u}}$, $\hat{\mathbf{v}}$ are two unit vectors in any two directions. Take any point O as origin and let **OP** = **r**. Draw a triangle OPA with OA, AP parallel to the directions of $\hat{\mathbf{u}}$, $\hat{\mathbf{v}}$ respectively (Fig. 5.9).

Then $$\mathbf{OP} = \mathbf{OA}+\mathbf{AP}.$$

This resolution into the vector components **OA**, **AP** is unique since only one triangle with sides parallel to the given directions can be constructed with **OP** as side.

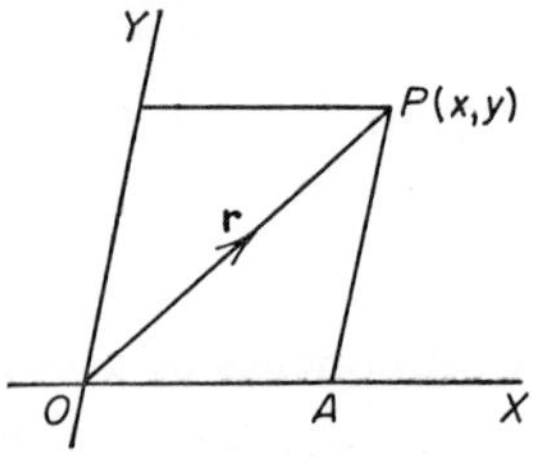

Fig. 5.9

Through O draw OX, OY with the same direction and sense as $\hat{\mathbf{u}}$, $\hat{\mathbf{v}}$. Then taking OX, OY as axes let P have the co-ordinates (x, y). We now have

$$\mathbf{OA} = x\hat{\mathbf{u}}, \quad \mathbf{AP} = y\hat{\mathbf{v}},$$

and hence we can write $\quad \mathbf{r} = x\hat{\mathbf{u}}+y\hat{\mathbf{v}}.$

Here $x\hat{\mathbf{u}}$, $y\hat{\mathbf{v}}$ are known as the vector components of **r** and the numbers x, y are known as the components of **r** for the given directions.

As we have seen it is convenient to denote the vector $x\hat{\mathbf{u}}+y\hat{\mathbf{v}}$ by the number-pair (x, y). Thus the vector $(3, -4)$ denotes the vector with components $(3, -4)$ for the given directions, i.e. the vector $3\hat{\mathbf{u}}-4\hat{\mathbf{v}}$.

Addition of vectors

Consider now several vectors $\mathbf{r}_1, \mathbf{r}_2, \mathbf{r}_3, \ldots.$

In component form they are

$$\mathbf{r}_1 = x_1\hat{\mathbf{u}}+y_1\hat{\mathbf{v}} = (x_1, y_1),$$
$$\mathbf{r}_2 = x_2\hat{\mathbf{u}}+y_2\hat{\mathbf{v}} = (x_2, y_2),$$
$$\mathbf{r}_3 = x_3\hat{\mathbf{u}}+y_3\hat{\mathbf{v}} = (x_3, y_3).$$

Adding we have

$$\mathbf{r}_1+\mathbf{r}_2+\mathbf{r}_3+\ldots = (x_1+x_2+x_3+\ldots)\,\hat{\mathbf{u}}+(y_1+y_2+y_3+\ldots)\,\hat{\mathbf{v}}.$$

Thus the vector $(\mathbf{r}_1+\mathbf{r}_2+\mathbf{r}_3+\ldots)$ has components $(x_1+x_2+x_3+\ldots)$, $(y_1+y_2+y_3+\ldots)$. In general we see that the components of the sum of several vectors is obtained by adding up the corresponding components of the separate vectors.

Special case

The case of rectangular axes, i.e. axes at right angles is very important. In this case it is usual to indicate the unit vectors $\hat{\mathbf{u}}$, $\hat{\mathbf{v}}$ by **i**, **j** respectively, i.e. **i**, **j** are the unit vectors with the same direction and sense as the positive OX, OY axes.

In this case the length of **OP** is easily calculated by using Pythagoras's Theorem (Fig. 5.10):

$$OP = \sqrt{(OA^2+AP^2)} = \sqrt{(x^2+y^2)}.$$

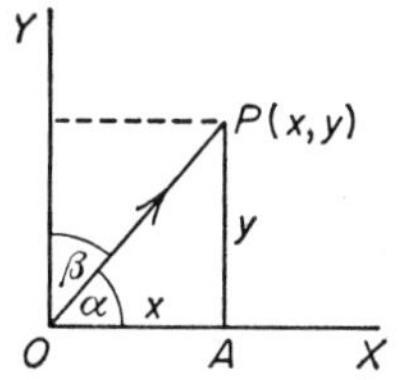

Fig. 5.10

Also if α, β are the angles that **OP** make with the positive OX, OY axes respectively, we have

$$\cos\alpha = \frac{x}{|\mathbf{OP}|}, \quad \cos\beta = \frac{y}{|\mathbf{OP}|}.$$

These are known as the direction cosines of **OP**.

Examples

(1) *If* $\mathbf{a} = 7\mathbf{i}+4\mathbf{j}$ *find* $|\mathbf{a}|$ *and the angle* **a** *makes with the x axis.*

$$\mathbf{a} = 7\mathbf{i}+4\mathbf{j},$$
$$\therefore \quad |\mathbf{a}|^2 = 7^2+4^2 = 65,$$
$$\therefore \quad |\mathbf{a}| = \sqrt{65}.$$

Angle is $\tan^{-1} y/x$, i.e. $\tan^{-1}\frac{4}{7}$.

(2) *If* $\mathbf{a} = 3\mathbf{i}+4\mathbf{j}$, $\mathbf{b} = 2\mathbf{i}-3\mathbf{j}$ *and* $\mathbf{c} = -\mathbf{i}+\mathbf{j}$ *show that* $\mathbf{a}+3\mathbf{b}+5\mathbf{c}$ *is parallel to the x axis.*

$$\begin{aligned}\mathbf{a}+3\mathbf{b}+5\mathbf{c} &= (3\mathbf{i}+4\mathbf{j})+3(2\mathbf{i}-3\mathbf{j})+5(-\mathbf{i}+\mathbf{j})\\ &= (3+6-5)\,\mathbf{i}+(4-9+5)\mathbf{j}\\ &= 4\mathbf{i}.\end{aligned}$$

Therefore $\mathbf{a}+3\mathbf{b}+5\mathbf{c}$ is parallel to the x axis.

Decomposition of a vector into three non-coplanar directions

We shall now show how any vector **r** can be expressed as the sum of three vectors which are parallel to any three vectors which are not in the same plane.

Let $\hat{\mathbf{u}}$, $\hat{\mathbf{v}}$, $\hat{\mathbf{w}}$ be unit vectors in the three given non-coplanar directions. Take any point O as origin and let **OP** = **r**. Draw a parallelepiped on **OP** as diagonal and with edges OA, OB, OC parallel to $\hat{\mathbf{u}}$, $\hat{\mathbf{v}}$, $\hat{\mathbf{w}}$ respectively. Referring to Fig. 5.11 we have

$$\mathbf{OP} = \mathbf{OA}+\mathbf{AD}+\mathbf{DP}.$$

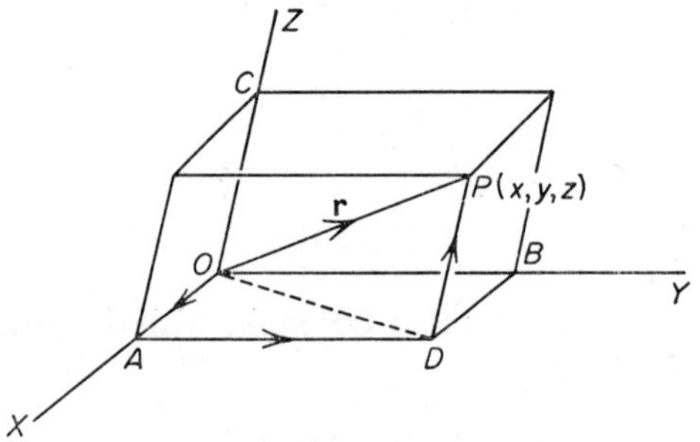

Fig. 5.11

Then **OP** has been expressed in terms of the vector components **OA**, **AD**, **DP**. This resolution of **r** is unique because only one parallelepiped can be drawn on **OP** as diagonal and with edges parallel to the given directions.

Through O draw OX, OY, OZ with the same direction and sense as $\hat{\mathbf{u}}$, $\hat{\mathbf{v}}$, $\hat{\mathbf{w}}$. Then taking OX, OY, OZ as axes let P have the co-ordinates (x, y, z). We now can write

$$\mathbf{OA} = x\hat{\mathbf{u}}, \quad \mathbf{AD} = y\hat{\mathbf{v}}, \quad \mathbf{DP} = z\hat{\mathbf{w}},$$

$$\therefore \quad \mathbf{r} = x\hat{\mathbf{u}}+y\hat{\mathbf{v}}+z\hat{\mathbf{w}}.$$

As before $x\hat{\mathbf{u}}$, $y\hat{\mathbf{v}}$, $z\hat{\mathbf{w}}$ are known as the vector components of **r** and the numbers x, y, z are known as the components of **r** for the given directions. Also as before we can denote the vector $x\hat{\mathbf{u}}+y\hat{\mathbf{v}}+z\hat{\mathbf{w}}$ by the number-triple (x, y, z).

Addition of vectors

Given several vectors $\mathbf{r}_1$, $\mathbf{r}_2$, $\mathbf{r}_3$, ... we can obtain the vector sum by expressing each in component form and adding.

$$\mathbf{r}_1 = x_1\hat{\mathbf{u}}+y_1\hat{\mathbf{v}}+z_1\hat{\mathbf{w}},$$

$$\mathbf{r}_2 = x_2\hat{\mathbf{u}}+y_2\hat{\mathbf{v}}+z_2\hat{\mathbf{w}},$$

$$\mathbf{r}_3 = x_3\hat{\mathbf{u}}+y_3\hat{\mathbf{v}}+z_3\hat{\mathbf{w}},$$

$$\therefore \quad (\mathbf{r}_1+\mathbf{r}_2+\mathbf{r}_3+\ldots) = (x_1+x_2+x_3+\ldots)\hat{\mathbf{u}}+(y_1+y_2+y_3+\ldots)\hat{\mathbf{v}} +(z_1+z_2+z_3+\ldots)\hat{\mathbf{w}}.$$

Thus the components of the sum of a number of vectors is obtained by adding up the corresponding components of the separate vectors.

Multiplication by a number

Suppose we have a vector $\mathbf{r} = x\hat{\mathbf{u}}+y\hat{\mathbf{v}}+z\hat{\mathbf{w}}$ and we require the components of the vector $m\mathbf{r}$ where m is any real number. We have

$$m\mathbf{r} = m(x\hat{\mathbf{u}}+y\hat{\mathbf{v}}+z\hat{\mathbf{w}}) = mx\hat{\mathbf{u}}+my\hat{\mathbf{v}}+mz\hat{\mathbf{w}}.$$

Hence each component of $m\mathbf{r}$ is obtained by multiplying the corresponding component of $\mathbf{r}$ by m.

Special case

The most important and common case of resolution of vectors is that in which the three directions form a right-handed rectangular Cartesian co-ordinate frame. In this case the axes OX, OY, OZ are mutually perpendicular and the resulting parallelepiped is a cuboid (Fig. 5.12).

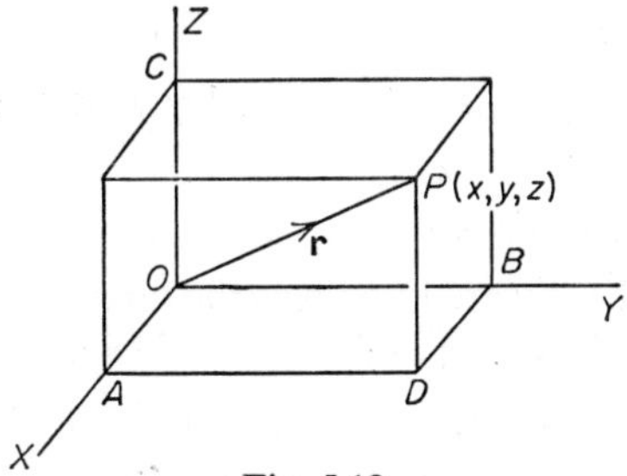

Fig. 5.12

If **i**, **j**, **k** are the unit vectors for this system then $\mathbf{i} = \hat{\mathbf{u}}, \mathbf{j} = \hat{\mathbf{v}}, \mathbf{k} = \hat{\mathbf{w}}$ and we write the vector **r** in component form as $\mathbf{r} = x\mathbf{i}+y\mathbf{j}+z\mathbf{k}$.

In this case the components x, y, z are also known as the projections, resolutes or resolved parts of **r** upon **i**, **j**, **k** respectively.

The sum of several vectors is given by

$$(\mathbf{r}_1+\mathbf{r}_2+\mathbf{r}_3+\ldots) = (x_1+y_1+z_1+\ldots)\,\mathbf{i}+(y_1+y_2+y_3+\ldots)\,\mathbf{j}$$
$$+(z_1+z_2+z_3+\ldots)\,\mathbf{k}.$$

The length of OP can be calculated by successive applications of Pythagoras's Theorem.

$$OP^2 = OD^2+DP^2 \text{ (Fig. 5.12)}$$
$$= OA^2+AD^2+DP^2$$
$$= x^2+y^2+z^2,$$
$$\therefore \quad OP = \sqrt{(x^2+y^2+z^2)}.$$

Thus the length of a vector is the square root of the sum of the squares of its rectangular components.

We make the following general observations:

(1) In all the above resolutions the number x is either positive or negative according as **OA** has the same sense as **i**, or the opposite sense. The same distinction of signs apply to the numbers y, z.

(2) The decomposition of a vector into three components is more useful than the decomposition into two components, for by the former decomposition we can deal with several vectors in space but the latter is only of use when the vectors are all coplanar.

(3) A vector may be resolved into three or more components in directions which are coplanar but this resolution is not unique because a polygon is not determined by its angles and one side.

In what follows the axes OX, OY, OZ are mutually perpendicular.

Direction cosines

Let $\mathbf{OP} = \mathbf{r}$ make angles of α, β and γ with the OX, OY and OZ axes respectively.

$$\therefore \quad x = r\cos\alpha, \quad y = r\cos\beta, \quad z = r\cos\gamma.$$

$\cos\alpha$, $\cos\beta$ and $\cos\gamma$ are known as the direction cosines of **OP** and are usually denoted by l, m and n respectively.

$$\therefore \quad l = x/r, \quad m = y/r \quad \text{and} \quad n = z/r.$$

Three useful facts involving direction cosines will now be obtained.

(1) $l^2+m^2+n^2 = 1.$

$$\mathbf{r} = x\mathbf{i}+y\mathbf{j}+z\mathbf{k},$$

$$\therefore \quad r^2 = x^2+y^2+z^2,$$

$$\therefore \quad 1 = \frac{x^2}{r^2}+\frac{y^2}{r^2}+\frac{z^2}{r^2}.$$

$$\therefore \quad l^2+m^2+n^2 = 1.$$

(2) *The coefficients of* **i**, **j** *and* **k** *of a unit vector are its direction cosines.*

Let $\hat{\mathbf{r}}$ be the unit vector.

$$\therefore \quad \hat{\mathbf{r}} = x\mathbf{i}+y\mathbf{j}+z\mathbf{k}.$$

Now $$x = |\hat{\mathbf{r}}|\, l, \quad y = |\hat{\mathbf{r}}|\, m, \quad z = |\hat{\mathbf{r}}|\, n.$$

But $$|\hat{\mathbf{r}}| = 1.$$

$$\therefore \quad x = l, \quad y = m, \quad z = n.$$

(3) *$\cos\theta = ll_1+mm_1+nn_1$ where θ is the angle between two vectors whose direction cosines are l, m, n and l_1, m_1, n_1, respectively.*

Let the position vectors of the points P and P_1 relative to the origin O of the axes be $\mathbf{r}$ and $\mathbf{r}_1$, and the angle between **OP** and $\mathbf{OP}_1$ be θ.

$$\mathbf{r} = x\mathbf{i}+y\mathbf{j}+z\mathbf{k} = r(l\mathbf{i}+m\mathbf{j}+n\mathbf{k}),$$

$$\mathbf{r}_1 = x_1\mathbf{i}+y_1\mathbf{j}+z_1\mathbf{k} = r_1(l_1\mathbf{i}+m_1\mathbf{j}+n_1\mathbf{k}).$$

$$\mathbf{PP}_1 = \mathbf{r}_1-\mathbf{r}$$

$$= (r_1 l_1-rl)\,\mathbf{i}+(r_1 m_1-rm)\,\mathbf{j}+(r_1 n_1-rn)\,\mathbf{k}.$$

Applying the cosine rule:

$$|\mathbf{PP}_1|^2 = |\mathbf{OP}|^2+|\mathbf{OP}_1|^2-2|\mathbf{OP}|\,|\mathbf{OP}_1|\cos\theta,$$

$$\therefore \quad \cos\theta = \frac{r^2+r_1^2-(r_1 l_1-rl)^2-(r_1 m_1-rm)^2-(r_1 n_1-rn)^2}{2rr_1}$$

$$= \frac{r^2+r_1^2-r^2(l^2+m^2+n^2)+2rr_1(ll_1+mm_1+nn_1)-r_1^2(l_1^2+m_1^2+n_1^2)}{2rr_1}.$$

Since $$l^2+m^2+n^2 = l_1^2+m_1^2+n_1^2 = 1,$$

$$\cos\theta = ll_1+mm_1+nn_1.$$

Modulus and direction cosines of $\mathbf{PP}_1$

Let the position vectors of the points P and P_1 relative to the origin O of the axes be $\mathbf{r}$ and $\mathbf{r}_1$. Then

$$\mathbf{r} = x\mathbf{i}+y\mathbf{j}+z\mathbf{k},$$

$$\mathbf{r}_1 = x_1\mathbf{i}+y_1\mathbf{j}+z_1\mathbf{k}.$$

$$\mathbf{PP}_1 = \mathbf{r}_1-\mathbf{r}$$

$$= (x_1-x)\,\mathbf{i}+(y_1-y)\,\mathbf{j}+(z_1-z)\,\mathbf{k},$$

$$\therefore\quad |\mathbf{PP}_1| = \sqrt{\{(x_1-x)^2+(y_1-y)^2+(z_1-z)^2\}}.$$

The direction cosines of $\mathbf{PP}_1$ are

$$\frac{x_1-x}{|\mathbf{PP}_1|},\quad \frac{y_1-y}{|\mathbf{PP}_1|},\quad \frac{z_1-z}{|\mathbf{PP}_1|}.$$

Angle between the vectors PQ and RS

Suppose we require the angle between the free vectors **PQ** and **RS** (Fig. 5.13). Consider the two corresponding localized vectors **OA** and **OB** passing through the origin O of the axes. Then the angle between **OA** and **OB** is the required angle. We have shown that this angle is given by

$$\cos\theta = ll_1+mm_1+nn_1,$$

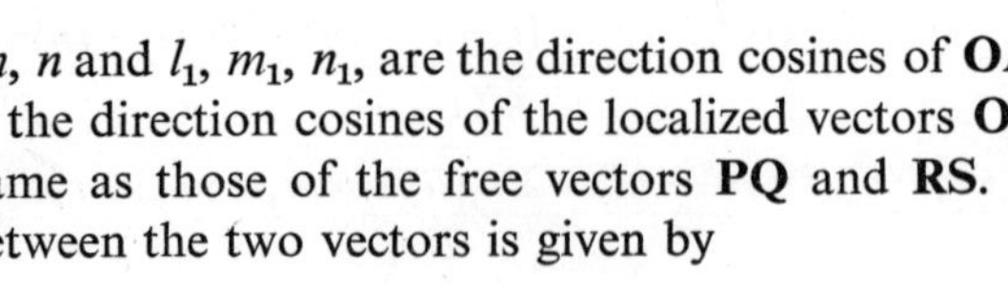

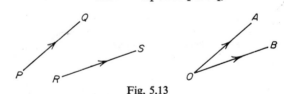

Fig. 5.13

where l, m, n and l_1, m_1, n_1, are the direction cosines of **OA** and **OB**. However, the direction cosines of the localized vectors **OA** and **OB** are the same as those of the free vectors **PQ** and **RS**. Hence the angle θ between the two vectors is given by

$$\cos\theta = ll_1+mm_1+nn_1,$$

where l, m, n and l_1, m_1, n_1 are the direction cosines of the vectors.

Examples

(1) *If the position vectors relative to the origin O of the axes of the points A and B are* $4\mathbf{i}+4\mathbf{j}-7\mathbf{k}$ *and* $5\mathbf{i}-2\mathbf{j}+6\mathbf{k}$ *respectively, find the direction cosines of* **OA, OB** *and* **AB** *and the angle between* **OA** *and* **AB**.

$$\mathbf{OA} = 4\mathbf{i}+4\mathbf{j}-7\mathbf{k} \quad \text{and} \quad \mathbf{OB} = 5\mathbf{i}-2\mathbf{j}+6\mathbf{k}.$$

$$\therefore \quad OA = \sqrt{(4^2+4^2+7^2)} \quad \text{and} \quad OB = \sqrt{(5^2+2^2+6^2)}$$

$$= 9, \qquad\qquad = \sqrt{65},$$

$$\therefore \quad \text{direction cosines are } \frac{4}{9}, \frac{4}{9}, \frac{-7}{9} \text{ and } \frac{5}{\sqrt{65}}, \frac{-2}{\sqrt{65}}, \frac{6}{\sqrt{65}}.$$

$$\mathbf{AB} = (5\mathbf{i}-2\mathbf{j}+6\mathbf{k})-(4\mathbf{i}+4\mathbf{j}-7\mathbf{k}) = \mathbf{i}-6\mathbf{j}+13\mathbf{k}.$$

$$\therefore \quad AB = \sqrt{(1^2+6^2+13^2)} = \sqrt{206},$$

$$\therefore \quad \text{direction cosines are } \frac{1}{\sqrt{206}}, \frac{-6}{\sqrt{206}}, \frac{13}{\sqrt{206}}.$$

$$\cos\theta = ll_1+mm_1+nn_1$$

$$= \frac{(4\times 1)+(4\times -6)+(-7\times 13)}{9\sqrt{206}},$$

$$\therefore \quad \text{angle is } \cos^{-1}\frac{-37}{3\sqrt{206}}.$$

(2) *Show that* $\mathbf{a} = 9\mathbf{i}+\mathbf{j}-6\mathbf{k}$ *and* $\mathbf{b} = 4\mathbf{i}-6\mathbf{j}+5\mathbf{k}$ *are at right angles to each other.*

Direction cosines of **a** are $\frac{9}{\sqrt{118}}, \frac{1}{\sqrt{118}}, \frac{-6}{\sqrt{118}}$.

Direction cosines of **b** are $\frac{4}{\sqrt{77}}, \frac{-6}{\sqrt{77}}, \frac{5}{\sqrt{77}}$.

$$\cos\theta = ll_1+mm_1+nn_1,$$

$$\therefore \quad \cos\theta = \frac{36-6-30}{\sqrt{118}.\sqrt{77}} = 0,$$

$$\therefore \quad \theta = 90^\circ.$$

Centroid of points

Let $A, B, C, \ldots$ be n points (x_1, y_1, z_1), (x_2, y_2, z_2), $(x_3, y_3, z_3)\ldots$, and O the origin of the axes.

Let **OA** = **a**, **OB** = **b**, **OC** = **c**, ...

$$\mathbf{a} = x_1\mathbf{i}+y_1\mathbf{j}+z_1\mathbf{k},$$
$$\mathbf{b} = x_2\mathbf{i}+y_2\mathbf{j}+z_2\mathbf{k},$$
$$\mathbf{c} = x_3\mathbf{i}+y_3\mathbf{j}+z_3\mathbf{k},$$
$$\dots\dots\dots\dots\dots$$

If G is the centroid of these points

$$\mathbf{OG} = \frac{\mathbf{a}+\mathbf{b}+\mathbf{c}\dots}{n}$$

$$= \frac{(x_1+x_2+x_3\dots)\mathbf{i}+(y_1+y_2+y_3\dots)\mathbf{j}+(z_1+z_2+z_3\dots)\mathbf{k}}{n}$$

$$= \frac{(\Sigma x)\mathbf{i}+(\Sigma y)\mathbf{j}+(\Sigma z)\mathbf{k}}{n}.$$

Therefore G is the point $\left(\frac{\Sigma x}{n}, \frac{\Sigma y}{n}, \frac{\Sigma z}{n}\right)$.

Example

Show that the centroid of the points

$A(4, 3, 2)$, $B(5, -4, -3)$, $C(8, 3, -2)$ *and* $D(-1, 6, -5)$

is the point $G(4, 2, -2)$. *Also show that* **AG** $= -\mathbf{j}-4\mathbf{k}$.

Let **a**, **b**, **c** and **d** be the position vectors of A, B, C and D respectively relative to the origin O of the axes.

$$\mathbf{a} = 4\mathbf{i}+3\mathbf{j}+2\mathbf{k},$$
$$\mathbf{b} = 5\mathbf{i}-4\mathbf{j}-3\mathbf{k},$$
$$\mathbf{c} = 8\mathbf{i}+3\mathbf{j}-2\mathbf{k},$$
$$\mathbf{d} = -\mathbf{i}+6\mathbf{j}-5\mathbf{k}.$$

$$\mathbf{OG} = \frac{\mathbf{a}+\mathbf{b}+\mathbf{c}+\mathbf{d}}{4}$$

$$= \frac{16\mathbf{i}+8\mathbf{j}-8\mathbf{k}}{4}$$

$$= 4\mathbf{i}+2\mathbf{j}-2\mathbf{k}.$$

Therefore G is the point $(4, 2, -2)$.

$$\begin{aligned}\mathbf{AG} &= \mathbf{g}-\mathbf{a} \quad \text{(where } \mathbf{g} \text{ is the position vector of } G)\\ &= (4\mathbf{i}+2\mathbf{j}-2\mathbf{k})-(4\mathbf{i}+3\mathbf{j}+2\mathbf{k})\\ &= -\mathbf{j}-4\mathbf{k}.\end{aligned}$$

Exercise 5

(1) Show that $|\mathbf{i}+\mathbf{j}| = \sqrt{2}$ and $|\mathbf{i}+\mathbf{j}+\mathbf{k}| = \sqrt{3}$.

(2) If $\mathbf{a} = 4\mathbf{i}+3\mathbf{j}-2\mathbf{k}$, $\mathbf{b} = 3\mathbf{i}-7\mathbf{j}+3\mathbf{k}$ and $\mathbf{c} = -2\mathbf{i}-5\mathbf{j}+\mathbf{k}$ find the values of m and n so that $\mathbf{a}+m\mathbf{b}+n\mathbf{c}$ is parallel to the x axis.

(3) $ABCD$ is a rectangle with $AB = 2AD = 2a$. E and F are the mid-points of BC and DC respectively. Show that the components in the directions AB and AD of the resultant of $\mathbf{AE}+\mathbf{AC}+\mathbf{AF}$ are $5a$ and $2\frac{1}{2}a$ respectively.

(4) OA, OB and OC are the diagonals of three adjacent faces of a cube and OD is a diagonal of the cube. Show that

$$\mathbf{OA}+\mathbf{OB}+\mathbf{OC} = 2\mathbf{OD}.$$

(5) If the position vectors of points A and B are $2\mathbf{i}-3\mathbf{j}+4\mathbf{k}$ and $3\mathbf{i}-7\mathbf{j}+12\mathbf{k}$ respectively, find the length of AB and its direction cosines.

(6) Calculate the modulus and the unit vector of the sum of the vectors $\mathbf{i}+4\mathbf{j}+2\mathbf{k}$, $3\mathbf{i}-3\mathbf{j}-2\mathbf{k}$ and $-2\mathbf{i}+2\mathbf{j}+6\mathbf{k}$.

(7) $A(2, -1, 3)$, $B(6, 3, -4)$ and $C(3, 1, 1)$ are the vertices of a triangle. Show that $AB = 3AC$ and the direction cosines of $\mathbf{BC}$ are $\frac{-3}{\sqrt{38}}, \frac{-2}{\sqrt{38}}, \frac{5}{\sqrt{38}}$.

(8) Show that the vectors $\mathbf{a} = 3\mathbf{i}-2\mathbf{j}-5\mathbf{k}$ and $\mathbf{b} = 6\mathbf{i}-\mathbf{j}+4\mathbf{k}$ are perpendicular to one another.

(9) The position vectors of the points A, B, C and D are $4\mathbf{i}+3\mathbf{j}-\mathbf{k}$, $5\mathbf{i}+2\mathbf{j}+2\mathbf{k}$, $2\mathbf{i}-2\mathbf{j}-3\mathbf{k}$ and $4\mathbf{i}-4\mathbf{j}+3\mathbf{k}$ respectively. Show that AB and CD are parallel.

(10) The position vectors of the points A, B and C are $2\mathbf{i}-\mathbf{j}+\mathbf{k}$, $3\mathbf{i}+2\mathbf{j}-\mathbf{k}$ and $6\mathbf{i}+11\mathbf{j}-7\mathbf{k}$ respectively. Show that A, B and C are collinear and that $AB:BC = 1:3$.

(11) Show that the angle between the vectors

$$4\mathbf{i}-4\mathbf{j}+7\mathbf{k} \quad \text{and} \quad -\mathbf{i}+4\mathbf{j}+8\mathbf{k}$$

is $\cos^{-1}\frac{4}{9}$.

(12) The position vectors of the points A, B and C are $8\mathbf{i}+4\mathbf{j}-3\mathbf{k}$, $6\mathbf{i}+3\mathbf{j}-4\mathbf{k}$ and $7\mathbf{i}+5\mathbf{j}-5\mathbf{k}$ respectively. Find the angle between **AB** and **BC**.

(13) Show that the centroid of the points $(2, -3, 3)$, $(6, -2, -2)$, $(-5, 1, 7)$ and $(1, -4, 4)$ is the point $(1, -2, 3)$.

(14) Show that the diagonals of a parallelepiped and the straight lines joining the mid-points of opposite edges are concurrent and bisect each other.

(15) If $\mathbf{r} = x\mathbf{i}+y\mathbf{j}+z\mathbf{k}$ show that the modulus of the sum of the vectors $\mathbf{r_1}, \mathbf{r_2}, \mathbf{r_3}, \ldots$ is $(\Sigma r^2+2\Sigma r_m r_n \cos r_{mn})^{\frac{1}{2}}$, where r_{mn} is the angle between the vectors $\mathbf{r_m}$ and $\mathbf{r_n}$.

6

APPLICATIONS IN MECHANICS

In this chapter we shall establish the vector nature of certain physical quantities and show how certain problems in Mechanics can be solved vectorially.

Vector quantities

Quantities such as displacement, velocity, acceleration, force and angular velocity are only fully specified when we know their magnitude and direction.

Let us consider velocity as an example. It is not enough to know how fast a particle is moving, that is its speed, but also in what direction it is moving. It is the combined speed–direction which determines the velocity. In dynamics we are at times concerned with the motion of a particle describing a circle with uniform speed. Although the speed is uniform its direction of motion which is in the direction of the tangent at any particular time is changing. Thus the velocity of the particle describing a circle with uniform speed is varying. So we see that for a velocity to be fully specified we must know its magnitude and direction.

Definition. *We define a vector quantity as one which has magnitude and direction and which obeys the triangle law of addition or its equivalent, the parallelogram law.*

Thus in order for a physical quantity having magnitude and direction to be a vector quantity, or briefly a vector, it is necessary to show that it obeys the triangle law of addition.

The following two examples will make this point clear. Consider displacements over the earth's surface (Fig. 6.1).

Suppose we start at point A and travel x miles south to B and then y miles east to C. Now suppose we again start at A but this time we travel y miles east to D and then x miles south to E.

Now obviously the final points C and E are not the same. This is because the longitude change depends on the latitude. However, we

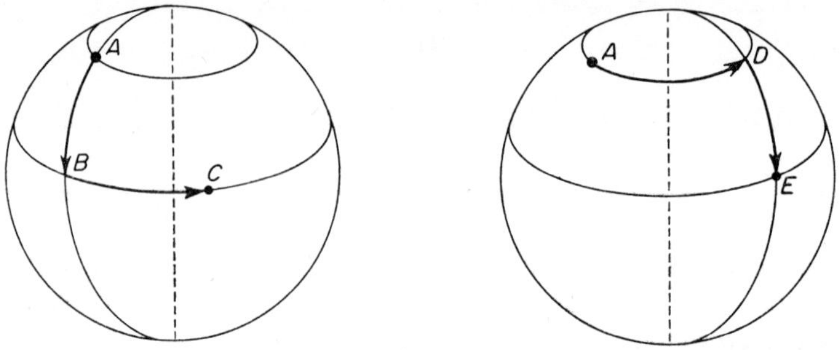

Fig. 6.1

have in each case made the same successive displacements but in the reverse order. Thus the successive displacements are not commutative. A consequence of the triangle law of addition is that the sum of vectors is commutative. We therefore conclude that displacements over the earth's surface although having magnitude and direction are not vectors.

As a second example we consider finite rotations of a rigid body about a fixed point in the body. A finite rotation has magnitude and direction since the angle turned through specifies the magnitude and the axis of rotation specifies the direction. The sense of direction is defined as the same as that moved by a right-handed corkscrew driven by the finite rotation along the axis of rotation.

Consider a book lying in the horizontal plane of the paper (Fig. 6.2*a*). We shall rotate the book in turn about two perpendicular horizontal axes XX', YY'.

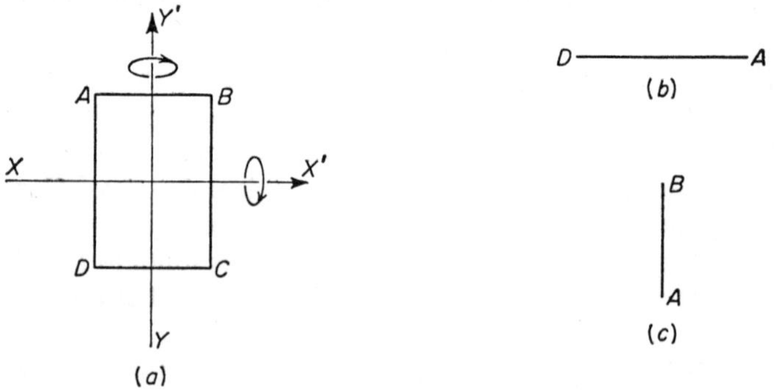

Fig. 6.2

Suppose the book is first rotated through a right angle about the axis XX', the sense of rotation being indicated by the arrow. Corners A and B will be above corners D and C, the book being in the vertical plane. Now we rotate it through another right angle about the axis YY', the sense of rotation being shown by the arrow. This will bring corners A and D above corners B and C, the plane of the book still being vertical (Fig. 6.2*b*).

We now repeat the rotations starting from the original position of the book, but in the reverse order, i.e. rotation through a right angle about the axis YY' and then about XX'. At the end of the two rotations the plane of the book is vertical and corners A and B are above corners D and C (Fig. 6.2*c*).

This clearly indicates that the order of performing finite rotations affects the final position of the book. Thus finite rotations do not commute and we conclude that a finite rotation although possessing magnitude and direction is not a vector.

We shall use the term 'directed quantity' for a physical quantity having magnitude and direction and the term 'vector quantity' or more briefly 'vector' for the same quantity when we have shown it to obey the triangle law of addition.

Representation of a vector quantity

Since we have seen that displacements have magnitude and direction and are added by the triangle law it follows that displacement is a vector. The representation of displacement by a directed line segment offers no difficulty since both displacement and the line segment have length as the common physical property.

However the magnitude of many vector quantities is not a length. By using a suitable scale a directed line segment can be used to represent any vector quantity whose magnitude is not a length, e.g. the directed line segment **AB** represents a velocity of 4 m.p.h. in the direction of A to B if the length of AB represents 4 m.p.h. in the chosen scale. Hence strictly speaking since we have not shown that velocity is a vector we are using the notation **AB** to imply that the velocity has the magnitude, direction and sense of **AB** but making no assumption about the nature of velocity itself.

As a consequence of the above geometrical representation of a physical quantity any vector quantity can be represented in the same way by directed line segments. Thus the algebra of vectors we have developed can also be applied to vector quantities of the physical world.

Displacement

A displacement from the point A to the point B is represented by the vector **AB**.

Two successive displacements are added vectorially.

A displacement from A to B followed by a displacement from B to C is the same as a displacement from A to C (Fig. 6.3). Thus

$$\mathbf{AB}+\mathbf{BC} = \mathbf{AC}.$$

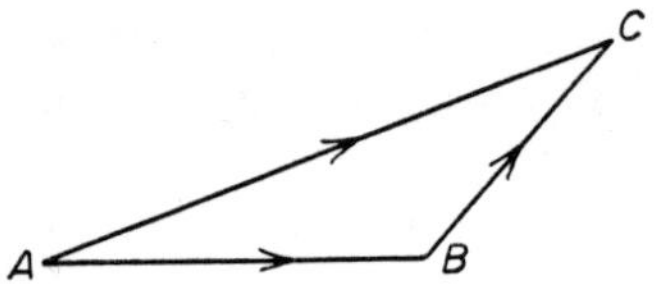

Fig. 6.3

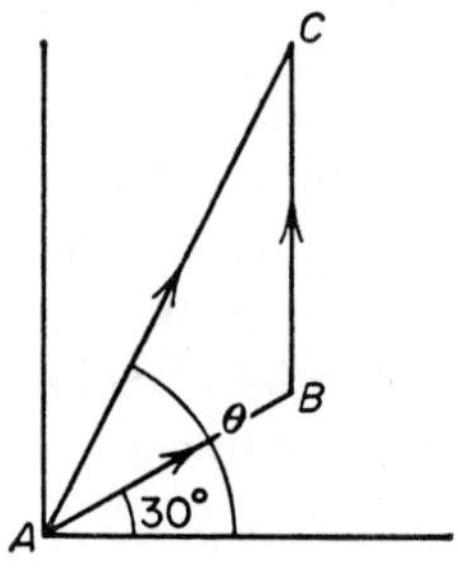

Fig. 6.4

Example

A ship starts from A, travels 4 *miles in the direction* N. 60° E. *to B, and then* 5 *miles* N *to C. Find its displacement from A.*

Let $\mathbf{i}$ and $\mathbf{j}$ be unit vectors towards east and north respectively. From Fig. 6.4,

$$\mathbf{AC} = \mathbf{AB}+\mathbf{BC}$$

$$= \left(\frac{4\sqrt{3}}{2}\mathbf{i}+4\cdot\frac{1}{2}\mathbf{j}\right)+5\mathbf{j}$$

$$= 2\sqrt{(3)}\,\mathbf{i}+7\mathbf{j},$$

$$\therefore \quad AC = \sqrt{(12+49)} = \sqrt{61} \text{ miles},$$

$$\tan\theta = \frac{7}{2\sqrt{3}}.$$

Therefore displacement is $\sqrt{61}$ miles at $\tan^{-1}\frac{7\sqrt{3}}{6}$ N. of E.

Velocity and acceleration

We assume that the reader is familiar with the idea of uniform velocity and acceleration, and with the idea that all velocities and accelerations are relative to some frame of reference.

The vector nature of velocity and acceleration when uniform will be established.

Resultant velocity and acceleration

Consider the following problem. A ship is steaming due north at 12 m.p.h. across a current which flows due east at 5 m.p.h. What is the actual velocity of the ship?

Now from the context we understand that the velocity of 12 m.p.h. due north is relative to an observer on the water, the velocity of 5 m.p.h. due east is relative to an observer on the land, and the actual velocity required is the velocity of the ship relative to the observer on the land. It is also convenient in this type of question to say that the ship has two velocities 'at the same time' or 'two simultaneous velocities'. The actual velocity is often called the resultant velocity.

Let in general, $\mathbf{u}$ be the velocity of the ship relative to the water, $\mathbf{v}$ be the velocity of the water relative to the land and $\mathbf{V}$ be the velocity of the ship relative to the land, all velocities being uniform.

In time t the whole of the water surface is displaced vt units in the direction of $\mathbf{v}$, and so if drifting the ship will have a displacement of $\mathbf{v}t$. However, in the same time on account of its motion the ship is displaced ut units in the direction of $\mathbf{u}$, i.e. it occurs a further displacement of $\mathbf{u}t$. Since displacement is a vector the resultant displacement is $\mathbf{u}t+\mathbf{v}t$ by the triangle law of addition.

Now since the velocities $\mathbf{u}$ and $\mathbf{v}$ are uniform it is reasonable to assume that the resultant velocity $\mathbf{V}$ is uniform. Hence in time t the resultant displacement is $\mathbf{V}t$.

$$\therefore \quad \mathbf{V}t = \mathbf{u}t+\mathbf{v}t,$$

$$\therefore \quad \mathbf{V} = \mathbf{u}+\mathbf{v}.$$

From this we see that uniform velocities obey the triangle law of addition, i.e. they are added vectorially. Hence we see that velocity when uniform is a vector.

We have since $\mathbf{V} = \mathbf{v}+\mathbf{u}$

velocity of ship relative to land = velocity of ship relative to water
+ velocity of water relative to land.

In general we have

$$\underset{A\,C}{\mathbf{v}} = \underset{A\,B}{\mathbf{v}} + \underset{B\,C}{\mathbf{v}},$$

where $\underset{A\,C}{\mathbf{v}}$, $\underset{A\,B}{\mathbf{v}}$, $\underset{B\,C}{\mathbf{v}}$ are velocities of A relative to C, A relative to B and B relative to C respectively.

We now consider uniform accelerations. Suppose a point has a uniform acceleration $\mathbf{a}_1$, and at the same time a uniform acceleration $\mathbf{a}_2$. Then after time t the gains in velocity are $a_1 t$, $a_2 t$ units in the direction of $\mathbf{a}_1$, $\mathbf{a}_2$ respectively. Since we have shown that velocity when uniform is a vector the resultant gain in the velocity of the particle is $\mathbf{a}_1 t+\mathbf{a}_2 t$.

Again, since the accelerations are uniform it is reasonable to assume that the resultant acceleration $\mathbf{a}$ is uniform. This being so the resultant gain in velocity in time t is $\mathbf{a}t$.

$$\therefore \quad \mathbf{a}t = \mathbf{a}_1 t+\mathbf{a}_2 t,$$

$$\therefore \quad \mathbf{a} = \mathbf{a}_1+\mathbf{a}_2.$$

Hence uniform accelerations are added vectorially and we can say that acceleration when uniform is a vector.

In general we can write

$$\underset{A\,C}{\mathbf{a}} = \underset{A\,B}{\mathbf{a}} + \underset{B\,C}{\mathbf{a}},$$

where $\underset{A\,C}{\mathbf{a}}$, $\underset{A\,B}{\mathbf{a}}$, $\underset{B\,C}{\mathbf{a}}$ are the uniform accelerations of A relative to C, A relative to B and B relative to C respectively.

The triangle law of addition when applied to velocities and acceleration is often known as the triangle of velocities or accelerations. The vector sum of velocities or accelerations is known as the resultant velocity or acceleration and the velocities or accelerations which are combined are known as the components of the resultant.

We shall in the next chapter show that velocity and acceleration are vectors even when they are variable.

Example

A ship whose course is due south is steaming across a current due west. After 2 *hours the ship has gone* 36 *miles in the direction* 15° *West of South. Find the velocity of the ship and current.*

Let the velocity of the ship and current be **u** m.p.h. and **v** m.p.h. and the resultant velocity be **V** m.p.h. (See Fig. 6.5.)

$$\therefore \quad \mathbf{V} = \mathbf{u}+\mathbf{v}.$$

If **i** and **j** are unit vectors in the directions due West and South.

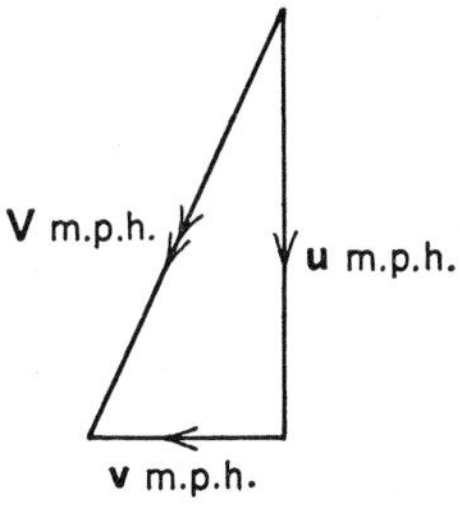

Fig. 6.5

$$\mathbf{V} = 18\sin 15°\mathbf{i}+18\cos 15°\mathbf{j},$$

$$\mathbf{u} = u\mathbf{j},$$

$$\mathbf{v} = v\mathbf{i}.$$

$$\therefore \quad 18\sin 15°\mathbf{i}+18\cos 15°\mathbf{j} = u\mathbf{j}+v\mathbf{i},$$

$$\therefore \quad v = 18\sin 15° = 4{\cdot}66,$$

$$\therefore \quad u = 18\cos 15° = 17{\cdot}4.$$

Therefore velocities of ship and current are 17·4 and 4·66 m.p.h. respectively.

Relative velocity and acceleration

Suppose points A and B are moving with uniform velocities ${}_{A}\mathbf{v}_{O}$ and ${}_{B}\mathbf{v}_{O}$ relative to a fixed origin O. Then the velocity of B relative to A denoted by ${}_{B}\mathbf{v}_{A}$ can be deduced from

$${}_{B}\mathbf{v}_{O} = {}_{B}\mathbf{v}_{A}+{}_{A}\mathbf{v}_{O},$$

from which we see that

$${}_{B}\mathbf{v}_{A} = {}_{B}\mathbf{v}_{O}-{}_{A}\mathbf{v}_{O},$$

i.e. velocity of B relative to A = vector sum of the velocities of B and the negative of A.

We give an alternative method of obtaining the relative velocity equation.

Let the velocities of two points A and B relative to a fixed point O be ${}_{A}\mathbf{v}_{O}$ and ${}_{B}\mathbf{v}_{O}$ respectively (Fig. 6.6).

Let $\mathbf{PR} = {}_{B}\mathbf{v}_{O}$ and let $\mathbf{PQ}$ and $\mathbf{QR}$ be the two components of $\mathbf{PR}$, $\mathbf{QR}$ being equal and parallel to ${}_{A}\mathbf{v}_{O}$, i.e. $\mathbf{QR} = {}_{A}\mathbf{v}_{O}$. Then $\mathbf{PQ}$ is the velocity of B relative to A.

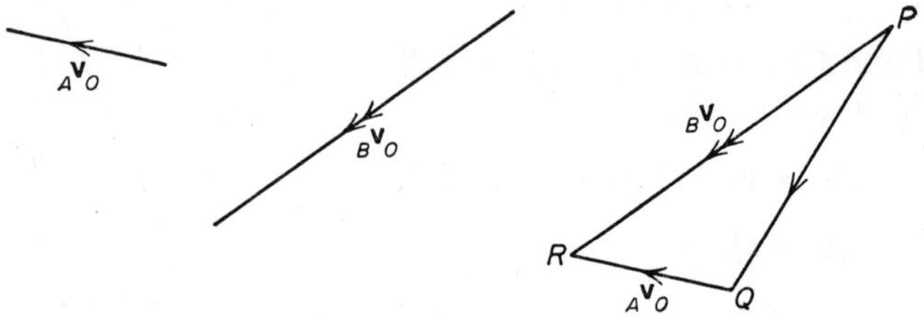

Fig. 6.6

But $$\mathbf{PQ}+\mathbf{QR} = \mathbf{PR},$$

$$\therefore \quad \mathbf{PQ} = \mathbf{PR}-\mathbf{QR},$$

$$\therefore {}_{B}\mathbf{v}_{A} = {}_{B}\mathbf{v}_{O} - {}_{A}\mathbf{v}_{O},$$

where ${}_{B}\mathbf{v}_{A}$ is the velocity of B relative to A.

The following deductions are important:

(1) If ${}_{A}\mathbf{v}_{O} = O$ we have ${}_{B}\mathbf{v}_{A} = {}_{B}\mathbf{v}_{O}$, i.e. the velocity of a point is the same relative to all fixed points.

(2) If O and B coincide we have ${}_{O}\mathbf{v}_{A} = -{}_{A}\mathbf{v}_{O}$, i.e. the velocity of A relative to O = $-$velocity of O relative to A.

By similar methods we can show that the corresponding result for uniform accelerations is

acceleration of B relative to A = acceleration of B relative to O
$-$ acceleration of A relative to O.

Examples.

(1) *The velocity of a particle A relative to B is* $3\mathbf{i}-4\mathbf{j}$ *and the velocity of B relative to a third particle C is* $\mathbf{i}+\mathbf{j}$. *Determine the*

magnitude and direction of the velocity of A relative to C, assuming that **i** *and* **j** *represent velocities of 1 ft./sec. horizontally and vertically respectively.*

$$\underset{AC}{\mathbf{v}} = \underset{AB}{\mathbf{v}} + \underset{BC}{\mathbf{v}} \quad \text{where} \quad \underset{AB}{\mathbf{v}} = 3\mathbf{i}-4\mathbf{j} \quad \text{and} \quad \underset{BC}{\mathbf{v}} = \mathbf{i}+\mathbf{j},$$

$$\therefore \quad \underset{AC}{\mathbf{v}} = 3\mathbf{i}-4\mathbf{j}+\mathbf{i}+\mathbf{j} = 4\mathbf{i}-3\mathbf{j},$$

Therefore magnitude $= \sqrt{(4^3+3^3)}$ ft./sec. $= 5$ ft./sec. Direction is $323^\circ\ 08'$ with direction of **i**.

(2) *A man on a ship steaming north-east at* 10 *m.p.h. observes the smoke issuing from the funnel in a south-east direction. He estimates the speed of the smoke to be the same as that of the ship. What is the magnitude and direction of the velocity of the wind?*

Let **i** and **j** represent velocities of 1 m.p.h. in the directions due east and north respectively.

Let **u** and **v** be the velocities of the ship and wind respectively, and **V** the velocity of the smoke relative to the ship.

Then

$$\mathbf{u} = \frac{10}{\sqrt{2}}\mathbf{i}+\frac{10}{\sqrt{2}}\mathbf{j},$$

$$\mathbf{v} = x\mathbf{i}+y\mathbf{j},$$

$$\mathbf{V} = \frac{10}{\sqrt{2}}\mathbf{i}-\frac{10}{\sqrt{2}}\mathbf{j}.$$

But

$$\mathbf{V} = \mathbf{v}-\mathbf{u},$$

$$\therefore \quad 5\sqrt{(2)}\mathbf{i}-5\sqrt{(2)}\mathbf{j} = (x\mathbf{i}+y\mathbf{j})-\{5\sqrt{(2)}\mathbf{i}+5\sqrt{(2)}\mathbf{j}\},$$

$$\therefore \quad 10\sqrt{(2)}\mathbf{i} = x\mathbf{i}+y\mathbf{j},$$

$$\therefore \quad x = 10\sqrt{2} \quad \text{and} \quad y = 0.$$

Therefore magnitude of velocity is $10\sqrt{2}$ m.p.h. and direction is from the west.

Angular velocity

Angular velocity about an axis is a directed quantity. Its magnitude is the magnitude of the angular velocity, and its direction is defined as being along the axis of rotation, the sense being the same as that moved by a right-handed corkscrew driven by the angular velocity along the axis of rotation (Fig. 6.7).

In order to show that angular velocity is a vector we must show that two angular velocities are added by the triangle law or its equivalent the parallelogram law.

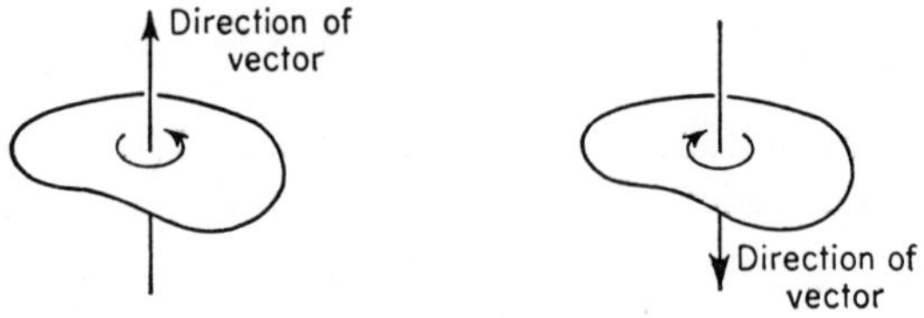

Fig. 6.7

Suppose OA is rotating about a point O with uniform angular velocity ω (Fig. 6.8). Then the velocity of the point A is $\omega.\ OA$ and is at right angles to OA.

Let **AB** and **AC** represent two angular velocities (Fig. 6.9).

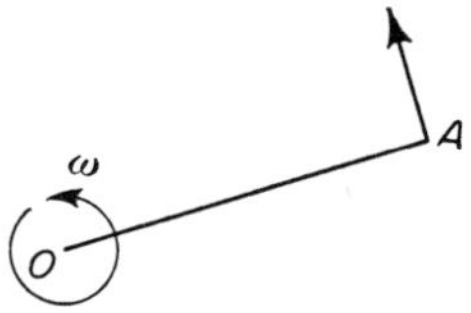

Fig. 6.8

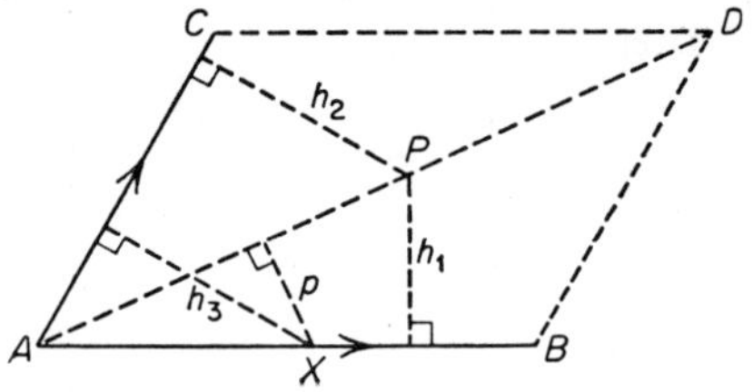

Fig. 6.9

Complete the parallelogram $ABDC$ and take P any point on AD.

Magnitude of velocity of P due to

$$\text{angular velocity } \mathbf{AB} = h_1.AB = 2\triangle APB.$$

Direction of this velocity is out of the paper.

Magnitude of velocity of P due to

$$\text{angular velocity } \mathbf{AC} = h_2.AC = 2\triangle APC.$$

Direction of this velocity is into the paper.

Since velocity is a vector we have from the triangle law of addition,

$$\text{resultant velocity of } P = 2\triangle APC - 2\triangle APB, \text{ into the paper.}$$

Since $\triangle APB$ and $\triangle APC$ have the same base AP and the altitudes from B and C respectively are equal

$$\triangle APB = \triangle APC,$$

therefore resultant velocity of $P = 0$.

Thus P must lie on the axis of the resultant angular velocity, i.e. angular velocities in the direction AB and AC combine to give an angular velocity in the direction of the diagonal.

Now consider the velocity of any point X on AB. Its velocity is the resultant of the velocities due to the angular velocities **AB** and **AC**.

Magnitude of velocity of X due to $\mathbf{AB} = 0$.

Magnitude of velocity of X due to $\mathbf{AC} = h_3 . AC$

$$= 2\triangle ACX,$$

$\therefore$ resultant velocity of $X = 2\triangle ACX$, direction being into the paper.

But if ω is the magnitude of the resultant angular velocity about AD,

$$\text{velocity of } X \text{ due to } \omega = \omega . p = \frac{2\omega \triangle ADX}{AD},$$

where p = perpendicular from X to AD.

$$\therefore \quad 2\triangle ACX = \frac{2\omega \triangle ADX}{AD}.$$

Now $\triangle ACX = \triangle ADX$, same base AX, same parallels,

$$\therefore \quad \omega = AD.$$

Since the direction of the resultant velocity of X is into the paper the sense of the resultant angular velocity must be in the sense A to D. Thus the sum of the angular velocities **AB, AC** is the angular velocity **AD**, i.e.

$$\mathbf{AB}+\mathbf{AC} = \mathbf{AD}.$$

We therefore conclude that angular velocity is a vector since the parallelogram law of addition is obeyed.

Example

Find the angular velocity vector $\boldsymbol{\omega}$ *of modulus* 14 *radians per sec. about an axis whose direction cosines are*

$$\frac{2}{7}, \frac{-3}{7}, \frac{6}{7}.$$

The vector is $x\mathbf{i}+y\mathbf{j}+z\mathbf{k}$, where

$$x = \frac{2}{7}.14, \quad y = \frac{-3}{7}.14, \quad z = \frac{6}{7}.14.$$

$$\therefore \quad \boldsymbol{\omega} = 4\mathbf{i}-6\mathbf{j}+12\mathbf{k}.$$

Force

Newton's First Law of Motion can be stated: *Every body continues in its state of rest or of uniform motion in a straight line, except in so far as it is compelled by impressed forces to change that state.*

Now if a body is not at rest or in uniform motion relative to a frame of reference we say that it is accelerating relative to this frame of reference. Thus the first law leads us to the idea that acceleration is caused by the action of force.

The Second Law of Motion is: *The rate of change of momentum is proportional to the impressed force and takes place in the direction of the straight line in which the force is impressed.*

For a constant mass this is equivalent to the statement that acceleration is proportional to the impressed force and is in the direction of the impressed force.

Now suppose that we have two particles *A* and *B* which are moving. Furthermore, suppose they are alike in every respect including the forces acting on them except that there is a force *P* acting on *A* but not on *B*.

Let *O* be any point and $\underset{AO}{\mathbf{a}}$ and $\underset{BO}{\mathbf{a}}$ the accelerations of *A* and *B* relative to *O* respectively. Then if $\underset{AB}{\mathbf{a}}$ is the acceleration of *A* relative to *B* we have $\underset{AO}{\mathbf{a}} = \underset{AB}{\mathbf{a}} + \underset{BO}{\mathbf{a}}$.

From this we see that the additional acceleration of *A* relative to *O* due to the force *P* is the acceleration of *A* relative to *B*. This leads to Newton's corollary to his Second Law: *Each of the forces acting on a particle is proportional in magnitude to the additional acceleration it produces and is in the same direction as the additional acceleration.*

By defining our unit of force as that which produces unit acceleration on a particle of unit mass, our force *P* will have the magnitude and direction of $m\mathbf{a}$ where m is the mass of the particle and $\mathbf{a}$ is the additional acceleration produced by *P*.

Although $\mathbf{a}$ is a vector and m a scalar we cannot assume that $m\mathbf{a}$ is a vector quantity since $m\mathbf{a}$ is a physical quantity of a different nature from $\mathbf{a}$. If we now write $\mathbf{P} = m\mathbf{a}$ we must understand this equation to specify the magnitude and direction of $\mathbf{P}$ as being ma and that of $\mathbf{a}$ respectively and to make no assumption about the nature of force. We shall now show that force is also a vector, assuming that acceleration is a vector.

Consider three particles A, B, C each of mass m.

Let A, B and C be acted upon by equal systems of forces.

Apply an extra force $\mathbf{P}$ to B and let the acceleration of B relative to A be $\mathbf{p}$. We can write $\mathbf{P} = m\mathbf{p}$ bearing in mind that this equation gives the magnitude and direction of the directed quantity $\mathbf{P}$. Now apply additional forces $\mathbf{P}$ and $\mathbf{Q}$ to C and let the acceleration of C relative to B be $\mathbf{q}$. Then $\mathbf{Q} = m\mathbf{q}$.

Let the forces $\mathbf{P}$ and $\mathbf{Q}$ acting on C be replaced by a single force $\mathbf{R}$ and let the acceleration of C relative to A be $\mathbf{a}$. Then $\mathbf{R} = m\mathbf{a}$.

Since acceleration of C relative to A = acceleration of C relative to B + acceleration of B relative to A,

we have

$$\begin{aligned} \mathbf{a} &= \mathbf{q}+\mathbf{p}, \\ \therefore \quad \mathbf{R} &= m(\mathbf{q}+\mathbf{p}) \\ &= m\mathbf{q}+m\mathbf{p}, \\ \therefore \quad \mathbf{R} &= \mathbf{Q}+\mathbf{P}. \end{aligned}$$

From this we see that the resultant force $\mathbf{R}$ is obtained by the vector addition of the forces $\mathbf{P}$ and $\mathbf{Q}$. Thus force is a vector. We can now state that if O is an origin, $\mathbf{P}$ the vector sum of all forces acting on a particle A and $\mathbf{a}$ the acceleration of A relative to O then we have the vector equation $\mathbf{P} = m\mathbf{a}$.

Care must be taken in dealing with a system of forces. If the forces are acting on a single particle or if they are concurrent when acting on a rigid body, then they may be treated as free vectors. However, if the forces acting on a rigid body do not meet at a point then they must be treated as localized vectors, and their lines of action need to be known for the effect of the forces to be understood.

Concurrent forces

If there are several forces $\mathbf{F}_1, \mathbf{F}_2, \mathbf{F}_3, \ldots$ acting on a point or on a single particle their net effect is the same as that of a single force equivalent to the vector sum of the forces and acting at the point or particle.

This equivalent single force is known as the resultant. If this resultant is represented by the vector **R** then

$$\mathbf{R} = \mathbf{F}_1+\mathbf{F}_2+\mathbf{F}_3+\ldots.$$

The forces $\mathbf{F}_1, \mathbf{F}_2, \mathbf{F}_3, \ldots$ are known as the components of the resultant **R**.

The resultant force is found by the vector polygon which has been already stated for finding the vector sum of several vectors.

Suppose $\mathbf{A}_0\mathbf{A}_1, \mathbf{A}_1\mathbf{A}_2, \mathbf{A}_2\mathbf{A}_3, \ldots, \mathbf{A}_{n-1}\mathbf{A}_n$ represent in magnitude and direction the forces

$$\mathbf{F}_1, \mathbf{F}_2, \mathbf{F}_3, \ldots, \mathbf{F}_n \quad \text{respectively (Fig. 6.10).}$$

If A_n does not coincide with A_0, that is the polygon is open, the resultant force is represented by the vector $\mathbf{A}_0\mathbf{A}_n$.

If A_n coincides with A_0, that is the polygon is closed, the resultant force is zero, and thus the forces are in equilibrium.

For a large number of forces the resultant is more quickly obtained by the method of resolution.

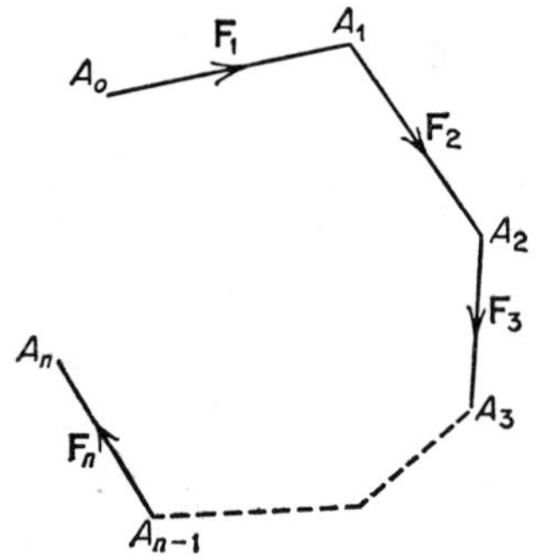

Fig. 6.10

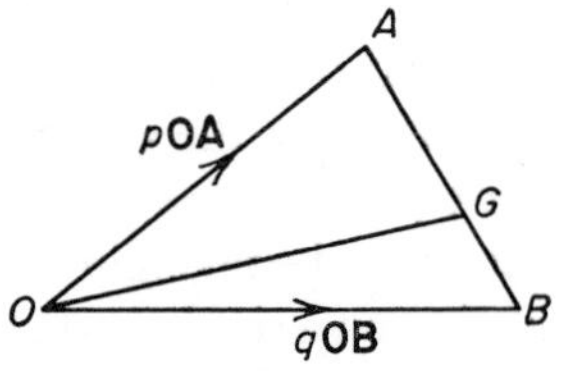

Fig. 6.11

Resultant of forces pOA and qOB

The resultant of two concurrent forces $p\mathbf{OA}$ and $q\mathbf{OB}$ is $(p+q)\,\mathbf{OG}$ where G is the point in AB such that $AG:GB = q:p$.

Proof. Referring to Fig. 6.11,

$$\begin{aligned} p\mathbf{OA}+q\mathbf{OB} &= p(\mathbf{OG}+\mathbf{GA})+q(\mathbf{OG}+\mathbf{GB}) \\ &= (p+q)\,\mathbf{OG}+p\mathbf{GA}+q\mathbf{GB}. \end{aligned}$$

But we are given $p\mathbf{AG} = q\mathbf{GB}$,

$$\therefore \quad p\mathbf{GA}+q\mathbf{GB} = 0,$$

$$\therefore \quad p\mathbf{OA}+q\mathbf{OB} = (p+q)\mathbf{OG}.$$

Examples

(1) *ABCDEF is a regular hexagon. Forces* **AB, AC, AD, AE, AF** *act at the vertices A. If O is the centre of the hexagon prove that the resultant is a force* 6**AO**.

Method I

Let BF and CE meet AD at P and Q respectively (Fig. 6.12). From geometry P and Q are mid-points of FB and EC respectively.

$$\begin{aligned}\mathbf{AB}+\mathbf{AC}+\mathbf{AD}+\mathbf{AE}+\mathbf{AF} &= (\mathbf{AB}+\mathbf{AF})+(\mathbf{AC}+\mathbf{AE})+\mathbf{AD}\\ &= 2\mathbf{AP}+2\mathbf{AQ}+\mathbf{AD}\\ &= 2.\tfrac{1}{2}\mathbf{AO}+2.1\tfrac{1}{2}\mathbf{AO}+2\mathbf{AO}\\ &= 6\mathbf{AO}.\end{aligned}$$

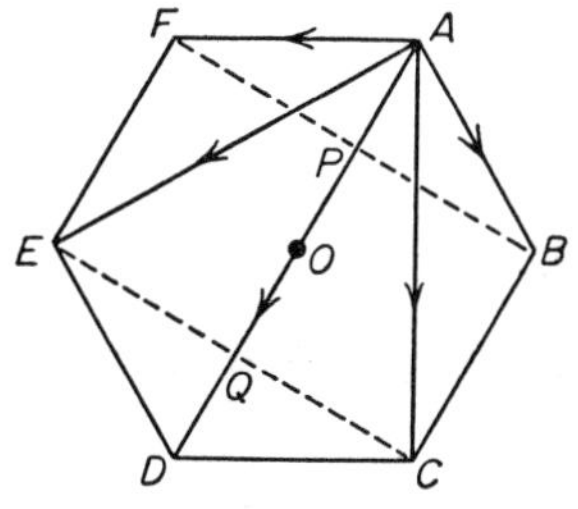

Fig. 6.12

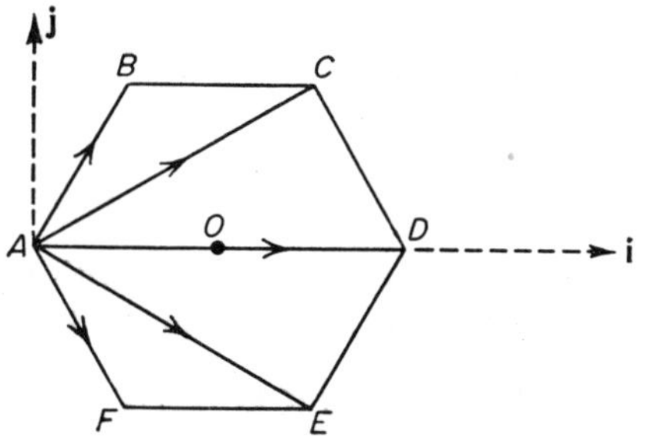

Fig. 6.13

Method II

Let **i** and **j** be unit forces in the directions AD and perpendicular to AD (Fig. 6.13). Let $AO = r$.

$$\begin{aligned}\mathbf{AB}+\mathbf{AC}+\mathbf{AD}+\mathbf{AE}+\mathbf{AF} &= (r\cos 60^\circ\mathbf{i}+r\sin 60^\circ\mathbf{j})\\ &\quad+(\sqrt{3}r\cos 30^\circ\mathbf{i}+\sqrt{3}r\sin 30^\circ\mathbf{j})\\ &\quad+(2r\mathbf{i})\\ &\quad+(\sqrt{3}r\cos 30^\circ\mathbf{i}-\sqrt{3}r\sin 30^\circ\mathbf{j})\\ &\quad+(r\cos 60^\circ\mathbf{i}-r\sin 60^\circ\mathbf{j})\\ &= (2r\cos 60^\circ+2\sqrt{3}r\cos 30^\circ+2r)\mathbf{i}\\ &= (r+3r+2r)\mathbf{i}\\ &= 6\mathbf{AO}.\end{aligned}$$

(2) *Find the resultant of the forces* **3BA**, **4BC**, **6CA** *which act along the sides of a triangle ABC.*

$$\mathbf{3BA}+\mathbf{4BC} = \mathbf{7BD} \quad \text{where} \quad AD:DC = 4:3. \quad \text{(See Fig. 6.14}a\text{.)}$$

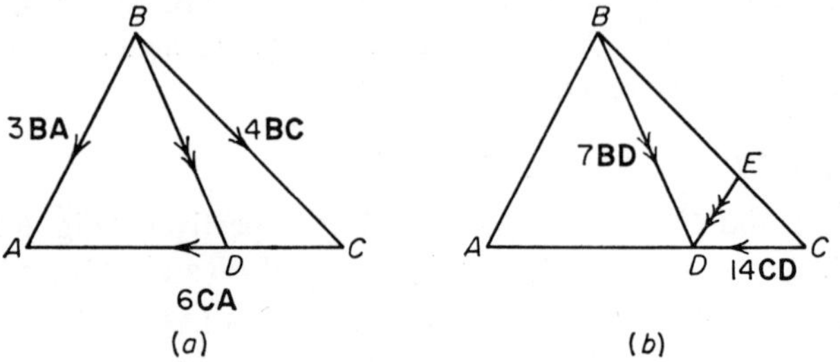

Fig. 6.14

We now have to combine **7BD** and **6CA**.

Now

$$CA:CD = 7:3,$$

$$\therefore \quad \mathbf{CA} = \tfrac{7}{3}\mathbf{CD},$$

$$\therefore \quad \mathbf{6CA} = \mathbf{14CD}.$$

We can now combine **7BD** with **14CD** since they both terminate at the same point D. (See Fig. 6.14*b*.)

$$\mathbf{7BD}+\mathbf{14CD} = \mathbf{21ED} \quad \text{where} \quad BE:EC = 2:1.$$

Therefore resultant is **21ED** where $BE:EC = 2:1$ and $AD:DC = 4:3$.

Centre of mass

Let masses of $m_1, m_2, m_3, \ldots$ be situated at the points $A, B, C, \ldots$ whose position vectors relative to an origin O are **a**, **b**, **c**, ... (Fig. 6.15).

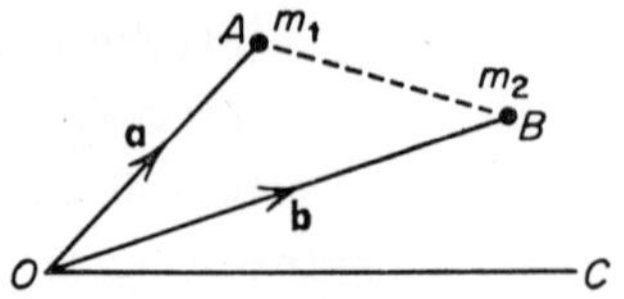

Fig. 6.15

Centre of mass of m_1 and m_2 is defined as the point P which divides AB in the ratio $m_2 : m_1$.

$$\therefore \quad \text{position vector of c. of m. of } m_1 \text{ and } m_2 = \frac{m_1\mathbf{a}+m_2\mathbf{b}}{m_1+m_2}.$$

C. of m. of (m_1+m_2) and m_3 divides PC in ratio $m_3 : (m_1+m_2)$.

$\therefore$ position vector of c. of m. of m_1, m_2 and m_3

$$= \frac{(m_1+m_2)\dfrac{m_1\mathbf{a}+m_2\mathbf{b}}{m_1+m_2}+m_3\mathbf{c}}{m_1+m_2+m_3}$$

$$= \frac{m_1\mathbf{a}+m_2\mathbf{b}+m_3\mathbf{c}}{m_1+m_2+m_3}.$$

Hence,

$$\text{position vector of c. of m. of all particles} = \frac{m_1\mathbf{a}+m_2\mathbf{b}+m_3\mathbf{c}+\dots}{m_1+m_2+m_3+\dots}$$

$$= \frac{\Sigma m\mathbf{a}}{\Sigma m}.$$

Thus the c. of m. of a system of particles of masses $m_1, m_2, m_3, \dots$ at points $A, B, C, \dots$ is the same as the centroid of the points $A, B, C, \dots$ with associated numbers $m_1, m_2, m_3, \dots$.

Centre of gravity

The centre of gravity of a system of particles is defined as the point through which the line of action of the resultant of the system of parallel forces acting on the particles passes, the forces being proportional to the masses of the particles. With this definition the centre of gravity can be shown to be identical with the centre of mass.

Example

Masses of 5, 3, 2 *lb. are situated at the points* (0, 2, 0), (6, −4, −8), (1, 6, −3). *Show that the centre of mass is the point* (2, 1, −3).

Let O be the origin and G the centre of mass.

$$\mathbf{OG} = \frac{\Sigma m\mathbf{a}}{\Sigma m}$$

$$= \frac{5(0\mathbf{i}+2\mathbf{j}+0\mathbf{k})+3(6\mathbf{i}-4\mathbf{j}-8\mathbf{k})+2(1\mathbf{i}+6\mathbf{j}-3\mathbf{k})}{10}$$

$$= \frac{20\mathbf{i}+10\mathbf{j}-30\mathbf{k}}{10}$$

$$= 2\mathbf{i}+\mathbf{j}-3\mathbf{k}.$$

Therefore centre of mass is the point (2, 1, −3).

Exercise 6

(1) If the components parallel to the x and y axes of the displacement $\mathbf{a}$ are 1 and -2 units, of the displacement $\mathbf{b}$ are -1 and 3 units and of the displacement $\mathbf{c}$ are 4 and 2 units, find the magnitude and direction of the displacements $\mathbf{a}+\mathbf{b}+\mathbf{c}$ and $\mathbf{a}-2\mathbf{b}+3\mathbf{c}$.

(2) If $\mathbf{a}$ is 4 units north, $\mathbf{b}$ is 7 units east and $\mathbf{c}$ is 4 units vertically upwards, find $\mathbf{a}+\mathbf{b}+\mathbf{c}$ and $\mathbf{a}+\mathbf{b}-\mathbf{c}$.

(3) A person travelling due east at 4 m.p.h. finds that the wind appears to blow directly from the north. When he doubles his speed the wind appears to come from the north-east. Find the velocity of the wind.

(4) The velocity of a particle A relative to a particle B is $5\mathbf{i}+2\mathbf{j}$, and the velocity of B relative to a third particle C is $2\mathbf{i}-5\mathbf{j}$. Find the magnitude and direction of the velocity of A relative to C assuming that $\mathbf{i}$ and $\mathbf{j}$ represent velocities of 1 ft./sec. horizontally and vertically respectively.

(5) At a certain instant two particles P and Q occupy positions A and B respectively 20 ft. apart. P moves towards Q with uniform velocity of 3 ft./sec., while Q moves in a direction perpendicular to AB with uniform velocity of 4 ft./sec. Determine: (i) velocity of Q relative to P; (ii) the shortest distance apart of the particles; (iii) the time taken to reach this shortest distance.

(6) Two particles move with speeds v and $2v$ respectively in opposite directions on the circumference of a circle. Show that their relative velocity has a maximum value of $3v$ when they cross one another, and a minimum value of v when they are at opposite ends of a diameter.

(7) Two particles P and Q are moving with the same speed v. P moves in a circle of centre O. Q moves along a fixed diameter AB of the circle and in the direction AB. If angle POB is θ show that the velocity of Q relative to P is $v\sqrt{(2+2\sin\theta)}$ at an angle $\frac{1}{2}\theta-\frac{1}{4}\pi$ with AB.

(8) A rigid body is rotating with an angular velocity of 6 radians per second about an axis OR where R is the point $(2, -2, 1)$. Find the angular velocity vector $\boldsymbol{\omega}$.

(9) A, B, C, D are the points $(2, -1, -1)$, $(5, 2, -1)$, $(2, -4, 2)$, $(3, -2, 3)$ respectively. Forces of 3, 1, 2 lb. wt. act along AB, AC, AD respectively. Find their resultant.

(10) Forces of 1, 2 and 3 lb. wt. act at the corner O of a cube one

along each of the diagonals of the faces which meet at O. Find the magnitude of the resultant and its inclination to each of the edges which meet at O.

(11) $ABCD$ is a quadrilateral. Show that the resultant of the forces **AB, AD, CB, CD** is **4PQ** where P, Q are the mid-points of AC, BD respectively.

(12) If G is the centroid of a triangle ABC, prove that the resultant of forces completely represented by **GA, 2GB, 3GC** is **3GD** where D is the point in BC such that $BD = 2DC$.

(13) B and E are the mid-points of the sides AC and DF of a quadrilateral $ACDF$. Show that the system of forces completely represented by **AD, BF, CE, DB, EA, FC** is in equilibrium.

(14) Forces represented by **BA, CA, 2BC** act along the sides of a triangle ABC. Show that their resultant is represented by **6DE**, where D bisects BC and E is the point of trisection of CA nearer C.

(15) Show that the resultant of forces represented by **PA, 2PB, 3PC** is **6PG** where G is the mid-point of the line joining C to a point of trisection of AB.

(16) $ABCD$ is a cyclic quadrilateral. Forces act on a particle at A in directions AB, AD their magnitudes being kDC and kBC respectively. Show that their resultant is of magnitude kBD in the direction AC.

(17) Masses of $m, 2m, \ldots, 6m$ are situated at the angular points O, A, B, C, D, E respectively of a regular hexagon $OABCDE$ of side a. Show that the distances of the centre of mass from OA and OD are $\frac{9\sqrt{3}a}{14}$ and $\frac{5a}{14}$ respectively.

(18) Masses of 2, 4, 6, 8 lb. are situated at the points $(2, -3, 4)$, $(0, 4, 5)$, $(1, -1, 2)$, $(3, 0, -2)$ respectively. Find the co-ordinates of the centre of mass.

7

DIFFERENTIATION AND INTEGRATION

Definition of the derivative of a vector

Suppose **r** is a continuous and single-valued function of a scalar variable t. Let **r** become $\mathbf{r}+\delta\mathbf{r}$ when t becomes $t+\delta t$, δt being small.

The differential coefficient, or the derivative, of **r** with respect to t is defined as

$$\operatorname*{Lt}_{\delta t\to 0}\frac{\delta\mathbf{r}}{\delta t}, \text{ providing this limit exists.}$$

It is written as $d\mathbf{r}/dt$. Thus

$$\frac{d\mathbf{r}}{dt} = \operatorname*{Lt}_{\delta t\to 0}\frac{\delta\mathbf{r}}{\delta t}.$$

Let $\mathbf{OP} = \mathbf{r}$ and $\mathbf{OP}' = \mathbf{r}+\delta\mathbf{r}$ (Fig. 7.1).

$$\therefore\quad \mathbf{OP}+\mathbf{PP}' = \mathbf{OP}',$$

$$\therefore\quad \mathbf{r}+\mathbf{PP}' = \mathbf{r}+\delta\mathbf{r},$$

$$\therefore\quad \mathbf{PP}' = \delta\mathbf{r},$$

$$\therefore\quad \frac{\delta\mathbf{r}}{\delta t} = \frac{\mathbf{PP}'}{\delta t}.$$

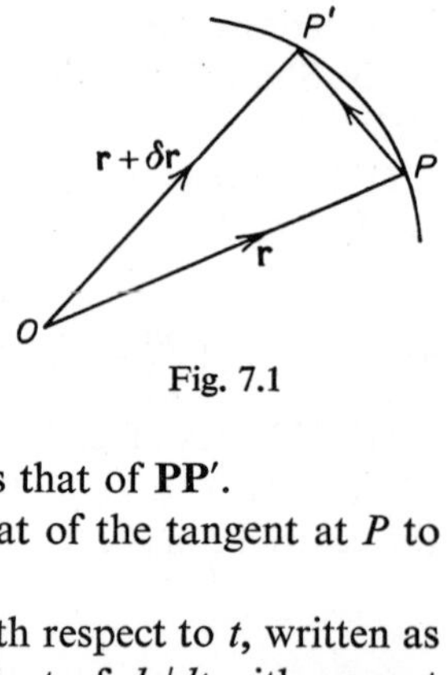

Fig. 7.1

Hence $\delta\mathbf{r}/\delta t$ is a vector whose direction is that of $\mathbf{PP}'$.

In the limit as $\delta t \to 0$ this direction is that of the tangent at P to the locus of P as t varies.

The second differential coefficient of **r** with respect to t, written as $d^2\mathbf{r}/dt^2$, is defined as the differential coefficient of $d\mathbf{r}/dt$ with respect to t.

If the scalar variable t is the time then as we shall see $d\mathbf{r}/dt$ and $d^2\mathbf{r}/dt^2$ represent the velocity and acceleration respectively, of a point at any time t. It is often convenient to write the velocity and acceleration of a point **r** as $\dot{\mathbf{r}}$ and $\ddot{\mathbf{r}}$ respectively.

Rules for the differentiation of vectors

(*a*) *Derivative of a constant vector*

$$\frac{d\mathbf{c}}{dt} = 0 \quad (\mathbf{c} \text{ is a constant}).$$

Proof. If **c** is a constant, an increment δt in t will produce no change in **c**.

$$\therefore \quad \frac{d\mathbf{c}}{dt} = 0.$$

(*b*) *Derivative of the product of a constant scalar and a vector*

$$\frac{d}{dt}(a\mathbf{r}) = a\frac{d\mathbf{r}}{dt}.$$

Proof. Let $\mathbf{b} = a\mathbf{r}$.

Suppose $\delta\mathbf{r}$ and $\delta\mathbf{b}$ are the increments in **r** and **b** respectively due to an increment δt in t.

Then
$$\mathbf{b}+\delta\mathbf{b} = a(\mathbf{r}+\delta\mathbf{r})$$
$$= a\mathbf{r}+a\delta\mathbf{r},$$
$$\therefore \quad \delta\mathbf{b} = a\delta\mathbf{r},$$
$$\therefore \quad \frac{\delta\mathbf{b}}{\delta t} = a\frac{\delta\mathbf{r}}{\delta t}.$$
$$\therefore \quad \operatorname*{Lt}_{\delta t\to 0}\frac{\delta\mathbf{b}}{\delta t} = \operatorname*{Lt}_{\delta t\to 0} a\frac{\delta\mathbf{r}}{\delta t},$$
$$\therefore \quad \frac{d\mathbf{b}}{dt} = a\frac{d\mathbf{r}}{dt},$$
$$\therefore \quad \frac{d}{dt}(a\mathbf{r}) = a\frac{d\mathbf{r}}{dt}.$$

(*c*) *Derivative of the sum of two vectors*

$$\frac{d}{dt}(\mathbf{r}+\mathbf{s}) = \frac{d\mathbf{r}}{dt}+\frac{d\mathbf{s}}{dt}.$$

Proof. Let $\mathbf{p} = \mathbf{r}+\mathbf{s}$

Suppose $\delta\mathbf{p}$, $\delta\mathbf{r}$ and $\delta\mathbf{s}$ are the increments in **p**, **r** and **s** respectively due to an increment δt in t.

Then

$$(\mathbf{p}+\delta\mathbf{p}) = (\mathbf{r}+\delta\mathbf{r})+(\mathbf{s}+\delta\mathbf{s}),$$

$$\therefore \quad \delta\mathbf{p} = \delta\mathbf{r}+\delta\mathbf{s},$$

$$\therefore \quad \frac{\delta\mathbf{p}}{\delta t} = \frac{\delta\mathbf{r}}{\delta t}+\frac{\delta\mathbf{s}}{\delta t},$$

$$\therefore \quad \underset{\delta t\to 0}{\mathrm{Lt}} \frac{\delta\mathbf{p}}{\delta t} = \underset{\delta t\to 0}{\mathrm{Lt}} \left(\frac{\delta\mathbf{r}}{\delta t}+\frac{\delta\mathbf{s}}{\delta t}\right),$$

$$\therefore \quad \frac{d\mathbf{p}}{dt} = \frac{d\mathbf{r}}{dt}+\frac{d\mathbf{s}}{dt},$$

$$\therefore \quad \frac{d}{dt}(\mathbf{r}+\mathbf{s}) = \frac{d\mathbf{r}}{dt}+\frac{d\mathbf{s}}{dt}.$$

(*d*) *Derivative of a vector function of a scalar function*

$$\frac{d\mathbf{r}}{dt} = \frac{d\mathbf{r}}{ds}\cdot\frac{ds}{dt} \quad \text{where} \quad s = f(t).$$

Proof. Let $\mathbf{r}$ be a function of the scalar variable s and s a function of t.

Suppose $\delta\mathbf{r}$ and δs are the increments in $\mathbf{r}$ and s due to an increment δt in t.

Then

$$\frac{\delta\mathbf{r}}{\delta t} = \frac{\delta\mathbf{r}}{\delta s}\cdot\frac{\delta s}{\delta t},$$

$$\therefore \quad \underset{\delta t\to 0}{\mathrm{Lt}} \frac{\delta\mathbf{r}}{\delta t} = \underset{\delta t\to 0}{\mathrm{Lt}} \frac{\delta\mathbf{r}}{\delta s}\cdot\frac{\delta s}{\delta t},$$

$$\therefore \quad \frac{d\mathbf{r}}{dt} = \frac{d\mathbf{r}}{ds}\cdot\frac{ds}{dt}.$$

(*e*) *Derivative of the product of a variable scalar and vector*

$$\frac{d}{dt}(u\mathbf{v}) = u\frac{d\mathbf{v}}{dt}+\mathbf{v}\frac{du}{dt} \quad (u, \mathbf{v} \text{ are variables}).$$

Proof. Let u be a scalar function of t.

Let $\mathbf{a} = u\mathbf{v}$.

Suppose δu, $\delta\mathbf{v}$ and $\delta\mathbf{a}$ are the increments in u, $\mathbf{v}$ and $\mathbf{a}$ respectively due to an increment δt in t.

Then

$$\mathbf{a}+\delta\mathbf{a} = (u+\delta u)(\mathbf{v}+\delta\mathbf{v})$$

$$= u\mathbf{v}+u\delta\mathbf{v}+\mathbf{v}\delta u+\delta u\,\delta\mathbf{v},$$

$$\therefore\quad \delta\mathbf{a} = u\delta\mathbf{v}+\mathbf{v}\delta u+\delta u\,\delta\mathbf{v},$$

$$\therefore\quad \frac{\delta\mathbf{a}}{\delta t} = u\frac{\delta\mathbf{v}}{\delta t}+\mathbf{v}\frac{\delta u}{\delta t}+\frac{\delta u}{\delta t}\delta\mathbf{v},$$

$$\therefore\quad \underset{\delta t\to 0}{\mathrm{Lt}}\frac{\delta\mathbf{a}}{\delta t} = \underset{\delta t\to 0}{\mathrm{Lt}}\left(u\frac{\delta\mathbf{v}}{\delta t}+\mathbf{v}\frac{\delta u}{\delta t}+\frac{\delta u}{\delta t}\delta\mathbf{v}\right),$$

$$\therefore\quad \frac{d\mathbf{a}}{dt} = u\frac{d\mathbf{v}}{dt}+\mathbf{v}\frac{du}{dt}.$$

$$\therefore\quad \frac{d}{dt}(u\mathbf{v}) = u\frac{d\mathbf{v}}{dt}+\mathbf{v}\frac{du}{dt}.$$

Derivative of a vector in terms of its components

Let $\mathbf{r} = x\mathbf{i}+y\mathbf{j}+z\mathbf{k}$.

Since the unit vectors $\mathbf{i}$, $\mathbf{j}$ and $\mathbf{k}$ are constant in magnitude and direction

$$\frac{d\mathbf{r}}{dt} = \frac{dx}{dt}\mathbf{i}+\frac{dy}{dt}\mathbf{j}+\frac{dz}{dt}\mathbf{k}.$$

Hence the components of the derivative of a vector are the derivatives of its components for fixed directions.

Higher derivatives may be obtained in the same way. Thus

$$\frac{d^2\mathbf{r}}{dt^2} = \frac{d^2x}{dt^2}\mathbf{i}+\frac{d^2y}{dt^2}\mathbf{j}+\frac{d^2z}{dt^2}\mathbf{k}.$$

Velocity

We now consider the case of a particle moving with variable velocity. Let the position of the particle relative to an origin O at time t be $\mathbf{OP} = \mathbf{r}$ and at time $t+\delta t$ be $\mathbf{OP}' = \mathbf{r}+\delta\mathbf{r}$ (Fig. 7.2).

Then $\mathbf{PP}' = \mathbf{OP}'-\mathbf{OP} = \delta\mathbf{r}$.

The average velocity of the particle relative to O during the time interval δt is defined as $\mathbf{PP}'/\delta t$, i.e. $\delta\mathbf{r}/\delta t$.

The instantaneous velocity, or briefly the velocity, of the particle relative to O at the instant t is defined as the rate of change of its position relative to O, i.e. $d\mathbf{r}/dt$ which can be written as $\dot{\mathbf{r}}$.

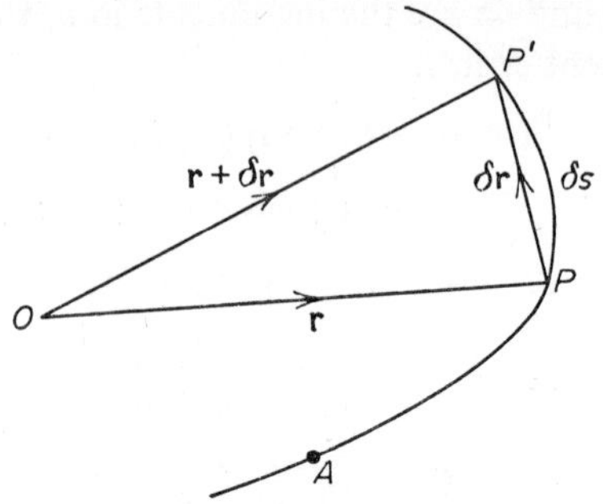

Fig. 7.2

Suppose A is any fixed point on the path of the particle and let arc $AP = s$ where s is positive if the particle after passing through A passes through P. Then we can write arc $PP' = \delta s$. We define the average speed of the particle during the interval of time δt as $\delta s/\delta t$. Now

$$\frac{d\mathbf{r}}{dr} = \underset{\delta t \to 0}{\mathrm{Lt}} \frac{\delta \mathbf{r}}{\delta t} = \underset{\delta t \to 0}{\mathrm{Lt}} \frac{\delta \mathbf{r}}{\delta s} \cdot \frac{\delta s}{\delta t}.$$

As $\delta t \to 0$, i.e. as P' approaches P, $(\delta s/\delta t) \to (ds/dt)$ which being the rate of increase of the distance of the particle from a fixed point in its path is its speed at time t. Also as $\delta t \to 0$, $|\delta \mathbf{r}|/\delta s \to 1$ and the direction of $\delta \mathbf{r}/\delta t \to$ the direction of the tangent at P, the sense of direction being the same as that of s increasing. If $\hat{\mathbf{t}}$ is the unit vector parallel to and having the same sense as this tangent we can write

$$\frac{d\mathbf{r}}{dt} = \frac{ds}{dt}\hat{\mathbf{t}}.$$

Thus the magnitude of the instantaneous velocity $\dot{\mathbf{r}}$ at the instant t is the positive value of the speed and its direction is along the tangent to the path at P.

We now show that velocity as defined by $d\mathbf{r}/dt$ is a vector. Suppose the motion of the particle P is compared by two observers moving relatively to one another. Each observer will have his own frame of reference which is fixed relative to himself. Suppose $OXYZ$, $O'X'Y'Z'$ are the two frames of reference which have no rotation relative to one another, i.e. the frames have different origins O, O' but the same initial directions (Fig. 7.3). This being so it will be sufficient when describing the relative motion to say 'relative to the origin' instead of 'relative to the frame'.

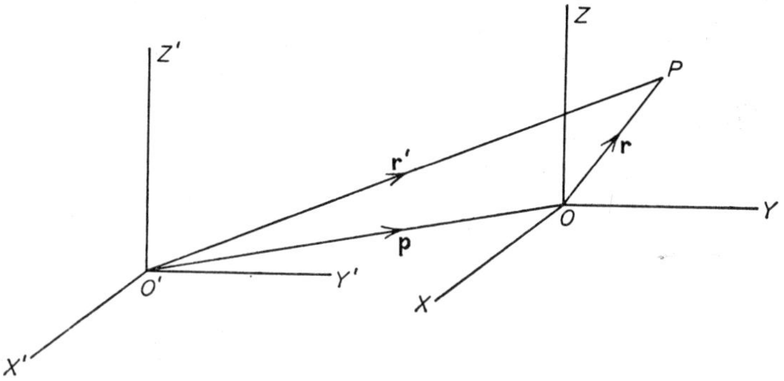

Fig. 7.3

Let **r**, **r**′ be the position vectors of P relative to O and O' respectively at the instant t. Also let **p** be the position vector of O relative to O' at the same time. Then we have

$$\mathbf{r}' = \mathbf{r}+\mathbf{p}.$$

This tells us that the position of P relative to O' is the vector sum of the position of P relative to O and the position of O relative to O'.

Differentiating with respect to the time t we have

$$\dot{\mathbf{r}}' = \dot{\mathbf{r}}+\dot{\mathbf{p}},$$

i.e. velocity of P relative to O' = velocity of P relative to O
+ velocity of O relative to O'.

This shows that in general velocities are added vectorially, a result we have shown previously for uniform velocities. Hence we conclude that velocity is a vector.

We note again that when $\dot{\mathbf{p}} = 0$ the velocity of a particle is the same relative to all fixed points.

Acceleration

Let **v** be the velocity relative to an origin O of a particle P at time t (Fig. 7.4). Take **v** to be the position vector of a point Q relative to a frame of reference with Ω as its origin. Now as **v** varies with time the point Q will also vary in position and trace out a locus which is known as the hodograph of the motion of the particle P. Suppose during the interval of time δt the particle moves from P to P' and its velocity changes from $\mathbf{v}$ to $\mathbf{v}+\delta\mathbf{v}$. Then the point Q will move along the hodograph to Q' where $\mathbf{\Omega Q'} = \mathbf{v}+\delta\mathbf{v}$ (Fig. 7.4).

The average acceleration during the interval of time δt is defined by $\mathbf{QQ'}/\delta t$, i.e. $\delta\mathbf{v}/\delta t$.

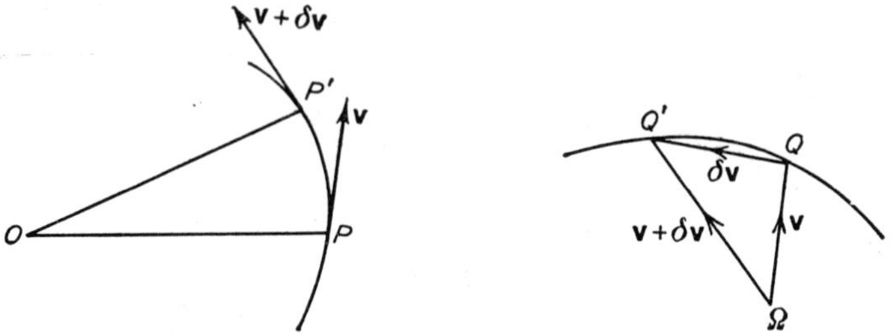

Fig. 7.4

The instantaneous acceleration, or briefly the acceleration, of the particle at the instant t is defined as the rate of change of its velocity, i.e. $d\mathbf{v}/dt$ which can be written as $\dot{\mathbf{v}}$ or $\ddot{\mathbf{r}}$.

Now

$$\frac{d\mathbf{v}}{dt} = \underset{\delta t \to 0}{\mathrm{Lt}} \frac{\delta\mathbf{v}}{\delta t} = \underset{\delta t \to 0}{\mathrm{Lt}} \frac{\mathbf{QQ'}}{\delta t}.$$

We see that as $\delta t \to 0$, $Q' \to Q$ and hence the direction of the instantaneous acceleration is that of the tangent at the point Q on the hodograph.

As before we compare the motion of P relative to two frames of reference. We have shown in the previous section that

$$\dot{\mathbf{r}}' = \dot{\mathbf{r}}+\dot{\mathbf{p}}.$$

Differentiating again with respect to the time t we have,

$$\ddot{\mathbf{r}}' = \ddot{\mathbf{r}}+\ddot{\mathbf{p}},$$

i.e. acceleration of P relative to O' = acceleration of P relative to O
+ acceleration of O relative to O'.

Since this shows that accelerations are added vectorially we conclude that acceleration is a vector.

We note that when $\ddot{\mathbf{p}} = 0$ the acceleration of a particle is the same relative to all points moving with constant velocity.

Derivative of a unit vector

Let $\mathbf{OP} = \hat{\mathbf{u}}$ be the position of a unit vector at a time t and $\mathbf{OP}' = \hat{\mathbf{u}}+\delta\hat{\mathbf{u}}$ be its position at a time $t+\delta t$ (Fig. 7.5). We then have

$$\mathbf{OP}' = \mathbf{OP}+\mathbf{PP}',$$

$$\therefore \quad \hat{\mathbf{u}}+\delta\hat{\mathbf{u}} = \hat{\mathbf{u}}+\mathbf{PP}',$$

$$\therefore \quad \delta\hat{\mathbf{u}} = \mathbf{PP}',$$

$$\therefore \quad \frac{\delta\hat{\mathbf{u}}}{\delta t} = \frac{\mathbf{PP}'}{\delta t},$$

$$\therefore \quad \frac{d\hat{\mathbf{u}}}{dt} = \operatorname*{Lt}_{\delta t\to 0} \frac{\mathbf{PP}'}{\delta t}.$$

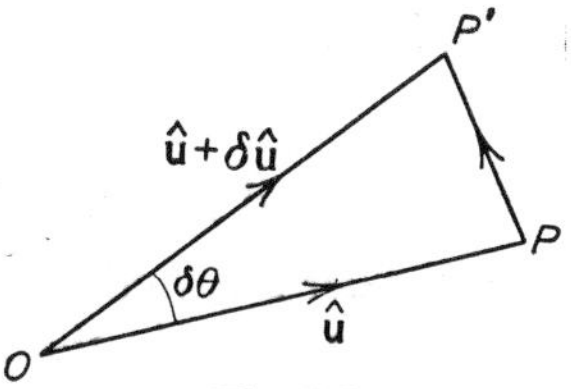

Fig. 7.5

Since $\quad |\mathbf{OP}| = |\mathbf{OP}'| = 1,$

$$|\mathbf{PP}'| = 2\sin\tfrac{1}{2}\delta\theta \text{ where angle } POP' = \delta\theta,$$

$$\therefore \quad \frac{|\mathbf{PP}'|}{\delta t} = \frac{2\sin\frac{1}{2}\delta\theta}{\delta t}$$

$$= \frac{\sin\frac{1}{2}\delta\theta}{\frac{1}{2}\delta\theta}\frac{\delta\theta}{\delta t}.$$

As $\delta t \to 0$, $\delta\theta \to 0$,

$$\frac{\sin\frac{1}{2}\delta\theta}{\frac{1}{2}\delta\theta} \to 1 \quad \text{and} \quad \frac{\delta\theta}{\delta t} \to \frac{d\theta}{dt}.$$

Hence in the limit $\mathbf{PP}'/\delta t$ has the magnitude $d\theta/dt$ and its direction is perpendicular to $\mathbf{OP}$. If $\hat{\mathbf{p}}$ is the unit vector perpendicular to the unit vector $\hat{\mathbf{u}}$ in the plane of motion and in the direction of θ increasing we have

$$\frac{d\hat{\mathbf{u}}}{dt} = \frac{d\theta}{dt}\hat{\mathbf{p}} \quad \text{or} \quad \dot{\hat{\mathbf{u}}} = \dot{\theta}\hat{\mathbf{p}}.$$

It is important to note that the direction of $\hat{\mathbf{p}}$ is the direction of $\hat{\mathbf{u}}$ when $\hat{\mathbf{u}}$ is rotated anticlockwise through a right angle, since the convention for positive angles is anticlockwise rotation.

Thus if $\hat{\mathbf{u}}$ is a unit vector which rotates in a plane with angular velocity $\dot{\theta}$ then $d\hat{\mathbf{u}}/dt$ is a vector of magnitude $\dot{\theta}$ and in a direction at right angles to $\hat{\mathbf{u}}$ in the plane.

If $\hat{\mathbf{p}}$ is rotated again in the positive direction the direction is that of $-\hat{\mathbf{u}}$. Thus

$$\dot{\hat{\mathbf{p}}} = -\dot{\theta}\hat{\mathbf{u}}.$$

Motion of a particle in two dimensions

An important application of differentiation of vectors is in the consideration of the motion of a particle in two dimensions. This motion can be referred in terms of Cartesian, polar or intrinsic co-ordinates.

Velocity and acceleration in Cartesian co-ordinates

Consider the motion of a particle in a plane curve (Fig. 7.6). Let O be a fixed point in the plane and OX, OY rectangular axes in the plane. Denoting the position vector of P by $\mathbf{r}$ and the unit vectors in the OX, OY directions by $\mathbf{i}$, $\mathbf{j}$ we have

$$\mathbf{r} = x\mathbf{i}+y\mathbf{j},$$

$$\therefore \quad \dot{\mathbf{r}} = \dot{x}\mathbf{i}+\dot{y}\mathbf{j},$$

and $$\ddot{\mathbf{r}} = \ddot{x}\mathbf{i}+\ddot{y}\mathbf{j}.$$

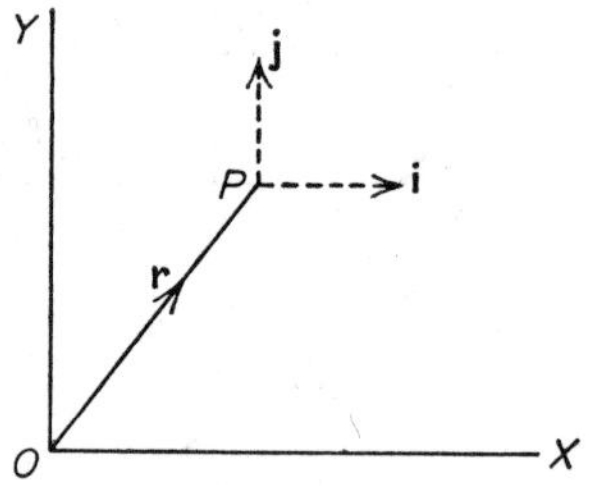

Fig. 7.6

Thus the velocity components parallel to the OX and OY axes are $\dot{x}$ and $\dot{y}$ respectively, and the acceleration components in these directions are $\ddot{x}$ and $\ddot{y}$.

$$\therefore \quad \text{velocity} = \sqrt{(\dot{x}^2+\dot{y}^2)},$$

$$\text{and acceleration} = \sqrt{(\ddot{x}^2+\ddot{y}^2)}.$$

Examples

(1) *The position vector of a particle at time t is given by*

$$\mathbf{r} = (\tfrac{1}{2}at^2)\,\mathbf{i}+(\tfrac{1}{2}bt^2+ut)\,\mathbf{j},$$

where a, b, u are constants and **i**, **j** *are unit vectors in the direction of the x-, y-axes respectively. Obtain its velocity at time t* = 0 *and show that its acceleration at any time has the constant value* $\sqrt{(a^2+b^2)}$. *Also show that its path is a parabola.*

$$\mathbf{r} = \frac{at^2}{2}\mathbf{i}+\left(\frac{bt^2}{2}+ut\right)\mathbf{j}.$$

Differentiating with respect to (t),

$$\dot{\mathbf{r}} = at\mathbf{i}+(bt+u)\,\mathbf{j}.$$

When $t = 0$, $$\dot{\mathbf{r}} = u\mathbf{j}.$$

Therefore velocity at $t = 0$ is u and in the direction of the y axis. Differentiating again

$$\ddot{\mathbf{r}} = a\mathbf{i}+b\mathbf{j}.$$

Therefore acceleration is independent of the time and is $\sqrt{(a^2+b^2)}$. We have

$$x = \frac{at^2}{2} \quad \text{and} \quad y = \frac{bt^2}{2}+ut.$$

Eliminating t,

$$y = \frac{b}{2}\frac{2x}{a}+u\sqrt{\frac{2x}{a}},$$

$$\therefore \quad y-\frac{bx}{a} = u\sqrt{\frac{2x}{a}},$$

$$\therefore \quad \left(y-\frac{bx}{a}\right)^2 = \frac{2u^2x}{a}.$$

This equation represents a parabola. Therefore the path of the particle is a parabola.

(2) *A particle moves in a plane and its co-ordinates at any time t are* $(a\cos nt,\, b\sin nt)$. *Show that its acceleration is always directed towards the origin of the co-ordinate system.*

Let $\mathbf{r}$ be the position vector of the particle relative to the origin and x, y the components of $\mathbf{r}$ in the direction of the unit vectors $\mathbf{i}$, $\mathbf{j}$ respectively. Then

$$\begin{aligned} \mathbf{r} &= x\mathbf{i}+y\mathbf{j} \\ &= a\cos nt\mathbf{i}+b\sin nt\mathbf{j}, \\ \therefore \quad \dot{\mathbf{r}} &= -na\sin nt\mathbf{i}+nb\cos nt\mathbf{j} \\ \therefore \quad \ddot{\mathbf{r}} &= -n^2a\cos nt\mathbf{i}-n^2b\sin nt\mathbf{j} \\ &= -n^2(a\cos nt\mathbf{i}+b\sin nt\mathbf{j}) \\ &= -n^2\mathbf{r}. \end{aligned}$$

Therefore its acceleration is always directed towards the origin.

Velocity and acceleration in polar co-ordinates

Let the path of a moving particle P be a plane curve (Fig. 7.7). Let O be a fixed origin and θ the inclination of OP to a fixed direction in the plane. Then the polar co-ordinates of P are (r, θ).

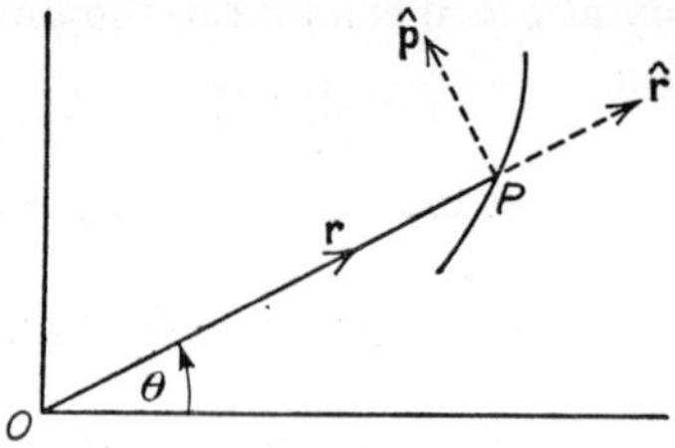

Fig. 7.7

Denote the position vector of P relative to the origin O by $\mathbf{r}$, the unit vector in the direction of $\mathbf{r}$ by $\hat{\mathbf{r}}$ and the unit vector in the plane perpendicular to $\hat{\mathbf{r}}$ by $\hat{\mathbf{p}}$, the right angle between $\hat{\mathbf{r}}$ and $\hat{\mathbf{p}}$ being measured in the conventional anticlockwise notation from $\hat{\mathbf{r}}$. It is important to note that $\hat{\mathbf{p}}$ is not in the direction of the tangent at P unless the path is a circle with O its centre.

We have

$$\mathbf{r} = r\hat{\mathbf{r}},$$

$$\therefore \quad \dot{\mathbf{r}} = \dot{r}\hat{\mathbf{r}} + r\frac{d\hat{\mathbf{r}}}{dt}$$

$$= \dot{r}\hat{\mathbf{r}} + r\dot{\theta}\hat{\mathbf{p}} \quad \text{(using differentiation of a unit vector).}$$

Therefore radial component of velocity $= \dot{r}$,

and transverse component of velocity $= r\dot{\theta}$.

For a particle moving in a circle centre O $\dot{r} = 0$, therefore the velocity $= r\dot{\theta}$ and is along the tangent.

Differentiating again,

$$\ddot{\mathbf{r}} = \ddot{r}\hat{\mathbf{r}} + \dot{r}\frac{d\hat{\mathbf{r}}}{dt} + \dot{r}\dot{\theta}\hat{\mathbf{p}} + r\ddot{\theta}\hat{\mathbf{p}} + r\dot{\theta}\frac{d\hat{\mathbf{p}}}{dt}$$

$$= \ddot{r}\hat{\mathbf{r}} + \dot{r}\dot{\theta}\hat{\mathbf{p}} + \dot{r}\dot{\theta}\hat{\mathbf{p}} + r\ddot{\theta}\hat{\mathbf{p}} - r\dot{\theta}^2\hat{\mathbf{r}}$$

$$= (\ddot{r} - r\dot{\theta}^2)\,\hat{\mathbf{r}} + (2\dot{r}\dot{\theta} + r\ddot{\theta})\,\hat{\mathbf{p}}.$$

Therefore radial component of acceleration $= \ddot{r} - r\dot{\theta}^2$,

and transverse component of acceleration $= 2\dot{r}\dot{\theta} + r\ddot{\theta}$

$$= \frac{1}{r}(2r\dot{r}\dot{\theta} + r^2\ddot{\theta})$$

$$= \frac{1}{r}\frac{d}{dt}(r^2\dot{\theta}).$$

For a particle moving in a circle centre O with uniform speed, $\dot{r} = 0$ and $\ddot{\theta} = 0$. Therefore the acceleration consists of the component $-r\dot{\theta}^2$, that is, it has an acceleration of $r\dot{\theta}^2$ directed towards the centre of the circle.

Example

A point moves along the equiangular spiral $r = e^\theta$ with uniform angular velocity about the origin. Prove that the acceleration is everywhere at right angles to the radius vector and proportional to its length.

Let the position vector of the point P relative to the origin be $\mathbf{r}$ and the unit vectors in the directions OP and perpendicular to OP be $\hat{\mathbf{r}}$ and $\hat{\mathbf{p}}$ respectively.

Since the angular velocity is uniform, $\dot{\theta} = \omega$ (say) and $\ddot{\theta} = 0$.

$$r = e^\theta,$$

$$\therefore \quad \dot{r} = e^\theta . \dot{\theta} = r\omega,$$

and
$$\ddot{r} = \dot{r}\omega = r\omega^2.$$

Now
$$\ddot{\mathbf{r}} = (\ddot{r} - r\dot{\theta}^2)\,\hat{\mathbf{r}} + (2\dot{r}\dot{\theta} + r\ddot{\theta})\,\hat{\mathbf{p}}$$
$$= (r\omega^2 - r\omega^2)\,\hat{\mathbf{r}} + 2r\omega^2\hat{\mathbf{p}}$$
$$= 2r\omega^2\hat{\mathbf{p}}.$$

Therefore acceleration is at right angles to the radius vector $\mathbf{r}$ and is proportional to its length r.

Velocity and acceleration in intrinsic co-ordinates

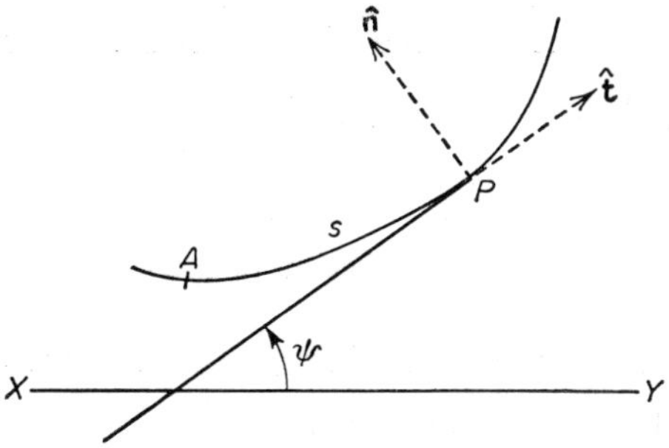

Fig. 7.8

Let A be a fixed point on the path of a moving particle and P the position of the particle at any time t (Fig. 7.8). Let arc $AP = s$ and let the tangent at P be inclined at an angle ψ to a fixed straight line XY. Then the intrinsic co-ordinates of P are (s, ψ). Let $P(s, \psi)$ be the position of the particle at a time t and $P'(s+\delta s, \psi+\delta\psi)$ its position at a time $t+\delta t$ (Fig. 7.9).

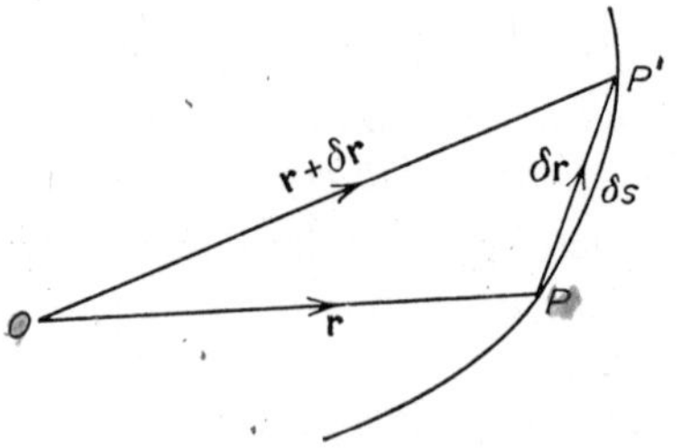

Fig. 7.9

Then $$\text{arc } PP' = \delta s.$$

Let the position vectors of P and P' relative to the origin O be $\mathbf{r}$ and $\mathbf{r}+\delta\mathbf{r}$ respectively.

The velocity $\mathbf{v}$ of P is defined as

$$\mathbf{v} = \underset{\delta t\to 0}{\mathrm{Lt}} \frac{\mathbf{PP'}}{\delta t}$$

$$= \underset{\delta t\to 0}{\mathrm{Lt}} \frac{\delta\mathbf{r}}{\delta t}$$

$$= \underset{\delta t\to 0}{\mathrm{Lt}} \frac{\delta\mathbf{r}}{\delta s}\cdot\frac{\delta s}{\delta t}.$$

As $\delta t \to 0$, the modulus of $\delta\mathbf{r} \to \delta s$, i.e. $\delta r/\delta s \to 1$ and the direction of $\delta\mathbf{r} \to$ the direction of the tangent at P.

Let $\hat{\mathbf{t}}$ be the unit vector in the direction of the tangent at P. Therefore in the limit,

$$\mathbf{v} = \frac{ds}{dt}\hat{\mathbf{t}},$$

$$\therefore \quad \mathbf{v} = \dot{s}\hat{\mathbf{t}}.$$

Thus the velocity is in the direction of the tangent and there is no normal component.

Let $\hat{\mathbf{n}}$ be the unit vector in the direction of the positive normal at P.

$$\therefore \quad \frac{d\hat{\mathbf{t}}}{dt} = \frac{d\psi}{dt}\hat{\mathbf{n}} = \dot{\psi}\hat{\mathbf{n}}.$$

Differentiating $\mathbf{v} = \dot{s}\hat{\mathbf{t}}$ we get

$$\dot{\mathbf{v}} = \ddot{s}\hat{\mathbf{t}} + \dot{s}\frac{d\hat{\mathbf{t}}}{dt}$$

$$= \ddot{s}\hat{\mathbf{t}} + \dot{s}\dot{\psi}\hat{\mathbf{n}}.$$

Therefore tangential component of acceleration $= \ddot{s}$,

and normal component of acceleration $= \dot{s}\dot{\psi}$.

The normal component can be written in terms of the radius of curvature of the path at P since

$$\dot{s}\dot{\psi} = \dot{s}\frac{d\psi}{ds}\cdot\frac{ds}{dt}$$

$$= \dot{s}^2 \Big/ \frac{ds}{d\psi}$$

$$= \frac{\dot{s}^2}{\rho},$$

where ρ = radius of curvature $= ds/d\psi$ by definition.

For a particle moving with constant speed u along the circumference of a circle of radius a, $\ddot{s} = \dot{u} = 0$ and $\rho = a$. Thus the acceleration is u^2/a and is directed towards the centre of the circle.

Example

A particle moves in the curve whose equation is $s = f(\psi)$ in such a way that the tangent to the curve rotates uniformly. Prove that the normal acceleration is proportional to the radius of curvature.

$$s = f(\psi),$$

$$\therefore \quad \dot{s} = f'(\psi).\dot{\psi}, \quad \text{where} \quad f'(\psi) = \frac{ds}{d\psi}.$$

Normal acceleration $= \dot{s}\dot{\psi}$

$$= f'(\psi).\dot{\psi}^2.$$

Radius of curvature $= \dfrac{ds}{d\psi}$ (by definition)

$$= f'(\psi),$$

therefore normal acceleration $= \rho\dot{\psi}^2$.

Since $\dot{\psi}$ = constant,

normal acceleration is proportional to ρ.

Summary

Velocity components

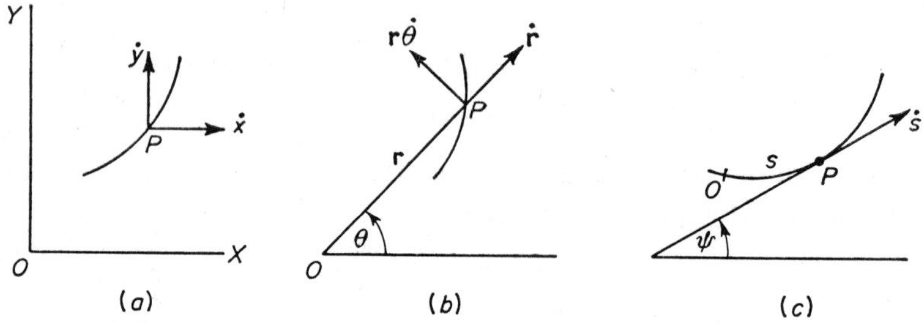

Fig. 7.10. (*a*) Cartesian, (*b*) Polar, (*c*) Intrinsic

Acceleration components

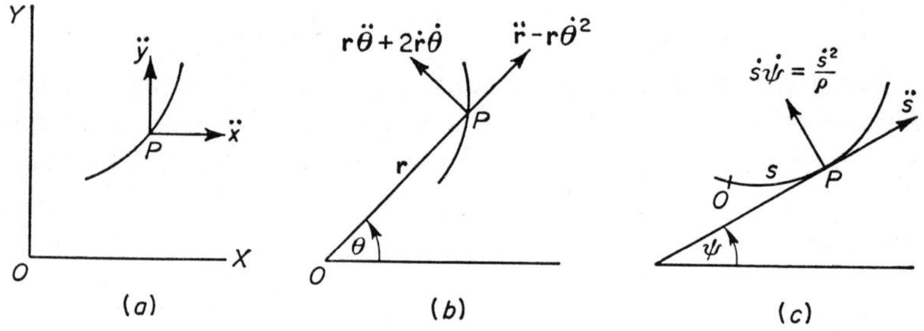

Fig. 7.11. (*a*) Cartesian, (*b*) Polar, (*c*) Intrinsic

Motion of a particle on a rotating plane

Consider the motion of a particle which is itself moving on a rotating plane. Let the plane rotate about a fixed point O with uniform angular velocity ω.

Let perpendicular axes Ox, Oy be drawn in the plane.

Let the position vector of the particle be

$$\mathbf{r} = x\mathbf{i}+y\mathbf{j},$$

where $\mathbf{i}$ and $\mathbf{j}$ are unit vectors in the Ox and Oy directions respectively which themselves rotate with the plane.

$$\therefore \quad \dot{\mathbf{r}} = \dot{x}\mathbf{i}+x\frac{d\mathbf{i}}{dt}+\dot{y}\mathbf{j}+y\frac{d\mathbf{j}}{dt}.$$

Now $$\frac{d\mathbf{i}}{dt} = \omega\mathbf{j} \quad \text{and} \quad \frac{d\mathbf{j}}{dt} = -\omega\mathbf{i},$$

from the differentiation of a unit vector.

$$\therefore \quad \dot{\mathbf{r}} = \dot{x}\mathbf{i} + \omega x\mathbf{j} + \dot{y}\mathbf{j} - \omega y\mathbf{i}$$

$$= (\dot{x} - \omega y)\mathbf{i} + (\dot{y} + \omega x)\mathbf{j}.$$

Thus the velocity of the particle consists of the two perpendicular components

$$\dot{x} - \omega y \quad \text{and} \quad \dot{y} + \omega x.$$

Differentiating again to obtain the acceleration,

$$\ddot{\mathbf{r}} = (\ddot{x} - \omega\dot{y})\mathbf{i} + (\dot{x} - \omega y)\frac{d\mathbf{i}}{dt} + (\ddot{y} + \omega\dot{x})\mathbf{j} + (\dot{y} + \omega x)\frac{d\mathbf{j}}{dt}$$

$$= (\ddot{x} - \omega\dot{y})\mathbf{i} + (\dot{x} - \omega y)\omega\mathbf{j} + (\ddot{y} + \omega\dot{x})\mathbf{j} - (\dot{y} + \omega x)\omega\mathbf{i}$$

$$= (\ddot{x} - 2\omega\dot{y} - \omega^2 x)\mathbf{i} + (\ddot{y} + 2\omega\dot{x} - \omega^2 y)\mathbf{j}.$$

The acceleration can be written as

$$\ddot{\mathbf{r}} = (\ddot{x}\mathbf{i} + \ddot{y}\mathbf{j}) + 2\omega(-\dot{y}\mathbf{i} + \dot{x}\mathbf{j}) - \omega^2(x\mathbf{i} + y\mathbf{j}).$$

$\ddot{x}\mathbf{i} + \ddot{y}\mathbf{j}$ is the acceleration of the particle with respect to the rotating co-ordinate system. If $\omega = 0$, i.e. the plane is stationary, this will be the only acceleration of the particle.

$2\omega(-\dot{y}\mathbf{i} + \dot{x}\mathbf{j})$ is the acceleration due to the velocity of the particle relative to the rotating co-ordinate system. This acceleration is known as the Coriolis acceleration and it vanishes if the particle is at rest relative to the plane.

$-\omega^2(x\mathbf{i} + y\mathbf{j}) = -\omega^2\mathbf{r}$ is the acceleration of the particle toward the centre of the rotation.

Example

An insect crawls outwards along a spoke of a bicycle wheel which is rotating uniformly at ω radians per second. If the insect crawls with uniform speed u find the magnitude and direction of its velocity and acceleration when it is a distance a from the centre.

Velocity is given by

$$\dot{\mathbf{r}} = (\dot{x} - \omega y)\mathbf{i} + (\dot{y} + \omega x)\mathbf{j},$$

where $x = a$, $\dot{x} = u$, $y = 0$, $\dot{y} = 0$, taking the rotating Ox axis as the spoke on which the insect crawls.

$$\therefore \quad \dot{\mathbf{r}} = u\mathbf{i}+\omega a\mathbf{j},$$

$$\therefore \quad \text{velocity} = \sqrt{(u^2+\omega^2a^2)} \text{ at } \tan^{-1} \omega a/u \text{ to the spoke.}$$

The acceleration is given by

$$\ddot{\mathbf{r}} = (\ddot{x}-2\omega\dot{y}-\omega^2x)\mathbf{i}+(\ddot{y}+2\omega\dot{x}-\omega^2y)\mathbf{j},$$

where $x = a$, $\dot{x} = u$, $\ddot{x} = 0$, $y = 0$, $\dot{y} = 0$, $\ddot{y} = 0$.

$$\therefore \quad \ddot{\mathbf{r}} = -\omega^2a\mathbf{i}+2\omega u\mathbf{j},$$

$$\therefore \quad \text{acceleration} = \omega\sqrt{(\omega^2a^2+4u^2)} \text{ at } \tan^{-1}-2u/\omega a \text{ to the spoke.}$$

Fig. 7.12 shows the directions of the velocity and acceleration.

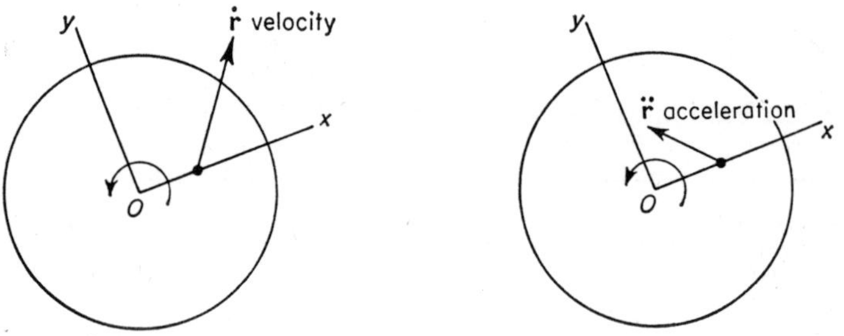

Fig. 7.12

This problem can also be solved by expressing the velocity and acceleration in terms of polar co-ordinates and this is left as an exercise.

Integration

Integration of a vector is the reverse process of the differentiation of a vector.

If $$\frac{d\mathbf{a}}{dt} = \mathbf{b} \quad \text{then} \quad \int \mathbf{b}\,dt = \mathbf{a}+\mathbf{c},$$

where $\mathbf{c}$ is an arbitary constant vector.

Examples

(1) *If at any time t after projection the position vector of a projectile relative to the point of projection is* $\mathbf{r}$ *and* $\mathbf{u}$ *its velocity of projection, obtain* $\mathbf{r}$ *in terms of* $\mathbf{u}$ *and t.*

If there are no resistances on the projectile and $\mathbf{g}$ is the acceleration due to gravity,

$$\ddot{\mathbf{r}} = \mathbf{g},$$

$$\therefore \quad \dot{\mathbf{r}} = \mathbf{g}t+\mathbf{a} \quad (\mathbf{a} = \text{constant of integration}).$$

When $t = 0$, $\dot{\mathbf{r}} = \mathbf{u}$,

$$\therefore \quad \mathbf{a} = \mathbf{u},$$

$$\therefore \quad \dot{\mathbf{r}} = \mathbf{g}t+\mathbf{u}.$$

Integrating again,

$$\mathbf{r} = \tfrac{1}{2}\mathbf{g}t^2+\mathbf{u}t+\mathbf{b} \quad (\mathbf{b} = \text{constant of integration}).$$

When $t = 0$, $\mathbf{r} = 0$ $\quad \therefore \quad \mathbf{b} = 0$

$$\therefore \quad \mathbf{r} = \tfrac{1}{2}\mathbf{g}t^2+\mathbf{u}t.$$

(2) *If* $d^2\mathbf{r}/dt^2 = -2\sin t\mathbf{i}-3\cos t\mathbf{j}$, *and if* $d\mathbf{r}/dt = 2\mathbf{i}$ *when* $t = 0$ *and* $\mathbf{r} = 3\mathbf{j}$ *when* $t = 0$, *show that the particle whose position vector is* $\mathbf{r}$ *is moving in an ellipse.*

$$\frac{d^2\mathbf{r}}{dt^2} = -2\sin t\mathbf{i}-3\cos t\mathbf{j},$$

$$\therefore \quad \frac{d\mathbf{r}}{dt} = 2\cos t\mathbf{i}-3\sin t\mathbf{j}+\mathbf{a} \quad (\mathbf{a} = \text{constant of integration}).$$

When $t = 0$, $d\mathbf{r}/dt = 2\mathbf{i}$,

$$\therefore \quad \mathbf{a} = 0,$$

$$\therefore \quad \frac{d\mathbf{r}}{dt} = 2\cos t\mathbf{i}-3\sin t\mathbf{j}.$$

Integrating again,

$$\mathbf{r} = 2\sin t\mathbf{i}+3\cos t\mathbf{j}+\mathbf{b} \quad (\mathbf{b} = \text{constant of integration}).$$

When $t = 0$, $\mathbf{r} = 3\mathbf{j}$,

$$\therefore \quad \mathbf{b} = 0,$$

$$\therefore \quad \mathbf{r} = 2\sin t\mathbf{i}+3\cos t\mathbf{j},$$

$$\therefore \quad x = 2\sin t \quad \text{and} \quad y = 3\cos t,$$

$$\therefore \tfrac{1}{4}x^2+\tfrac{1}{9}y^2 = 1.$$

Therefore path of particle is an ellipse.

Exercise 7

(1) The position vector of a particle at time t is $\mathbf{r}$, $\mathbf{v}$ is its velocity and $\mathbf{a}$ is its acceleration which is constant. Show that if $\mathbf{r}_0$ and $\mathbf{v}_0$ are the initial values of $\mathbf{r}$ and $\mathbf{v}$ respectively

$$\mathbf{v} = \mathbf{v}_0 + \mathbf{a}t \quad \text{and} \quad \mathbf{r} - \mathbf{r}_0 = \mathbf{v}_0 t + \tfrac{1}{2}\mathbf{a}t^2.$$

(2) The position vector of a point at any time t relative to a fixed origin is $\mathbf{a}\cos\omega t + \mathbf{b}\sin\omega t$ where $\mathbf{a}$ and $\mathbf{b}$ are constant vectors and ω is a constant scalar. Show that the acceleration is everywhere towards the origin and proportional to the distance from the origin.

(3) If $d^2\mathbf{r}/dt^2 = 4\mathbf{i}$ and if $\mathbf{r} = 0$ when $t = 0$ and $d\mathbf{r}/dt = 4\mathbf{j}$ when $t = 0$, prove that the point whose position vector is $\mathbf{r}$ is describing a parabola.

(4) The position vector of a particle at time t with respect to fixed axes is $(t^2+1)\mathbf{i} - 2t\mathbf{j} + t^2\mathbf{k}$. Find the magnitude of the velocity and acceleration when $t = 2$.

(5) If $d^2\mathbf{r}/dt^2 = \mathbf{p}\cos wt$ and if $\mathbf{r} = 0$ when $t = 0$ and $d\mathbf{r}/dt = \mathbf{u}$ when $t = 0$, show that $\mathbf{r} = \mathbf{u}t + (\mathbf{p}/\omega^2)(1 - \cos wt)$.

(6) If $\mathbf{p}$ and $\mathbf{q}$ are two unit vectors whose directions make angles of θ and $\theta + \frac{1}{2}\pi$ respectively with a fixed direction, prove

$$d^2\mathbf{p}/dt^2 = \mathbf{q}\ddot{\theta} - \mathbf{p}\dot{\theta}^2.$$

(7) A point moves from the origin with velocities after a time t of $a\cos t$ and $a\sin t$, parallel to the Ox and Oy axes respectively. Prove that its acceleration is a and that the equation of its path is

$$x^2 + y^2 = 2ay.$$

(8) A particle is moving in a curve whose equation is $xy = c^2$. If at any point in its path its acceleration is at right angles to the x-axis, prove that the magnitude of its acceleration varies as y^3.

(9) A point P moves along the equiangular spiral $r = ae^{k\theta}$. If its acceleration is always in the direction OP where O is the origin, prove that the magnitude of its acceleration varies as r^{-3}.

(10) An insect crawls outward along a spoke of a bicycle wheel which is itself rolling on the ground with constant velocity v. If the insect crawls with constant velocity u relative to the wheel, find the radial and transverse components of the acceleration of the insect when it is a distance d from the centre of the wheel.

(11) A lamp is at a height d above the ground. A man of height h starts from a point immediately below the lamp and walks at a speed u in a circle of radius a. Show that the velocity of the end of his shadow after a time t is $ud/(d-h)$ at an angle of ut/a with his initial direction and the acceleration is $u^2d/[a(d-h)]$ at an angle of $\frac{1}{2}\pi+(ut/a)$.

(12) A smooth horizontal tube OA of length a can rotate about O. A particle is placed in the tube at a distance b from O and the tube is then set rotating with constant angular velocity ω.

Show that the particle leaves the tube after a time

$$\frac{1}{\omega}\log_e\frac{a+\sqrt{(a^2-b^2)}}{b}$$

with a velocity of $\omega\sqrt{(2a^2-b^2)}$ in a direction $\tan^{-1}a/\sqrt{(a^2-b^2)}$ with the tube.

(13) P and O are two opposite points on the banks of a river of width d, PO being perpendicular to the direction of flow of the river. A boat whose speed in still water is u starts from P and is rowed across the river with its bow always directed towards O. If the speed of the river is u show that the actual path of the boat is a parabola whose vertex is the point where the boat meets the opposite bank and whose semi latus rectum is PO. Also show that this point is at a distance $\frac{1}{2}d$ below O.

(14) A point A is moving along the circumference of a fixed circle of radius a with constant angular velocity ω about the centre. A point B is also moving along the circumference of the circle and the radii on which A and B lie are always at right angles to one another. Show that the acceleration of B relative to A is always directed towards A and is of magnitude $\sqrt{2}\omega^2a$.

(15) A particle moves on the curve $y = \log\sec x$ in such a way that the tangent rotates uniformly. Show that the magnitude of the acceleration varies as ρ^2 and is in the direction parallel to the y axis.

8

THE SCALAR PRODUCT

Introduction

The aim of this chapter is to create the algebra for a product of two vectors. We shall try to do this by developing a meaning for the product of two vectors which is capable of a geometrical interpretation.

In chapter 3 we have seen that the multiplication of a vector by a number is another vector to which we can give a precise meaning. No matter how we define the product of two vectors the product will not obviously have the same meaning as the product of two numbers, for a vector is not a number.

Consider the vectors

$$\mathbf{a} = x_1\mathbf{i}+y_1\mathbf{j}+z_1\mathbf{k} = (x_1, y_1, z_1)$$

and

$$\mathbf{b} = x_2\mathbf{i}+y_2\mathbf{j}+z_2\mathbf{k} = (x_2, y_2, z_2).$$

It is reasonable to expect that any definition of the product of two vectors **a** and **b** will involve the product of their components. Now there are various product combinations of the components of **a** with the components of **b**. Our aim is to combine these components in some way which is capable of some interpretation. Once we have done this we can frame a definition and investigate the structure of our definition more closely particularly as to its meaning. Finally we have to show whether our product definition obeys the usual multiplicative laws of algebra.

Rotation of a vector

Consider the vector $\mathbf{OA} = 2\mathbf{i}+5\mathbf{j} = (2, 5)$ as in Fig. 8.1. If **OA** is rotated anticlockwise through a right angle we obtain the vector $\mathbf{OB} = (-5, 2)$. This can be seen by considering the rotation of a triangle AON through 90° anticlockwise when OM, MB will be the new positions of ON, NA.

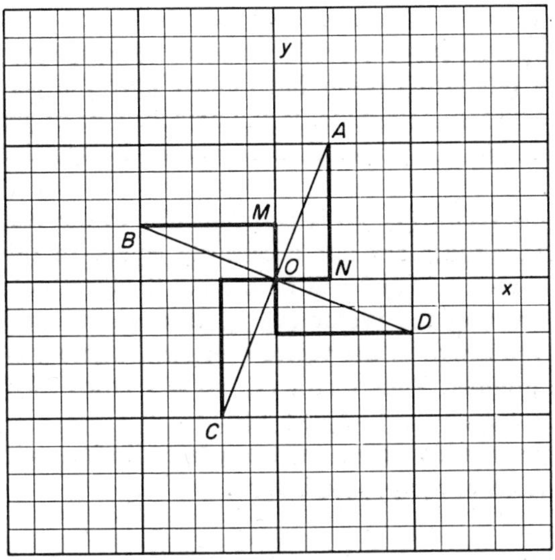

Fig. 8.1

If we rotate **OB** anticlockwise through 90° we obtain

$$\mathbf{OC} = (-2, -5).$$

A further rotation of 90° anticlockwise gives us $\mathbf{OD} = (5, -2)$.

Writing the vectors in the order of obtaining them we have

$$\mathbf{OA} = (2, 5), \quad \mathbf{OB} = (-5, 2), \quad \mathbf{OC} = (-2, -5), \quad \mathbf{OD} = (5, -2).$$

From these we can deduce that if the vector $x_1\mathbf{i}+y_1\mathbf{j} = (x_1, y_1)$ is rotated anticlockwise through 90° we obtain the vector $(-y_1, x_1)$.

Returning to the numerical examples we make the following observation about the components:

$$\mathbf{OA} = (2, 5), \quad \mathbf{OB} = (-5, 2), \quad (2\times -5)+(5\times 2) = 0,$$
$$\mathbf{OB} = (-5, 2), \quad \mathbf{OC} = (-2, -5), \quad (-5\times -2)+(2\times -5) = 0,$$
$$\mathbf{OC} = (-2, -5), \quad \mathbf{OD} = (5, -2), \quad (-2\times 5)+-(5\times -2) = 0.$$

This suggests investigating the value of $x_1x_2+y_1y_2$ for the general vectors $\mathbf{a} = (x_1, y_1)$, $\mathbf{b} = (x_2, y_2)$, where **b** is obtained by rotating **a** through 90° anticlockwise. In this case we have

$$x_2 = -y_1,$$

and

$$y_2 = x_1,$$

$$\therefore \quad x_1x_2+y_1y_2 = x_1(-y_1)+y_1x_1 = 0.$$

Thus we see that if we have two perpendicular vectors (x_1, y_1), (x_2, y_2) of equal lengths the product defined by $x_1x_2+y_1y_2$ is zero.

This is an interesting result but limited since the perpendicular vectors are equal in magnitude. It will obviously be of greater value if it is true for all perpendicular vectors irrespective of their magnitudes.

Suppose the vector (x_2, y_2) is perpendicular to the vector (x_1, y_1) and their magnitudes are not necessarily equal. In this case the length of the vector (x_2, y_2) will be k times the length of the vector formed by rotating the vector (x_1, y_1) through 90° anticlockwise, i.e. k times the length of the vector $(-y_1, x_1)$, where k is a positive or negative number. Thus vector (x_2, y_2) = vector $(-ky_1, kx_1)$ and we have $x_1x_2+y_1y_2 = x_1(-ky_1)+y_1(kx_1) = 0$.

Thus we see that if we have any two perpendicular vectors (x_1, y_1), (x_2, y_2) the value of $x_1x_2+y_1y_2$ is zero.

The scalar product: definition and notation

The study of perpendicular vectors has produced a meaning for $x_1x_2+y_1y_2$, namely that if $x_1x_2+y_1y_2 = 0$ the vectors (x_1, x_2), (y_1, y_2) are perpendicular. This leads us to the idea of $x_1x_2+y_1y_2$ as being a promising definition of a product of two vectors (x_1, y_1), (x_2, y_2). Extending this idea to vectors in space we shall consider a product of the vectors (x_1, y_1, z_1), (x_2, y_2, z_2) to be defined by

$$x_1x_2+y_1y_2+z_1z_2.$$

Now the components $x_1, x_2, y_1, y_2, z_1, z_2$ are all numbers representing the lengths of the component vectors. Therefore our product of two vectors defined by $x_1x_2+y_1y_2+z_1z_2$ is a number. We have previously discussed vector quantities. Distinct from these are quantities which possess only magnitude, such as length, mass and area and these are called scalar quantities. We can therefore think of numbers as scalar quantities or briefly scalars. For this reason our defined product $x_1x_2+y_1y_2+z_1z_2$ is called the scalar product of two vectors.

The scalar product of the vectors **a**, **b** is denoted symbolically by placing a dot between the vectors **a**, **b**, i.e. **a**.**b**. Hence it is sometimes known as the 'dot' product. The dot must never be omitted since we are not dealing with the product of two numbers.

We now state our definition of the scalar product.

Definition. *The scalar product of the vectors* $\mathbf{a} = (x_1, y_1, z_1)$, $\mathbf{b} = (x_2, y_2, z_2)$ *is defined by the number* $\mathbf{a}.\mathbf{b} = x_1x_2+y_1y_2+z_1z_2$.

Immediate consequences of the definition

(1) For the mutually perpendicular vectors

$$\mathbf{i} = (1, 0, 0), \quad \mathbf{j} = (0, 1, 0), \quad \mathbf{k} = (0, 0, 1),$$

$$\mathbf{j}.\mathbf{k} = \mathbf{k}.\mathbf{i} = \mathbf{i}.\mathbf{j} = 0.$$

(2) If $\mathbf{a} = (x, y, z)$

$$\mathbf{a}.\mathbf{a} = x^2+y^2+z^2 = a^2,$$

or writing $\mathbf{a}.\mathbf{a}$ as $\mathbf{a}^2$ we have $\mathbf{a}^2 = a^2$, i.e. the scalar product of a vector by itself is the square of its magnitude.

In particular for the unit vectors **i, j, k,**

$$\mathbf{i}.\mathbf{i} = \mathbf{j}.\mathbf{j} = \mathbf{k}.\mathbf{k} = 1, \quad \text{i.e.} \quad \mathbf{i}^2 = \mathbf{j}^2 = \mathbf{k}^2 = 1.$$

(3) Suppose **a, b** are parallel vectors. Let

$$\mathbf{a} = (a_1, a_2, a_3), \mathbf{b} = (b_1, b_2, b_3).$$

Since **a, b** are parallel $\quad \mathbf{b} = (ka_1, ka_2, ka_3),$

where k is a positive or negative number.

Then

$$\begin{aligned} \mathbf{a}.\mathbf{b} &= a_1ka_1+a_2ka_2+a_3ka_3 \\ &= k(a_1^2+a_2^2+a_3^2) \\ &= ka^2. \end{aligned}$$

Now

$$b^2 = k^2(a_1^2+a_2^2+a_3^2) = k^2a^2,$$

$$\therefore \quad b = ka,$$

$$\therefore \quad \mathbf{a}.\mathbf{b} = ab,$$

that is the scalar product of parallel vectors is the product of their magnitudes.

The commutative and distributive laws

We now investigate whether the following laws hold for scalar products:

$$\mathbf{a}.\mathbf{b} = \mathbf{b}.\mathbf{a} \qquad \text{(Commutative Law),*}$$

$$\mathbf{a}.(\mathbf{b}+\mathbf{c}) = \mathbf{a}.\mathbf{b}+\mathbf{a}.\mathbf{c} \qquad \text{(Distributive Law),}$$

$$\mathbf{a}.(m\mathbf{b}) = m(\mathbf{a}.\mathbf{b}) \qquad \text{(Distributive Law).}$$

* Those familar with matrix theory will know that the Commutative Law does not hold for the multiplication of two matrices A, B, i.e. $AB \neq BA$.

Before doing so we point out that since $\mathbf{a}.(\mathbf{b}.\mathbf{c})$ has no meaning, $\mathbf{b}.\mathbf{c}$ being a number, there is no question of an associative law for scalar products.

Let

$$\mathbf{a} = (a_1, a_2, a_3),\ \mathbf{b} = (b_1, b_2, b_3),\ \mathbf{c} = (c_1, c_2, c_3).$$

We use our definition of a scalar product namely,

$$\mathbf{a}.\mathbf{b} = a_1 b_1 + a_2 b_2 + a_3 b_3.$$

The Commutative Law

$$\mathbf{a}.\mathbf{b} = a_1 b_1 + a_2 b_2 + a_3 b_3,$$

$$\mathbf{b}.\mathbf{a} = b_1 a_1 + b_2 a_2 + b_3 a_3,$$

$$\therefore \quad \mathbf{a}.\mathbf{b} = \mathbf{b}.\mathbf{a}.$$

The Distributive Laws

$$\mathbf{b}+\mathbf{c} = (b_1+c_1,\ b_2+c_2,\ b_3+c_3),$$

$$\begin{aligned} \therefore \quad \mathbf{a}.(\mathbf{b}+\mathbf{c}) &= a_1(b_1+c_1)+a_2(b_2+c_2)+a_3(b_3+c_3) \\ &= a_1 b_1 + a_1 c_1 + a_2 b_2 + a_2 c_2 + a_3 b_3 + a_3 c_3. \end{aligned}$$

$$\mathbf{a}.\mathbf{b}+\mathbf{a}.\mathbf{c} = (a_1 b_1 + a_2 b_2 + a_3 b_3) + (a_1 c_1 + a_2 c_2 + a_3 c_3),$$

$$\therefore \quad \mathbf{a}.(\mathbf{b}+\mathbf{c}) = \mathbf{a}.\mathbf{b}+\mathbf{a}.\mathbf{c}.$$

$$m\mathbf{b} = (mb_1,\ mb_2,\ mb_3),$$

$$\begin{aligned} \therefore \quad \mathbf{a}.(m\mathbf{b}) &= a_1 m b_1 + a_2 m b_2 + a_3 m b_3 \\ &= m(a_1 b_1 + a_2 b_2 + a_3 b_3) \\ &= m(\mathbf{a}.\mathbf{b}). \end{aligned}$$

In the same way by repeated application of the above results we can show that the commutative and distributive laws hold for scalar products involving the sum of several vectors. For example,

$$\begin{aligned} (\mathbf{a}+\mathbf{b}+\mathbf{c}+\ldots).(\mathbf{p}+\mathbf{q}+\mathbf{r}+\ldots) = {} & \mathbf{a}.\mathbf{p}+\mathbf{a}.\mathbf{q}+\mathbf{a}.\mathbf{r}+\mathbf{b}.\mathbf{p}+\mathbf{b}.\mathbf{q}+\mathbf{b}.\mathbf{r} \\ & + \mathbf{c}.\mathbf{p}+\mathbf{c}.\mathbf{q}+\mathbf{c}.\mathbf{r}+\ldots. \end{aligned}$$

Applications of the commutative and distributive laws

Knowing that the commutative and distributive laws apply to scalar products we can perform operations involving them just as in number algebra we can simplify the following

$$(p+q)(r+s) = p(r+s)+q(r+s)$$
$$= pr+ps+qr+qs,$$
$$(x+y)^2 = (x+y)(x+y)$$
$$= x(x+y)+y(x+y)$$
$$= x^2+xy+yx+y^2$$
$$= x^2+2xy+y^2.$$

because numbers obey the commutative and distributive laws. The following two examples illustrate the simplification of scalar products:

(1) $$(\mathbf{a}+\mathbf{b}).(\mathbf{a}-2\mathbf{b}) = \mathbf{a}.(\mathbf{a}-2\mathbf{b})+\mathbf{b}.(\mathbf{a}-2\mathbf{b})$$
$$= \mathbf{a}.\mathbf{a}+\mathbf{a}.(-2\mathbf{b})+\mathbf{b}.\mathbf{a}+\mathbf{b}.(-2\mathbf{b})$$
$$= \mathbf{a}^2-2\mathbf{a}.\mathbf{b}+\mathbf{a}.\mathbf{b}-2\mathbf{b}^2$$
$$= \mathbf{a}^2-\mathbf{a}.\mathbf{b}-2\mathbf{b}^2,$$

(2) If $\mathbf{a} = 3\mathbf{i}+5\mathbf{j}+2\mathbf{k}$ *and* $\mathbf{b} = 2\mathbf{i}+2\mathbf{j}-8\mathbf{k}$ *where* **i, j, k** *are three mutally perpendicular vectors, show that* **a, b** *are perpendicular.*

$$\mathbf{a}.\mathbf{b} = (3\mathbf{i}+5\mathbf{j}+2\mathbf{k}).(2\mathbf{i}+2\mathbf{j}-8\mathbf{k})$$
$$= 6\mathbf{i}^2+6\mathbf{i}.\mathbf{j}-24\mathbf{k}.\mathbf{i}+10\mathbf{i}.\mathbf{j}+10\mathbf{j}^2-40\mathbf{j}.\mathbf{k}+4\mathbf{k}.\mathbf{i}+4\mathbf{j}.\mathbf{k}-16\mathbf{k}^2.$$

Since $\quad \mathbf{j}.\mathbf{k} = \mathbf{k}.\mathbf{i} = \mathbf{i}.\mathbf{j} = 0$ and $\mathbf{i}^2 = \mathbf{j}^2 = \mathbf{k}^2 = 1,$

$$\mathbf{a}.\mathbf{b} = 6+10-16 = 0,$$

therefore **a, b** are perpendicular.

Otherwise, using the definition of scalar product directly

$$\mathbf{a}.\mathbf{b} = 3\times 2+5\times 2+2\times -8$$
$$= 0,$$

therefore **a, b** are perpendicular.

Meaning of the scalar product of any two vectors

We have seen that if two vectors are parallel their scalar product is the product of their lengths. It is reasonable to assume that the scalar product of two vectors in space depends on the lengths of the vectors and the angle between them. Suppose we have vectors **OP**, **OQ**. The relation between their lengths and the angle between them is given by the cosine rule. So by considering the problem of two vectors geometrically we hope to obtain further meaning of our definition of the scalar product.

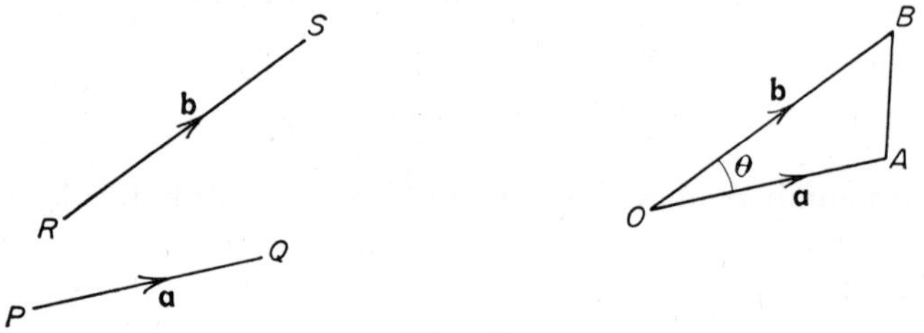

Fig. 8.2

Referring to Fig. 8.2 suppose we have two vectors

$$\mathbf{PQ} = \mathbf{a} = (x_1, y_1, z_1), \quad \mathbf{RS} = \mathbf{b} = (x_2, y_2, z_2),$$

which are inclined at an angle θ with one another. Let the two associated vectors located at the origin O be **OA**, **OB**, i.e. $\mathbf{OA} = \mathbf{a}$, $\mathbf{OB} = \mathbf{b}$, angle $AOB = \theta$.

We have
$$\mathbf{AB} = \mathbf{b}-\mathbf{a} = (x_2-x_1, y_2-y_1, z_2-z_1)$$

and applying the cosine rule to the triangle AOB,

$$AB^2 = OA^2+OB^2-2OA.OB\cos\theta,$$

$$\therefore \quad (x_2-x_1)^2+(y_2-y_1)^2+(z_2-z_1)^2$$
$$= x_1^2+y_1^2+z_1^2+x_2^2+y_2^2+z_2^2-2OA.OB\cos\theta,$$

$$\therefore \quad -2x_1x_2-2y_1y_2-2z_1z_2 = -2OA.OB\cos\theta,$$

$$\therefore \quad x_1x_2+y_1y_2+z_1z_2 = |\mathbf{a}|\,|\mathbf{b}|\cos\theta.$$

But
$$\mathbf{a}.\mathbf{b} = x_1x_2+y_1y_2+z_1z_2, \text{ by definition,}$$

$$\therefore \quad \mathbf{a}.\mathbf{b} = |\mathbf{a}||\mathbf{b}|\cos\theta.$$

Another way of obtaining this result is to make use of the commutative and distributive laws which have been proved to hold for scalar products.

By the cosine rule

$$AB^2 = OA^2+OB^2-2OA.OB\cos\theta = a^2+b^2-2ab\cos\theta. \qquad (1)$$

Remembering that $\mathbf{AB}.\mathbf{AB} = \mathbf{AB}^2 = AB^2$ we express AB^2 in vector form.

$$\mathbf{AB} = \mathbf{b}-\mathbf{a},$$

$$\therefore \quad \mathbf{AB}.\mathbf{AB} = (\mathbf{b}-\mathbf{a}).(\mathbf{b}-\mathbf{a}),$$

$$\therefore \quad \mathbf{AB}^2 = \mathbf{a}^2+\mathbf{b}^2-2\mathbf{a}.\mathbf{b},$$

$$\therefore \quad AB^2 = a^2+b^2-2\mathbf{a}.\mathbf{b}. \qquad (2)$$

Comparing (1) and (2) $\quad \mathbf{a}.\mathbf{b} = ab\cos\theta.$

The result $\mathbf{a}.\mathbf{b} = |\mathbf{a}|\,|\mathbf{b}|\cos\theta$ expressed in words means that the scalar product of two vectors is the product of their lengths and the cosine of the included angle. Thus the scalar product has a trigonometrical meaning.

The interpretation of the scalar product given by $\mathbf{a}.\mathbf{b} = |\mathbf{a}|\,|\mathbf{b}|\cos\theta$ is of great value since we can find the angle between the vectors **a, b** no matter where they are located by using

$$\cos\theta = \frac{\mathbf{a}.\mathbf{b}}{|\mathbf{a}|\,|\mathbf{b}|}.$$

We have previously found the angle between two vectors by using direction cosines, and it will be seen later on that the angle is more easily and neatly obtained by using the scalar product.

Care however must be exercised in dealing with the included angle θ.

Referring back to Fig. 8.2 we see that the included angle θ is the angle between the vectors **OA, OB** when **OA, OB** are both directed outward from the point O. The sense of measurement of the angle is unimportant since $\cos\theta = \cos(-\theta)$.

In Fig. 8.3 the angle between the vectors **a, b** is denoted by θ. We see that the angle is either acute or obtuse. If θ is obtuse, $\cos\theta$ is negative and the scalar product is therefore negative.

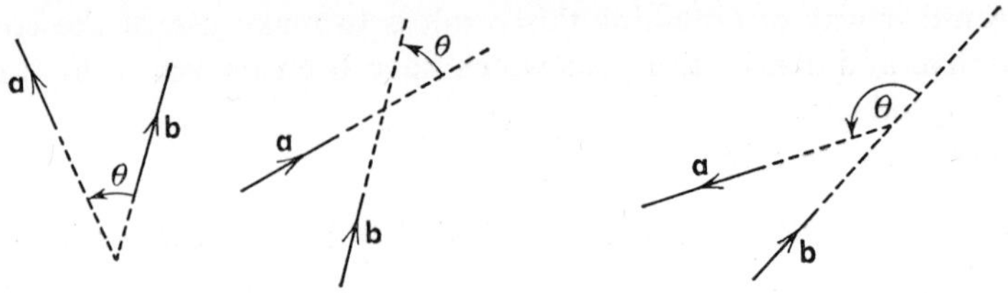

Fig. 8.3

Geometrical meaning of $\mathbf{a}.\mathbf{b} = |\mathbf{a}|\,|\mathbf{b}| \cos \theta$

In chapter 5 we defined the projection of **b** on **a** as $|\mathbf{b}|\cos\theta$ where θ is the angle between the vectors. Thus $|\mathbf{a}|\,|\mathbf{b}|\cos\theta$ can be regarded as the projection of **b** on **a** or of **a** on **b**. This leads to the following geometrical interpretation of the scalar product:

The scalar product of two vectors is the product of the length of one vector and the projection of the other upon it.

As we have seen the projection can be positive (θ acute) or negative (θ obtuse) and hence the scalar product is positive or negative, agreeing with the previous section.

Consequences of $\mathbf{a}.\mathbf{b} = |\mathbf{a}|\,|\mathbf{b}| \cos \theta$

(1) When **a**, **b** are parallel $\cos\theta = \cos 0 = 1$,

$$\therefore \quad \mathbf{a}.\mathbf{b} = |\mathbf{a}|\,|\mathbf{b}| = ab.$$

In particular if $\mathbf{a} = \mathbf{b}$, $\quad \mathbf{a}.\mathbf{a} = a^2$.

We have had these results before by using the definition

$$\mathbf{a}.\mathbf{b} = x_1x_2+y_1y_2+z_1z_2.$$

(2) When **a**, **b** are perpendicular, $\cos\theta = \cos 90° = 0$,

$$\therefore \quad \mathbf{a}.\mathbf{b} = 0.$$

We have had this result before but only for two vectors **a**, **b** in the x-y plane. We now see that our definition $\mathbf{a}.\mathbf{b} = x_1x_2+y_1y_2+z_1z_2$ leads to the meaning of perpendicularity for any two vectors $\mathbf{a} = (x_1, y_1, z_1)$, $\mathbf{b} = (x_2, y_2, z_2)$ in space if $x_1x_2+y_1y_2+z_1z_2 = 0$.

The scalar product of a vector and the zero vector

So far we have considered $\mathbf{a} \neq \mathbf{0}$, $\mathbf{b} \neq \mathbf{0}$.

If $\mathbf{a} = \mathbf{0} = (0, 0, 0)$ then from our definition

$$\mathbf{0}.\mathbf{b} = 0+0+0 = 0.$$

Similarly, $$\mathbf{a}.\mathbf{0} = 0.$$

These results can also be obtained from $\mathbf{a}.\mathbf{b} = |\mathbf{a}|\,|\mathbf{b}|\cos\theta$ for if $\mathbf{a} = \mathbf{0}$, $|\mathbf{a}| = 0$ or if $\mathbf{b} = \mathbf{0}$, $|\mathbf{b}| = 0$ and in either case

$$|\mathbf{a}|\,|\mathbf{b}|\cos\theta = 0.$$

Thus in general $\mathbf{0}.\mathbf{p} = \mathbf{p}.\mathbf{0} = 0$.

Thus the scalar product of a vector and the zero vector is the number zero.

Alternative treatment of the scalar product

Some authors prefer a different treatment of the scalar product from the one developed here. We shall give an outline of this alternative procedure.

(1) The scalar product $\mathbf{a}.\mathbf{b}$ is defined as the number given by

$$\mathbf{a}.\mathbf{b} = |\mathbf{a}|\,|\mathbf{b}|\cos\theta,$$

where θ is the angle between the vectors **a**, **b**.

The special cases for perpendicular, parallel and equal vectors are then obtained by putting $\theta = 90°$, $\theta = 0$ and $\mathbf{a} = \mathbf{b}$, $\theta = 0$ respectively into the definition.

(2) The commutative and distributive laws are proved for scalar products by a method involving projections. (See Ex. 8, Question 2.)

(3) A formula for calculating the scalar product in terms of its components is deduced in the following way:

Let
$$\mathbf{a} = x_1\mathbf{i}+y_1\mathbf{j}+z_1\mathbf{k}, \quad \mathbf{b} = x_2\mathbf{i}+y_2\mathbf{j}+z_2\mathbf{k}.$$
Then

$$\begin{aligned}(\mathbf{a}.\mathbf{b}) &= (x_1\mathbf{i}+y_1\mathbf{j}+z_1\mathbf{k}).(x_2\mathbf{i}+y_2\mathbf{j}+z_2\mathbf{k}) \\ &= x_1x_2\mathbf{i}^2+y_1y_2\mathbf{j}^2+z_1z_2\mathbf{k}^2+\text{terms involving the scalar} \\ &\qquad \text{product of the perpendicular vectors } \mathbf{i}.\mathbf{j}, \text{ etc.}\end{aligned}$$

Since $$\mathbf{i}^2 = \mathbf{j}^2 = \mathbf{k}^2 = 1,$$

$$\mathbf{a}.\mathbf{b} = x_1x_2+y_1y_2+z_1z_2.$$

Thus no matter how the scalar product is evolved the same relations are obtained finally. For the purpose of reference we give a summary of the important relations.

Summary

(1) The scalar product of two vectors **a, b** is a number.

(2) If $\mathbf{a} = (x_1, y_1, z_1)$, $\mathbf{b} = (x_2, y_2, z_2)$,

$$\mathbf{a}.\mathbf{b} = x_1x_2+y_1y_2+z_1z_2.$$

(3) If θ is the angle between **a, b**

$$\mathbf{a}.\mathbf{b} = |\mathbf{a}|\,|\mathbf{b}|\cos\theta.$$

(4) If **a, b** are perpendicular, $\mathbf{a}.\mathbf{b} = 0$. In particular for the mutually perpendicular unit vectors

$$\mathbf{j}.\mathbf{k} = \mathbf{k}.\mathbf{i} = \mathbf{i}.\mathbf{j} = 0.$$

(5) If **a, b** are parallel, $\mathbf{a}.\mathbf{b} = |\mathbf{a}|\,|\mathbf{b}|$.

In particular $\mathbf{a}.\mathbf{a} = \mathbf{a}^2 = a^2$.

For the unit vectors $\mathbf{i}^2 = \mathbf{j}^2 = \mathbf{k}^2 = 1$.

(6) The Commutative and Distributive Laws apply.

$$\mathbf{a}.\mathbf{b} = \mathbf{b}.\mathbf{a},$$

$$\mathbf{a}.(\mathbf{b}+\mathbf{c}) = \mathbf{a}.\mathbf{b}+\mathbf{a}.\mathbf{c},$$

$$\mathbf{a}.(m\mathbf{b}) = m(\mathbf{a}.\mathbf{b}).$$

(7) If one of the vectors is the zero vector the scalar product is 0, i.e.

$$\mathbf{0}.\mathbf{a} = \mathbf{a}.\mathbf{0} = 0.$$

General examples

The scalar product is of great use in questions involving distances and angles. The two relations

$$\mathbf{a}.\mathbf{b} = x_1x_2+y_1y_2+z_1z_2,$$

$$\mathbf{a}.\mathbf{b} = |\mathbf{a}|\,|\mathbf{b}|\cos\theta$$

are often used, as will be seen from some of the following examples:

(1) *A, B, C, D are the points* (2, 3, 4), (−1, 0, 3), (2, −4, 1), (1, −2, −1) respectively. *Show that the projections of* **AB** *on* **CD** and **CD** *on* **AB** *are* $-\frac{1}{3}$ *and* $-1/\sqrt{19}$ *respectively.*

Let **a**, **b**, **c**, **d** be the position vectors of *A*, *B*, *C*, *D* respectively relative to the origin *O*.

$$\mathbf{a} = (2, 3, 4),\ \mathbf{b} = (-1, 0, 3),$$

$$\therefore\quad \mathbf{AB} = \mathbf{b}-\mathbf{a} = (-3, -3, -1);$$

$$\mathbf{c} = (2, -4, 1),\ \mathbf{d} = (1, -2, -1),$$

$$\therefore\quad \mathbf{CD} = \mathbf{d}-\mathbf{c} = (-1, 2, -2),$$

$$\therefore\quad \mathbf{AB}.\mathbf{CD} = 3-6+2 = -1;$$

$$|\mathbf{AB}| = \sqrt{(3^2+3^2+1)} = \sqrt{19},$$

$$|\mathbf{CD}| = \sqrt{(1^2+2^2+2^2)} = 3.$$

$\mathbf{AB}.\mathbf{CD} = |\mathbf{AB}|\,|\mathbf{CD}|\cos\theta$, where θ is the angle between **AB**, **CD**.

Projection of **AB** on **CD** $= |\mathbf{AB}|\cos\theta = \dfrac{-1}{3} = -\dfrac{1}{3}$.

Projection of **CD** on **AB** $= |\mathbf{CD}|\cos\theta = \dfrac{-1}{\sqrt{19}} = -\dfrac{1}{\sqrt{19}}$.

(2) *Prove that the line drawn from the vertex of an isosceles triangle to the mid-point of its base is perpendicular to the base.*

Let *O* be the mid-point of the base *BC* of the isosceles triangle *ABC* (Fig. 8.4).

Let **OA** = **p** and **OB** = **q**,

$$\therefore\quad \mathbf{OC} = -\mathbf{q}.$$

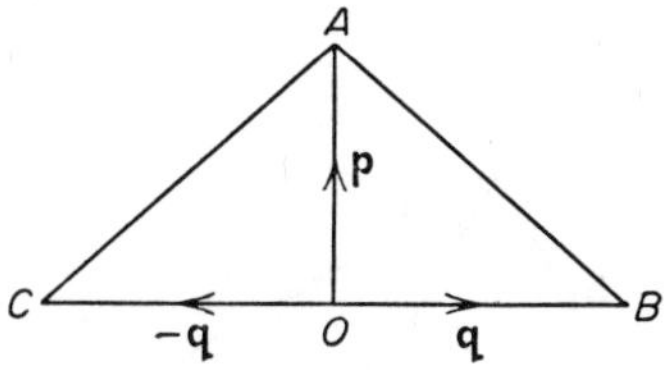

Fig. 8.4

We now make use of the fact that $BA = CA$.

$$\mathbf{BA} = \mathbf{p}-\mathbf{q},$$

$$\mathbf{CA} = \mathbf{p}+\mathbf{q}.$$

$$\mathbf{BA}.\mathbf{BA} = (\mathbf{p}-\mathbf{q}).(\mathbf{p}-\mathbf{q}) = \mathbf{p}^2-2\mathbf{p}.\mathbf{q}+\mathbf{q}^2,$$

$$\mathbf{CA}.\mathbf{CA} = (\mathbf{p}+\mathbf{q}).(\mathbf{p}+\mathbf{q}) = \mathbf{p}^2+2\mathbf{p}.\mathbf{q}+\mathbf{q}^2.$$

Now $\quad \mathbf{BA}.\mathbf{BA} = BA^2$ and $\mathbf{CA}.\mathbf{CA} = CA^2$,

since $\quad \mathbf{a}.\mathbf{a} = |\mathbf{a}|\,|\mathbf{a}|\cos 0 = |\mathbf{a}|^2 = a^2.$

Also since $BA = CA$ we have

$$p^2 - 2\mathbf{p}.\mathbf{q} + q^2 = p^2 + 2\mathbf{p}.\mathbf{q} + q^2,$$

$$\therefore \quad 4\mathbf{p}.\mathbf{q} = 0,$$

$$\therefore \quad \mathbf{p}.\mathbf{q} = 0$$

$$\therefore \quad \mathbf{p} \text{ is perpendicular to } \mathbf{q} \quad (\mathbf{p} \neq \mathbf{0}, \mathbf{q} \neq \mathbf{0}),$$

$$\therefore \quad AO \text{ is perpendicular to } BC.$$

(3) *AD is the median of a triangle. Prove $AB^2 + AC^2 = 2AD^2 + \frac{1}{2}BC^2$* (Apollonius's Theorem).

Let **b, c** be the position vectors of B, C relative to the origin A (Fig. 8.5).

Then $\mathbf{AD} = \frac{1}{2}(\mathbf{b}+\mathbf{c})$ and $\mathbf{BC} = \mathbf{c}-\mathbf{b}$.

We make use of the result $\mathbf{a}.\mathbf{a} = \mathbf{a}^2 = a^2$.

$$\mathbf{AD}.\mathbf{AD} = \tfrac{1}{4}(\mathbf{b}+\mathbf{c}).(\mathbf{b}+\mathbf{c}),$$

and

$$\mathbf{BC}.\mathbf{BC} = (\mathbf{c}-\mathbf{b}).(\mathbf{c}-\mathbf{b}),$$

$$\therefore \quad AD^2 = \tfrac{1}{4}(b^2 + c^2 + 2\mathbf{b}.\mathbf{c}),$$

$$\therefore \quad 4AD^2 = b^2 + c^2 + 2\mathbf{b}.\mathbf{c}.$$

Also

$$BC^2 = b^2 + c^2 - 2\mathbf{b}.\mathbf{c}.$$

Adding

$$4AD^2 + BC^2 = 2b^2 + 2c^2 = 2AB^2 + 2AC^2,$$

$$\therefore \quad AB^2 + AC^2 = 2AD^2 + \tfrac{1}{2}BC^2.$$

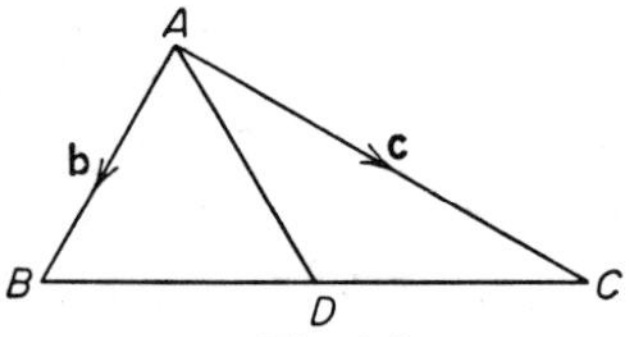

Fig. 8.5

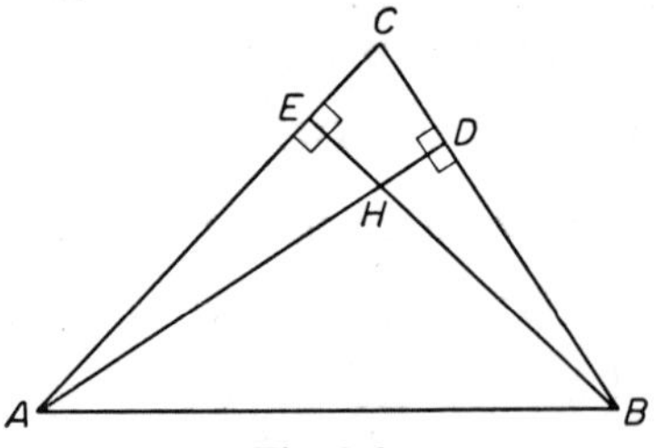

Fig. 8.6

(4) *Prove that the altitudes of a triangle are concurrent*

Let the altitudes AD, BE of a triangle meet at H (Fig. 8.6).

Let the position vectors of A, B, C with H as the origin be **a, b, c** respectively.

Since **HA** is perpendicular to **BC**,

$$\mathbf{HA}.\mathbf{BC} = 0,$$

$$\therefore \quad \mathbf{a}.(\mathbf{c}-\mathbf{b}) = 0,$$

$$\therefore \quad \mathbf{a}.\mathbf{c}-\mathbf{a}.\mathbf{b} = 0,$$

$$\therefore \quad \mathbf{a}.\mathbf{c} = \mathbf{a}.\mathbf{b}. \tag{1}$$

(Note here that we cannot cancel the vector **a** from each side since obviously **b** and **c** need not be equal. In general cancellation of a common vector from each side of a scalar product equation is not allowed.)

Similarly, since **HB** is perpendicular to **AC**

$$\mathbf{HB}.\mathbf{AC} = 0,$$

$$\therefore \quad \mathbf{b}.(\mathbf{c}-\mathbf{a}) = 0,$$

$$\therefore \quad \mathbf{b}.\mathbf{c} = \mathbf{a}.\mathbf{b}. \tag{2}$$

From (1) and (2) above we obtain

$$\mathbf{a}.\mathbf{c} = \mathbf{b}.\mathbf{c},$$

$$\therefore \quad \mathbf{c}.(\mathbf{a}-\mathbf{b}) = 0,$$

$$\therefore \quad \mathbf{HC}.\mathbf{BA} = 0,$$

∴ **HC** is perpendicular to **BA**,

∴ the altitude from C on to AB passes through H,

∴ the altitudes are concurrent.

(5) *In any triangle ABC,* $\mathbf{BC} = \mathbf{a}$, $\mathbf{CA} = \mathbf{b}$, $\mathbf{AB} = \mathbf{c}$. *Prove that* $|\mathbf{a}|^2 = |\mathbf{b}|^2+|\mathbf{c}|^2+2\mathbf{b}.\mathbf{c}$. *Comment on this result and discuss the result when* $\mathbf{b}.\mathbf{c} = 0$.

In Fig. 8.7, $\quad \mathbf{a} = -\mathbf{b}-\mathbf{c} = -(\mathbf{b}+\mathbf{c}),$

$$\therefore \quad \mathbf{a}.\mathbf{a} = -(\mathbf{b}+\mathbf{c}).-(\mathbf{b}+\mathbf{c})$$

$$= (\mathbf{b}+\mathbf{c}).(\mathbf{b}+\mathbf{c})$$

$$= \mathbf{b}.\mathbf{b}+\mathbf{c}.\mathbf{c}+2\mathbf{b}.\mathbf{c}.$$

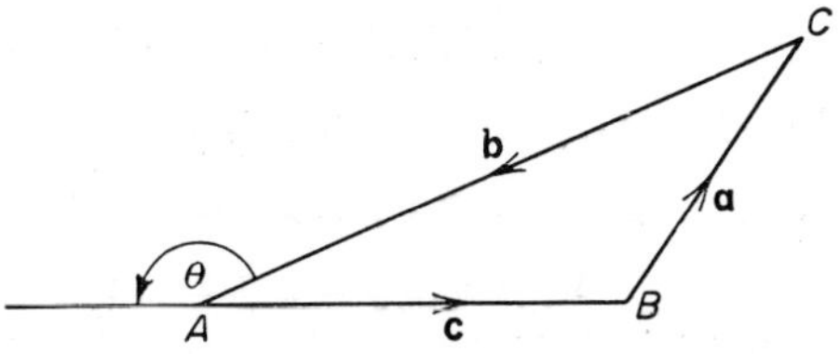

Fig. 8.7

Since $\mathbf{a}.\mathbf{a} = |\mathbf{a}|^2, \quad \mathbf{b}.\mathbf{b} = |\mathbf{b}|^2, \quad \mathbf{c}.\mathbf{c} = |\mathbf{c}|^2,$

$$|\mathbf{a}|^2 = |\mathbf{b}|^2+|\mathbf{c}|^2+2\mathbf{b}.\mathbf{c}.$$

Writing $|\mathbf{a}| = a, \quad |\mathbf{b}| = b, \quad |\mathbf{c}| = c$

we have $a^2 = b^2+c^2+2\mathbf{b}.\mathbf{c}.$

Geometrically this is the Extension of Pythagoras's Theorem in vector form.

It is also the vector form of the cosine rule which can be put into the usual form by writing

$$\begin{aligned} 2\mathbf{b}.\mathbf{c} &= 2|\mathbf{b}|\,|\mathbf{c}|\cos\theta = 2bc\cos\theta \\ &= 2bc\cos(180^\circ - A) \\ &= -2bc\cos A, \\ \therefore \quad a^2 &= b^2+c^2-2bc\cos A. \end{aligned}$$

When $\mathbf{b}.\mathbf{c} = 0$, $\mathbf{b}$ is perpendicular to $\mathbf{c}$, i.e. angle $BAC = 90^\circ$. The vector form of the cosine rule then becomes

$$a^2 = b^2+c^2,$$

which is in agreement with the well-known theorem of Pythagoras.

(6) *The position vectors of the points A, B, C are* (8, 4, −3), (6, 3, −4), (7, 5, −5) *respectively. Find the angle between* **AB** *and* **BC**. *Hence find the area of triangle ABC.*

$$\begin{aligned} \mathbf{AB} = \mathbf{b}-\mathbf{a} &= (6, 3, -4)-(8, 4, -3) \\ &= (-2, -1, -1), \\ \therefore \quad |\mathbf{AB}| &= \sqrt{(2^2+1^2+1^2)} = \sqrt{6}. \\ \mathbf{BC} = \mathbf{c}-\mathbf{b} &= (7, 5, -5)-(6, 3, -4) \\ &= (1, 2, -1), \\ \therefore \quad |\mathbf{BC}| &= \sqrt{(1^2+2^2+1^2)} = \sqrt{6}. \\ \mathbf{AB}.\mathbf{BC} &= |\mathbf{AB}|\,|\mathbf{BC}|\cos\theta, \\ \therefore \quad (-2, -1, -1).(1, 2, -1) &= \sqrt{6}.\sqrt{6}\cos\theta, \\ \therefore \quad -2-2+1 &= 6\cos\theta, \\ \therefore \quad \cos\theta &= -\tfrac{3}{6} = -\tfrac{1}{2}, \\ \therefore \quad \theta &= 120^\circ. \end{aligned}$$

This is the angle between **AB** and **BC**,

$$\therefore \quad \text{angle between } \mathbf{BA} \text{ and } \mathbf{BC} = 60°.$$

$$\therefore \quad \text{angle } ABC = 60°.$$

$$\text{Area of triangle } ABC = \tfrac{1}{2}.BA.BC\sin B$$

$$= \tfrac{1}{2}.\sqrt{6}.\sqrt{6}.\frac{\sqrt{3}}{2}$$

$$= \frac{3\sqrt{3}}{2}.$$

(7) *OABC is a tetrahedron. If the edge OC is perpendicular to the edge AB and the edge OB is perpendicular to the edge AC, show that the edge OA is perpendicular to the edge BC.*

Let the position vectors of A, B, C relative to O as origin be **a, b, c** respectively (Fig. 8.8).

Since **OC** is perpendicular to **AB** we have

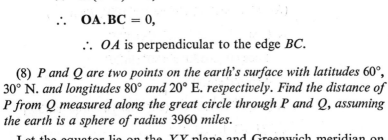

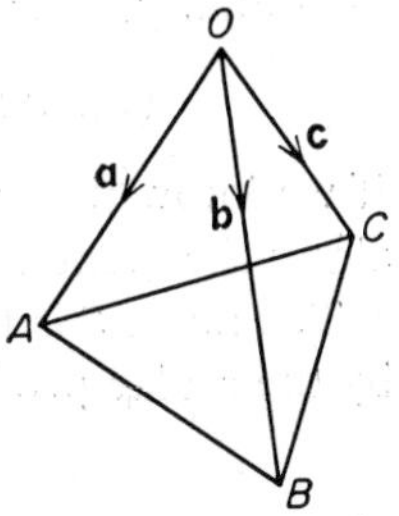

Fig. 8.8

$$\mathbf{OC}.\mathbf{AB} = \mathbf{c}.(\mathbf{b}-\mathbf{a}) = 0,$$

$$\therefore \quad \mathbf{b}.\mathbf{c} = \mathbf{a}.\mathbf{c}.$$

Similarly, $$\mathbf{OB}.\mathbf{AC} = \mathbf{b}.(\mathbf{c}-\mathbf{a}) = 0,$$

$$\therefore \quad \mathbf{b}.\mathbf{c} = \mathbf{a}.\mathbf{b},$$

$$\therefore \quad \mathbf{a}.\mathbf{c} = \mathbf{a}.\mathbf{b},$$

$$\therefore \quad \mathbf{a}.(\mathbf{c}-\mathbf{b}) = 0,$$

$$\therefore \quad \mathbf{OA}.\mathbf{BC} = 0,$$

$\therefore$ OA is perpendicular to the edge BC.

(8) *P and Q are two points on the earth's surface with latitudes* 60°, 30° N. *and longitudes* 80° *and* 20° E. *respectively. Find the distance of P from Q measured along the great circle through P and Q, assuming the earth is a sphere of radius* 3960 *miles.*

Let the equator lie on the XY plane and Greenwich meridian on the XZ plane. Let R be the radius of the earth.

Referring to Fig. 8.9, P is the point (ON, NM, MP), i.e. point ($R\cos 60° \cos 80°$, $R\cos 60° \sin 80°$, $R\sin 60°$).

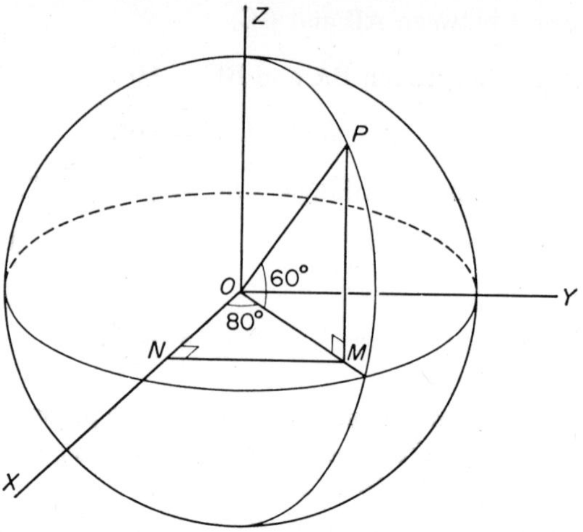

Fig. 8.9

Similarly, Q is the point

$$(R\cos 30^\circ \cos 20^\circ, \quad R\cos 30^\circ \sin 20^\circ, \quad R\sin 30^\circ).$$

If we know the angle $POQ = \theta$ in radians the length of the arc PQ along the great circle is given by $R\theta$.

The angle θ is the angle between the vectors **OP**, **OQ** and is given by the scalar product relation

$$\mathbf{OP}.\mathbf{OQ} = |\mathbf{OP}|\,|\mathbf{OQ}|\cos\theta.$$

Now

$$\begin{aligned}\mathbf{OP}.\mathbf{OQ} &= (R\cos 60^\circ \cos 80^\circ, R\cos 60^\circ \sin 80^\circ, R\sin 60^\circ).\\ &\quad (R\cos 30^\circ \cos 20^\circ, R\cos 30^\circ \sin 20^\circ, R\sin 30^\circ)\\ &= R^2 (\cos 60^\circ \cos 30^\circ \cos 80^\circ \cos 20^\circ\\ &\quad +\cos 60^\circ \cos 30^\circ \sin 80^\circ \sin 20^\circ\\ &\quad +\sin 60^\circ \sin 30^\circ)\\ &= R^2[\cos 60^\circ \cos 30^\circ \cos(80^\circ - 20^\circ) + \sin 60^\circ \sin 30^\circ]\\ &= R^2.\left(\frac{1}{2}.\frac{\sqrt{3}}{2}.\frac{1}{2} + \frac{\sqrt{3}}{2}.\frac{1}{2}\right)\\ &= \frac{3\sqrt{3}}{8}R^2.\end{aligned}$$

Also

$$|\mathbf{OP}||\mathbf{OQ}|\cos\theta = R^2\cos\theta,$$

$$\therefore \quad \cos\theta = \frac{3\sqrt{3}}{8},$$

$$\therefore \quad \theta = 0{\cdot}8639 \text{ radians.}$$

$$\therefore \quad \text{distance} = R\theta$$

$$= 3960\times 0{\cdot}8639 \text{ miles}$$

$$= 3420 \text{ miles.}$$

Differentiation of the scalar product

By proceeding as in chapter 7 we show that if $\mathbf{a} = f(t)$, $\mathbf{b} = f(t)$ then

$$\frac{d}{dt}(\mathbf{a}.\mathbf{b}) = \mathbf{a}.\frac{d\mathbf{b}}{dt}+\mathbf{b}.\frac{d\mathbf{a}}{dt}.$$

Let $y = \mathbf{a}.\mathbf{b}$ and δy, $\delta\mathbf{a}$, $\delta\mathbf{b}$ be the increments in y, $\mathbf{a}$, $\mathbf{b}$ respectively due to an increment of δt in t. Then

$$y+\delta y = (\mathbf{a}+\delta\mathbf{a}).(\mathbf{b}+\delta\mathbf{b})$$

$$= \mathbf{a}.\mathbf{b}+\mathbf{a}.\delta\mathbf{b}+\mathbf{b}.\delta\mathbf{a}+\delta\mathbf{a}.\delta\mathbf{b}.$$

But

$$y = \mathbf{a}.\mathbf{b},$$

$$\therefore \quad \delta y = \mathbf{a}.\delta\mathbf{b}+\mathbf{b}.\delta\mathbf{a}+\delta\mathbf{a}.\delta\mathbf{b},$$

$$\therefore \quad \operatorname*{Lt}_{\delta t\to 0}\frac{\delta y}{\delta t} = \operatorname*{Lt}_{\delta t\to 0}\left(\mathbf{a}.\frac{\delta\mathbf{b}}{\delta t}+\mathbf{b}.\frac{\delta\mathbf{a}}{\delta t}+\delta\mathbf{a}.\frac{\delta\mathbf{b}}{\delta t}\right),$$

$$\therefore \quad \frac{dy}{dt} = \mathbf{a}.\frac{d\mathbf{b}}{dt}+\mathbf{b}.\frac{d\mathbf{a}}{dt}.$$

The following is an important special case. If $\mathbf{a} \neq \mathbf{0}$,

$$\frac{d}{dt}(\mathbf{a}^2) = \frac{d}{dt}(\mathbf{a}.\mathbf{a}) = 2\mathbf{a}.\frac{d\mathbf{a}}{dt}.$$

But

$$\mathbf{a}^2 = a^2 \quad \text{and} \quad \frac{d}{dt}(a^2) = 2a\frac{da}{dt}.$$

$$\therefore \quad \mathbf{a}.\frac{d\mathbf{a}}{dt} = a\frac{da}{dt}.$$

Further if $\mathbf{a}$ is a vector of constant length but of changing direction, a is a constant and $da/dt = 0$,

$$\therefore \quad \mathbf{a}.\frac{d\mathbf{a}}{dt} = 0,$$

$$\therefore \quad \mathbf{a} \quad \text{and} \quad \frac{d\mathbf{a}}{dt} \text{ are perpendicular.}$$

Thus the derivative of a vector of constant length is perpendicular to the vector.

A special case of this result is when $\mathbf{a}$ is a unit vector, i.e. of constant length 1 and we have shown in chapter 7 that the derivative of a unit vector is perpendicular to the vector.

Integration

Regarding integration as the reverse of differentiation we have the following immediately from the previous section:

(1) $\displaystyle\int\left(\mathbf{a}.\frac{d\mathbf{b}}{dt}+\mathbf{b}.\frac{d\mathbf{a}}{dt}\right)dt = \mathbf{a}.\mathbf{b}+c.$

(2) $\displaystyle\int 2\mathbf{a}.\frac{d\mathbf{a}}{dt}\,dt = \mathbf{a}.\mathbf{a}+c = \mathbf{a}^2+c.$

The arbitrary constant c is a number since $\mathbf{a}.\mathbf{b}$ and $\mathbf{a}^2$ are numbers.

Examples

(1) *Differentiate the following in which* $\mathbf{r}$ *is a function of the time* t *and* $\mathbf{a}$, $\mathbf{b}$ *are constant vectors*:

(i) $\mathbf{r}^2+\dfrac{1}{\mathbf{r}^2}$, (ii) $\mathbf{r}.\dfrac{d\mathbf{r}}{dt}$, (iii) $\left(\dfrac{d\mathbf{r}}{dt}\right)^2$, (iv) $\dfrac{\mathbf{r}+\mathbf{a}}{\mathbf{r}^2+\mathbf{a}^2}$, (v) $(\mathbf{a}.\mathbf{r})\mathbf{b}$.

(i) $\displaystyle\frac{d}{dt}\left(\mathbf{r}^2+\frac{1}{\mathbf{r}^2}\right) = 2\mathbf{r}.\frac{d\mathbf{r}}{dt}-\frac{2}{\mathbf{r}^4}\mathbf{r}.\frac{d\mathbf{r}}{dt} = 2\mathbf{r}.\dot{\mathbf{r}}-\frac{2\mathbf{r}.\dot{\mathbf{r}}}{\mathbf{r}^4} = 2r\dot{r}-\frac{2\dot{r}}{r^3}.$

(ii) $\displaystyle\frac{d}{dt}\left(\mathbf{r}.\frac{d\mathbf{r}}{dt}\right) = \frac{d\mathbf{r}}{dt}.\frac{d\mathbf{r}}{dt}+\mathbf{r}.\frac{d^2\mathbf{r}}{dt^2} = \dot{\mathbf{r}}^2+\mathbf{r}.\ddot{\mathbf{r}}.$

(iii) $\displaystyle\frac{d}{dt}\left(\frac{d\mathbf{r}}{dt}\right)^2 = \frac{d}{dt}\left(\frac{d\mathbf{r}}{dt}.\frac{d\mathbf{r}}{dt}\right) = 2\frac{d\mathbf{r}}{dt}.\frac{d^2\mathbf{r}}{dt^2} = 2\dot{\mathbf{r}}.\ddot{\mathbf{r}}.$

(iv) $\displaystyle\frac{d}{dt}\left(\frac{\mathbf{r}+\mathbf{a}}{\mathbf{r}^2+\mathbf{a}^2}\right) = \frac{(\mathbf{r}^2+\mathbf{a}^2)d\mathbf{r}/dt-(\mathbf{r}+\mathbf{a})\,2\mathbf{r}.d\mathbf{r}/dt}{(\mathbf{r}^2+\mathbf{a}^2)^2}$

$$= \frac{\dot{\mathbf{r}}}{r^2+a^2}-\frac{2r\dot{r}(\mathbf{r}+\mathbf{a})}{(r^2+a^2)^2}.$$

(v) $\displaystyle\frac{d}{dt}(\mathbf{a}.\mathbf{r})\mathbf{b} = \left(\mathbf{a}.\frac{d\mathbf{r}}{dt}\right)\mathbf{b} = (\mathbf{a}.\dot{\mathbf{r}})\mathbf{b}.$

(2) *If* $d^2\mathbf{r}/dt^2+n^2\mathbf{r} = 0$, *show that* $(d\mathbf{r}/dt)^2 = c-n^2\mathbf{r}^2$ *where* n, c *are constants.*

$$\frac{d^2\mathbf{r}}{dt^2}+n^2\mathbf{r} = 0,$$

$$\therefore \quad \frac{d^2\mathbf{r}}{dt^2} = -n^2\mathbf{r}.$$

The right-hand side cannot be integrated immediately since we do not know $\mathbf{r}$ in terms of t.

To integrate the equation both sides are multiplied by $2(d\mathbf{r}/dt)$ to form scalar products. We then have

$$2\frac{d\mathbf{r}}{dt}\cdot\frac{d^2\mathbf{r}}{dt^2} = -2n^2\mathbf{r}.\frac{d\mathbf{r}}{dt},$$

$$\therefore \quad \int 2\frac{d\mathbf{r}}{dt}\cdot\frac{d^2\mathbf{r}}{dt^2}\,dt = -n^2\int 2\mathbf{r}.\frac{d\mathbf{r}}{dt}\,dt.$$

The left-hand integral is $(d\mathbf{r}/dt)^2$ from Ex. 1 (iii) and the right-hand integral is $\mathbf{r}^2$.

$$\therefore \quad (d\mathbf{r}/dt)^2 = -n^2\mathbf{r}^2+c,$$

where c is a constant number.

Work done by a constant force

We now consider an application of the scalar product in Mechanics.

Suppose a particle at A is displaced to B by a constant force $\mathbf{P}$, the angle between $\mathbf{P}$ and $\mathbf{AB}$ being θ (Fig. 8.10). The force $\mathbf{P}$ is then said to do work on the particle.

The work done by the force on the particle is defined as the product of the magnitude of the force and the resolved part of the displacement in the direction of the force.

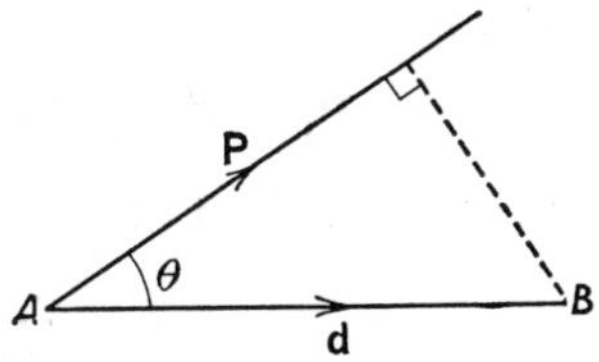

Fig. 8.10

If the work done $= W$ and $\mathbf{AB} = \mathbf{d}$ then

$$W = Pd\cos\theta,$$

where $P = |\mathbf{P}|$ and $d = |\mathbf{d}|$.

This is a scalar quantity. Since $d\cos\theta$ is the projection of $\mathbf{d}$ on $\mathbf{P}$ we have

$$W = \mathbf{P}.\mathbf{d}.$$

From this it is evident that if **P** and **d** are perpendicular the work done is zero.

Consider several forces $\mathbf{P}_1, \mathbf{P}_2, \ldots$ acting on the particle. Let the displacement be **d**. Then the total work done by the forces is

$$\mathbf{P}_1.\mathbf{d}+\mathbf{P}_2.\mathbf{d}+\ldots = (\mathbf{P}_1+\mathbf{P}_2+\ldots).\mathbf{d}.$$

Now $\mathbf{P}_1+\mathbf{P}_2+\ldots$ is the sum of the forces, that is, it is the resultant of the forces.

Thus the total work done is the same as the work done by the resultant of the system of forces.

Suppose

$$\mathbf{P} = X\mathbf{i}+Y\mathbf{j}+Z\mathbf{k} \quad \text{and} \quad \mathbf{d} = x\mathbf{i}+y\mathbf{j}+z\mathbf{k}.$$

Then work done by **P** is given by

$$\begin{aligned} W &= \mathbf{P}.\mathbf{d} \\ &= (X\mathbf{i}+Y\mathbf{j}+Z\mathbf{k}).(x\mathbf{i}+y\mathbf{j}+z\mathbf{k}) \\ &= Xx+Yy+Zz. \end{aligned}$$

Example

Find the work done by the forces 3, 6 *lb. wt. acting in the directions of the vectors* (1, 2, −2), (−2, −1, 2) *if a particle is displaced from a point* $A(3, 5, -2)$ *to a point* $B(-1, 3, 2)$, *the unit of length being* 1 *ft.*

The unit vectors in the given directions are

$$\tfrac{1}{3}(\mathbf{i}+2\mathbf{j}-2\mathbf{k}) \quad \text{and} \quad \tfrac{1}{3}(-2\mathbf{i}-\mathbf{j}+2\mathbf{k}).$$

The forces are

$$\mathbf{P}_1 = \mathbf{i}+2\mathbf{j}-2\mathbf{k} \quad \text{and} \quad \mathbf{P}_2 = 2(-2\mathbf{i}-\mathbf{j}+2\mathbf{k}).$$

Let the resultant of $\mathbf{P}_1$, $\mathbf{P}_2$ be **R**

$$\therefore \quad \mathbf{R} = -3\mathbf{i}+2\mathbf{k}.$$

The displacement **d** is given by $\mathbf{AB} = -4\mathbf{i}-2\mathbf{j}+4\mathbf{k}.$
The work done is given by

$$\begin{aligned} W &= \mathbf{R}.\mathbf{d} \\ &= (-3\mathbf{i}+2\mathbf{k}).(-4\mathbf{i}-2\mathbf{j}+4\mathbf{k}) \\ &= (12+8) \text{ ft. lb. wt.} \\ &= 20 \text{ ft. lb. wt.} \end{aligned}$$

Work done by a variable force

Let MN be the path along which a particle travels under the action of a variable force (Fig. 8.11). Take several points on the curve and join them up as shown forming sides of a polygon.

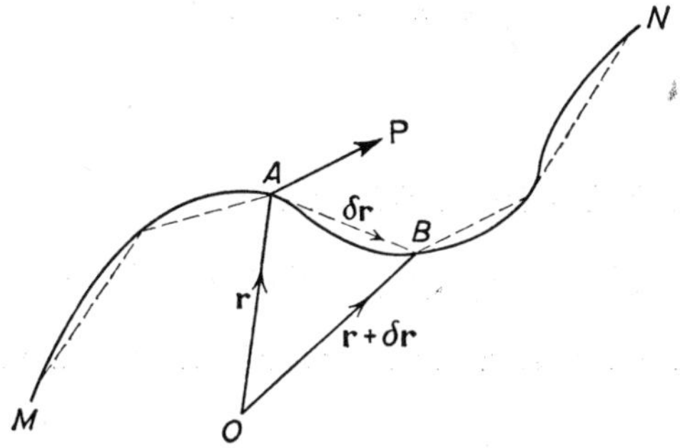

Fig. 8.11

Suppose at any time the particle is at the point A whose position vector relative to a fixed origin O is $\mathbf{r}$ and a short time later is at the point B, position vector $\mathbf{r}+\delta\mathbf{r}$. Then the particle has undergone a displacement $\mathbf{AB} = \delta\mathbf{r}$.

The work done by the force producing the displacement $\delta\mathbf{r}$ is approximately $\mathbf{P}.\delta\mathbf{r}$ where $\mathbf{P}$ is the value of the variable force at A. The work done by the variable force as the particle moves from M to N along the curved path is approximately the sum of all such terms as $\mathbf{P}.\delta\mathbf{r}$, i.e. $\Sigma(\mathbf{P}.\delta\mathbf{r})$, formed by considering the work done by the variable force producing displacements along the sides of the polygon.

If the number of the sides of the polygon is increased indefinitely then the length of each side tends to zero, and the work done by the variable force is the limiting value of the above sum. This is written in the usual way as

$$\int \mathbf{P}.d\mathbf{r}.$$

Thus if W is the work done from M to N we have

$$W = \int \mathbf{P}.d\mathbf{r}.$$

Suppose $\quad \mathbf{P} = X\mathbf{i}+Y\mathbf{j}+Z\mathbf{k} \quad$ and $\quad \mathbf{r} = x\mathbf{i}+y\mathbf{j}+z\mathbf{k}.$

Then $$W = \int \mathbf{P}.d\mathbf{r}$$

$$= \int (X\mathbf{i}+Y\mathbf{j}+Z\mathbf{k}).d(x\mathbf{i}+y\mathbf{j}+z\mathbf{k})$$

$$= \int (X\,dx+Y\,dy+Z\,dz).$$

Example

Find the work done by the field of force:

$$\text{(i) } \mathbf{P} = x^2\mathbf{i}+y^2\mathbf{j}, \qquad \text{(ii) } \mathbf{P} = y^2\mathbf{i}+x^2\mathbf{j}$$

on a particle constrained to move from (0, 0) *to* (2, 4) *along the parabola* $y = x^2$.

(i) $$\mathbf{P} = x^2\mathbf{i}+y^2\mathbf{j} \quad \text{and} \quad \mathbf{r} = x\mathbf{i}+y\mathbf{j}.$$

Work done

$$= \int \mathbf{P}.d\mathbf{r}$$

$$= \int_{(0,\,0)}^{(2,\,4)} (x^2\mathbf{i}+y^2\mathbf{j}).d(x\mathbf{i}+y\mathbf{j})$$

$$= \int_{(0,\,0)}^{(2,\,4)} (x^2dx+y^2dy)$$

$$= \int_0^2 (x^2dx+x^4.2x\,dx), \quad \text{since} \quad y = x^2 \quad \text{and} \quad dy = 2x\,dx$$

$$= \int_0^2 (x^2+2x^5)\,dx$$

$$= \left[\frac{x^3}{3}+\frac{x^6}{3}\right]_0^2$$

$$= \tfrac{1}{3}(8+64)$$

$$= \tfrac{72}{3}$$

$$= 24.$$

(ii) $$\mathbf{P} = y^2\mathbf{i}+x^2\mathbf{j} \quad \text{and} \quad \mathbf{r} = x\mathbf{i}+y\mathbf{j}.$$

Work done

$$= \int \mathbf{P}.d\mathbf{r}$$

$$= \int_{(0,\,0)}^{(2,\,4)} (y^2\mathbf{i}+x^2\mathbf{j}).(x\mathbf{i}+y\mathbf{j})$$

$$= \int_{(0,\,0)}^{(2,\,4)} (y^2 dx+x^2 dy)$$

$$= \int_0^2 (x^4 dx+x^2.2x\,dx), \quad \text{since} \quad y = x^2 \quad \text{and} \quad dy = 2xdx$$

$$= \int_0^2 (x^4+2x^3)dx$$

$$= \left[\frac{x^5}{5}+\frac{x^4}{2}\right]_0^2$$

$$= \tfrac{32}{5}+\tfrac{16}{2} = \tfrac{72}{5}.$$

Exercise 8

(1) If $\mathbf{a} = 2\mathbf{i}-2\mathbf{j}+\mathbf{k}$, $\mathbf{b} = \mathbf{i}+2\mathbf{j}-3\mathbf{k}$, $\mathbf{c} = 2\mathbf{i}-\mathbf{j}+4\mathbf{k}$, obtain $(\mathbf{b}+\mathbf{c})$, $3\mathbf{b}$ and the projections of $\mathbf{b}$, $\mathbf{c}$, $(\mathbf{b}+\mathbf{c})$, $3\mathbf{b}$ on $\mathbf{a}$. Hence verify that $p(\mathbf{b}+\mathbf{c}) = p(\mathbf{b})+p(\mathbf{c})$ and $p(3\mathbf{b}) = 3p(\mathbf{b})$ where $p(\mathbf{x})$ denotes the projection of $\mathbf{x}$ on $\mathbf{a}$.

(2) If $p(\mathbf{x})$ denotes the projection of $\mathbf{x}$ on $\mathbf{a}$ deduce that

$$\mathbf{a}.(\mathbf{b}+\mathbf{c}) = \mathbf{a}.\mathbf{b}+\mathbf{a}.\mathbf{c} \quad \text{and} \quad \mathbf{a}.(k\mathbf{b}) = k(\mathbf{a}.\mathbf{b})$$

by multiplying by $\mathbf{a}$ the results

$$p(\mathbf{b}+\mathbf{c}) = p(\mathbf{b})+p(\mathbf{c}) \quad \text{and} \quad p(k\mathbf{b}) = kp(\mathbf{b}).$$

(3) If $\mathbf{p} = -3\mathbf{i}+4\mathbf{j}+5\mathbf{k}$, $\mathbf{q} = 2\mathbf{i}-\mathbf{j}+3\mathbf{k}$, $\mathbf{r} = 4\mathbf{i}+3\mathbf{j}-2\mathbf{k}$ evaluate $\mathbf{p}.\mathbf{q}$ and $\mathbf{p}.\mathbf{r}$ and verify that $\mathbf{p}.(\mathbf{q}+\mathbf{r}) = \mathbf{p}.\mathbf{q}+\mathbf{p}.\mathbf{r}$. Also simplify $(\mathbf{p}.\mathbf{q})\mathbf{r}+(\mathbf{p}.\mathbf{r})\mathbf{q}$.

(4) If angle $ABC = 90°$ and $\mathbf{a}$, $\mathbf{b}$, $\mathbf{c}$ are the position vectors of A, B, C respectively, prove that $\mathbf{b}^2+2\mathbf{a}.\mathbf{c} = \mathbf{b}.\mathbf{c}+\mathbf{a}.\mathbf{c}+\mathbf{a}.\mathbf{b}$.

(5) In triangle AOB, angle $AOB = 90°$. If P and Q are points of trisection on AB, prove that $OP^2+OQ^2 = \frac{5}{9}AB^2$.

(6) $ABCD$ is a trapezium with $AB = a$, $DC = 2a$, $DA = b$. E is a point in BC such that $BE = \frac{1}{3}BC$. Show that $\mathbf{AC}.\mathbf{DE} = \frac{2}{3}(4a^2-b^2)$. Comment on the case of $b = 2a$.

(7) A, B, C are the points (1, 2, 3), (0, 6, 11), (5, −2, 10) respectively. Show that the angle between the vectors $\mathbf{AB}$, $\mathbf{AC}$ is $\cos^{-1}\frac{4}{9}$. Hence find the shortest distance from B to the line AC.

(8) Using scalar products prove that the angle between two lines with direction cosines (l_1, m_1, n_1) and (l_2, m_2, n_2) is

$$\cos^{-1}(l_1 l_2+m_1 m_2+n_1 n_2).$$

(*Hint*. Consider unit vectors $\hat{\mathbf{u}}_1$, $\hat{\mathbf{u}}_2$ at angle θ to each other.)

(9) Prove that the diagonals of a rhombus are perpendicular.

(10) Prove that the acute angles between the diagonals of a cube is $\cos^{-1}\frac{1}{3}$.

(11) Find the unit vectors which are perpendicular to the vectors

$$\mathbf{a} = 2\mathbf{i}-3\mathbf{j}+6\mathbf{k} \quad \text{and} \quad \mathbf{b} = -6\mathbf{i}+2\mathbf{j}+3\mathbf{k}.$$

(12) Prove that the sum of the squares of the diagonals of a parallelogram is equal to twice the sum of the squares on two adjacent sides.

(13) Prove that the angle in a semicircle is a right angle.

(14) $ABCD$ is any quadrilateral with P, Q the mid-points of the diagonals AC, BD respectively. Prove that

$$AB^2+BC^2+CD^2+DA^2 = AC^2+BD^2+4PQ^2.$$

(15) $OABC$ is a tetrahedron. The edges OA, OB are perpendicular to the edges BC, AC respectively. Prove that the edge OC is perpendicular to the edge AB and that

$$OA^2+BC^2 = OB^2+AC^2 = OC^2+AB^2.$$

(16) G is the centroid of a triangle ABC and X is any point in or out of the plane ABC. Prove that

$$XA^2+XB^2+XC^2 = GA^2+GB^2+GC^2+3XG^2.$$

(17) Find the angles, the sides and the area of the triangle whose vertices are at the points $A(1, 1, -1)$, $B(2, -1, 1)$, $C(-1, 1, 1)$.

(18) If $\mathbf{v} = \mathbf{v}_0+\mathbf{a}t$ and $\mathbf{r}-\mathbf{r}_0 = \mathbf{v}_0 t+\frac{1}{2}\mathbf{a}t^2$ prove that

$$\mathbf{v}^2 = \mathbf{v}_0^2+2\mathbf{a}.(\mathbf{r}-\mathbf{r}_0).$$

(19) **u**, **v** are two unit vectors lying in the **i**−**j** plane and making angles of θ, ϕ respectively with **i**. Show that $\mathbf{u} = \mathbf{i}\cos\theta+\mathbf{j}\sin\theta$ and $\mathbf{v} = \mathbf{i}\cos\phi+\mathbf{j}\sin\phi$. Obtain $\mathbf{u}.\mathbf{v}$ and hence show

$$\cos(\theta-\phi) = \cos\theta\cos\phi+\sin\theta\sin\phi.$$

(20) O is the circumcentre of triangle ABC, and R is the radius of the circumcircle. Show that

$$\mathbf{OB}.\mathbf{OC} = R^2\cos 2A,\quad \mathbf{OA}.\mathbf{OC} = R^2\cos 2B,\quad \mathbf{OA}.\mathbf{OB} = R^2\cos 2C.$$

Hence prove $bc\cos A = R^2(1+\cos 2A-\cos 2B-\cos 2C)$.

(21) (i) If $\mathbf{r}.(d\mathbf{r}/dt) = 0$ show that $|\mathbf{r}|$ is constant. (ii) If

$$\mathbf{r} = \mathbf{i}\cos nt+\mathbf{j}\sin nt$$

show that $d/dt\,(\mathbf{r}^2) = 0$.

(22) If $\hat{\mathbf{u}}$ is a unit vector show that $\hat{\mathbf{u}}.(d\hat{\mathbf{u}}/dt) = 0$ and

$$\hat{\mathbf{u}}.\left(\hat{\mathbf{u}}+\frac{d^2\hat{\mathbf{u}}}{dt^2}\right)+\left(\frac{d\hat{\mathbf{u}}}{dt}\right)^2 = 1.$$

(23) Prove that

$$\int \mathbf{u}.\frac{d\mathbf{v}}{dt}dt = \mathbf{u}.\mathbf{v}-\int \mathbf{v}.\frac{d\mathbf{u}}{dt}dt.$$

(24) Forces of 6, 12, 9 lb. wt. in the directions of the vectors $4\mathbf{i}+4\mathbf{j}-7\mathbf{k}$, $7\mathbf{i}-4\mathbf{j}+4\mathbf{k}$, $-4\mathbf{i}+7\mathbf{j}-4\mathbf{k}$ respectively act on a particle producing a displacement of $(2\mathbf{i}+3\mathbf{j}+6\mathbf{k})$ ft. Calculate the work done.

(25) Calculate the work done by the field of force

$$\mathbf{P} = (x+y)^2\,\mathbf{i}+(x-y)^2\mathbf{j}$$

on a particle moving from (1, 0) to (0, 1) along the circle

$$x = \cos t,\quad y = \sin t.$$

(26) Calculate the work done by the field of force

$$\mathbf{P} = \frac{x\mathbf{i}+y\mathbf{j}}{\sqrt{(x^2+y^2)}}$$

on a particle moving around a square whose sides are $x = 0$, $x = 1$, $y = 0$, $y = 1$.

(*Hint*. Consider the field of force along each side and hence calculate the work done on each of the 4 legs round the square, working anticlockwise.)

MISCELLANEOUS EXERCISES

(1) A vector of magnitude PQ in a direction P to Q is represented by $\mathbf{PQ}$.

(*a*) $\mathbf{OB}$ makes an angle of 30° with the x axis and $\mathbf{OC}$ makes an angle of 120° with the x axis. Calculate the magnitudes of $\mathbf{OB}$ and $\mathbf{OC}$ if $2\mathbf{OB}+3\mathbf{OC} = 6\mathbf{i}+4\mathbf{j}$, where $\mathbf{i}$ and $\mathbf{j}$ are unit vectors along the x axis and y axis respectively.

(*b*) The points H and K are the middle points of the sides BC and CD respectively of a parallelogram $ABCD$. Prove that

$$3(\mathbf{AB}+\mathbf{AC}+\mathbf{AD}) = 4(\mathbf{AH}+\mathbf{AK}). \qquad \text{(C.)}$$

(2) (*a*) A vector of magnitude OP in the direction from O to P is represented by $\mathbf{OP}$. If $\mathbf{OP}-3\mathbf{OQ}+2\mathbf{OR} = 0$ show that P, Q, R are collinear.

(*b*) A unit vector parallel to the x axis is represented by $\mathbf{i}$ and a unit vector parallel to the y axis by $\mathbf{j}$.

If $\mathbf{OP} = a\mathbf{i}+s\mathbf{j}$ and $\mathbf{OQ} = -a\mathbf{i}+t\mathbf{j}$, where a is a constant and s and t are variables, show that the locus of P and Q are parallel straight lines. In this case find $\mathbf{OQ}$ when $\mathbf{OP} = 2\mathbf{i}+3\mathbf{j}$ and OQ is perpendicular to OP. (C.)

(3) (*a*) Unit vectors along the Ox and Oy axes are represented by $\mathbf{i}$ and $\mathbf{j}$ respectively, and $\mathbf{OP}$ represents a vector of magnitude OP in the direction from O to P. A triangle PQR is formed by the extremities of the vectors $\mathbf{OP}$, $\mathbf{OQ}$ and $\mathbf{OR}$, where

$$\mathbf{OP} = 2\mathbf{i}, \quad \mathbf{OQ} = -3\mathbf{i}+\mathbf{j} \quad \text{and} \quad \mathbf{OR} = a\mathbf{i}+b\mathbf{j},$$

a and b being constants. There are particles of masses m, $2m$ and $3m$ at the points P, Q and R respectively. If the centre of mass of the particles is at G where $\mathbf{OG} = \frac{1}{6}(5\mathbf{i}+8\mathbf{j})$, find a and b.

(*b*) If $\mathbf{OA} = 2\mathbf{i}+3\mathbf{j}$ and $\mathbf{OB} = \lambda(-\mathbf{i}+5\mathbf{j})$, find $\mathbf{OM}$ where M is the middle point of AB, and find the locus of M as λ varies. (C.)

(4) Particles of equal mass m are placed, one each at the n points whose position vectors are $\mathbf{r}_1, \mathbf{r}_2, \ldots, \mathbf{r}_n$. Prove that the centre of mass of the system of particles is at the point whose position vector is $(\mathbf{r}_1+\mathbf{r}_2+\ldots+\mathbf{r}_n)/n$.

In a system of four particles of unit mass the position vectors of the particles are **a, b, c, d**. In a second system three particles of unit mass have position vectors $\frac{3}{2}\mathbf{a}$, $3\mathbf{b}$, $\frac{1}{2}(\mathbf{c}+\mathbf{d})$; and in a third system two particles of unit mass have position vectors of $2\mathbf{a}$ and $5\mathbf{b}$. Show that the centres of mass of the three systems are collinear. (C.)

(5) A, B, C are three given points and x, y are scalar constants. Prove that the sum of the vectors $x\mathbf{AB}$ and $y\mathbf{AC}$ is $(x+y)\mathbf{AD}$, the point D being such that $x\mathbf{BD} = y\mathbf{DC}$.

Three forces are represented completely by the vectors $p\mathbf{AD}$, $q\mathbf{BE}$, $r\mathbf{CF}$ where D, E, F are points on the sides BC, CA, AB respectively of the triangle ABC such that

$$\frac{BD}{DC} = l, \quad \frac{CE}{EA} = m, \quad \frac{AF}{FB} = n.$$

Show that the three forces are equivalent to three forces acting along the sides of the triangle, and find these equivalent forces.

If $p = q = r$ and $l = m = n$ show that the system reduces to a couple and find its magnitude in terms of p, l, and the area of the triangle. (C.)

(6) Find the radial and transverse components of acceleration referred to polar co-ordinates (r, θ) of a particle moving in a plane.

P is a point on the curve $r = a+b\cos\theta$, O is the origin and Q is the point on the initial line such that $OQ = PQ$ and the angle $POQ = \theta$. A particle describes the curve in such a manner that the radius vector OP rotates with constant angular velocity ω. Show that the radial and transverse components of acceleration of the particle when at P are $-\omega^2(a+2b\cos\theta)$ and $-2b\omega^2\sin\theta$ respectively.

Show also that the acceleration of the particle may be written as $a\omega^2\lambda+2b\omega^2\mu$ where λ, μ are unit vectors in the directions PO, PQ respectively. (C.)

(7) (i) If $\mathbf{OA} = \mathbf{a}$, $\mathbf{OB} = \mathbf{b}$ and $\mathbf{OC} = \mathbf{c}$ show that the condition for $\mathbf{OA}$ to be perpendicular to $\mathbf{BC}$ is $\mathbf{a}.(\mathbf{c}-\mathbf{b}) = 0$. Also show that if $\mathbf{OB}$ is perpendicular to $\mathbf{CA}$, then $\mathbf{OC}$ is perpendicular to $\mathbf{AB}$.

(ii) Given that $\mathbf{c} = \mathbf{a}+\mathbf{b}$ expand the right-hand side of each of the equations.

$$\mathbf{c}.\mathbf{c} = (\mathbf{a}+\mathbf{b}).\mathbf{c}, \quad \mathbf{c}.\mathbf{c} = (\mathbf{a}+\mathbf{b}).(\mathbf{a}+\mathbf{b}).$$

State the equivalent formulae in trigonometry.

(8) Prove that the sum of the squares on the edges of any tetrahedron is equal to four times the sum of the squares on the joins of the mid-points of opposite edges.

(9) $OABC$ is a tetrahedron. If G is the centroid of ABC prove that $3\mathbf{OG} = \mathbf{OA}+\mathbf{OB}+\mathbf{OC}$. Furthermore, if OA, OB, OC and the angles BOC, COA, AOB are denoted by a, b, c and α, β, γ respectively, prove that

$$(3OG)^2 = a^2+b^2+c^2+2bc\cos\alpha+2ca\cos\beta+2ab\cos\gamma.$$

(10) ABC is a triangle. P is a point on BC such that $BP:PC = l:m$. Q is a point on CA such that $CQ:QA = n:l$. If O is any fixed point obtain $\mathbf{OP}$ in terms of $\mathbf{OB}$, $\mathbf{OC}$ and $\mathbf{OQ}$ in terms of $\mathbf{OA}$, $\mathbf{OC}$. By eliminating $\mathbf{OC}$, show that R divides AB in the ratio $-m:n$ where R is the point of intersection of AB and PQ. Hence verify Menelaus's Theorem, namely,

$$\frac{BP}{PC}\cdot\frac{CQ}{QA}\cdot\frac{AR}{RB} = -1.$$

ANSWERS TO EXERCISES

Exercise 5 (p. 67)

(2) $\frac{7}{8}, -\frac{5}{8}$. (5) $9; \frac{1}{9}, -\frac{4}{9}, \frac{8}{9}$.

(6) $7, \frac{1}{7}(2\mathbf{i}+3\mathbf{j}+6\mathbf{k})$. (12) $120°$.

Exercise 6 (p. 86)

(1) $5, 36° 52'$ with x axis; $\sqrt{229}$, $352° 24'$ with x axis.

(2) 9 units, bearing $\tan^{-1}\frac{4}{7}$ N. of E., elevation $\sin^{-1}\frac{4}{9}$;
9 units, bearing $\tan^{-1}\frac{4}{7}$ N. of E. depression $\sin^{-1}\frac{4}{9}$.

(3) $4\sqrt{2}$ m.p.h. from N.W.

(4) $\sqrt{58}$ ft./sec., $336° 48'$ with horizontal.

(5) 5 ft./sec. at $\tan^{-1}(-\frac{4}{3})$ with AB; 16 ft.; 2·4 sec.

(8) $4\mathbf{i}-4\mathbf{j}+2\mathbf{k}$. (9) $\sqrt{\frac{43}{3}}$ lb. wt.

(10) 5 lb. wt.; direction cosines $\frac{3}{5\sqrt{2}}, \frac{4}{5\sqrt{2}}, \frac{1}{\sqrt{2}}$.

(18) 1·7, 0·2, 1·2.

Exercise 7 (p. 106)

(4) $6, 2\sqrt{2}$. (10) $-\frac{v^2d}{a^2}, \frac{2uv}{a}$.

Exercise 8 (p. 131)

(1) $\frac{-5}{3}, \frac{10}{3}, \frac{5}{3}, -5$. (3) $5, -10, 25\mathbf{j}-40\mathbf{k}$.

(6) AC, DE are perpendicular. (7) $\sqrt{65}$.

(11) $\pm\frac{1}{7}(3\mathbf{i}+6\mathbf{j}+2\mathbf{k})$.

(17) $\cos^{-1}\frac{1}{3\sqrt{2}}, \cos^{-1}\frac{7}{3\sqrt{13}}, \cos^{-1}\frac{3}{\sqrt{26}}$; $AB = 3$, $BC = \sqrt{13}$,
$CA = 2\sqrt{2}$; $\sqrt{17}$.

(24) 9 ft. lb. wt. (25) $\frac{-4}{3}$. (26) 0.

Miscellaneous exercises (p. 134)

(1) (*a*) $\dfrac{3\sqrt{3}+2}{2}, \dfrac{2\sqrt{3}-3}{3}$. (2) (*b*) $-2\mathbf{i}+\frac{4}{3}\mathbf{j}$.

(3) (*a*) $a = 3, b = 2$. (*b*) $\mathbf{OM} = \dfrac{2-\lambda}{2}\mathbf{i}+\dfrac{3+5\lambda}{2}\mathbf{j}$, $10x+2y = 13$.

(5) $\left(\dfrac{p}{1+l}-\dfrac{mq}{1+m}\right)$ **AB**, etc., $\dfrac{2p(1-l)\,\triangle}{1+l}$.

(8) $c = a\cos B+b\cos A$, $c^2 = a^2+b^2-2ab\cos C$.

INDEX